"*Overcoming Bipolar Disorder* is about more than just medication. New research shows that learning specific skills to manage bipolar disorder can significantly reduce symptoms and help to maintain long-term balance. Until now, these proven self-management programs have not been available outside of research centers. *Overcoming Bipolar Disorder* will help to spread this knowledge to a much broader audience. It should be an important resource for people living with bipolar disorder and for concerned family members."

—Gregory Simon, MD, MPH, psychiatrist and researcher at Group Health
Cooperative in Seattle, WA

"This self-help workbook for individuals with bipolar disorder is written in an engaging and practical style. Concise and extremely relevant 'modules' on key topics empower individuals to assess and problem-solve such diverse, yet common, challenges as coping with depression and anxiety, substance abuse, and binge eating. A focus on individual core values and goal-setting emphasize a personalized approach that is the opposite of one-size-fits-all treatment programs. The authors have done on outstanding job in producing a text that will help individuals and families dealing with bipolar disorder."

—Martha Sajatovic, MD, professor of psychiatry at Case Western Reserve
University in Cleveland, OH

"This book presents a marvelous compendium of approaches to managing life with bipolar disorder. The strategies outlined in this book enable a person to better understand the factors involved in their mood swings and include suggestions for recognizing and managing external stressors that trigger these swings. In each chapter, attention is paid to the biological, psychological and psychosocial aspects of potential mood dysregulation and the actions that one can take to maintain overall health. I highly recommend this book to any person with bipolar disorder who seeks to take charge of their illness.

—Lori Altshuler, MD, professor in mood disorders research at the
University of California, Los Angeles

Overcoming
Bipolar Disorder

A Comprehensive Workbook for Managing
Your Symptoms & Achieving Your Life Goals

MARK S. BAUER, MD
AMY M. KILBOURNE, PH.D., MPH
DEVRA E. GREENWALD, MPH
EVETTE J. LUDMAN, PH.D.
WITH LINDA McBRIDE, MSN

New Harbinger Publications, Inc.

Publisher's Note

Care has been taken to confirm the accuracy of the information presented and to describe generally accepted practices. However, the authors, editors, and publisher are not responsible for errors or omissions or for any consequences from application of the information in this book and make no warranty, express or implied, with respect to the contents of the publication.

The authors, editors, and publisher have exerted every effort to ensure that any drug selection and dosage set forth in this text are in accordance with current recommendations and practice at the time of publication. However, in view of ongoing research, changes in government regulations, and the constant flow of information relating to drug therapy and drug reactions, the reader is urged to check the package insert for each drug for any change in indications and dosage and for added warnings and precautions. This is particularly important when the recommended agent is a new or infrequently employed drug.

Some drugs and medical devices presented in this publication may have Food and Drug Administration (FDA) clearance for limited use in restricted research settings. It is the responsibility of the health care provider to ascertain the FDA status of each drug or device planned for use in their clinical practice.

Constructing Your Personal Mania Profile (exercise 8.2), Developing a Bio-Psychosocial List of Personal Triggers of Manic Symptoms (exercise 9.1), Personal Action Plan for Mania (exercise 15.4), Constructing Your Personal Depression Profile (exercise 16.2), Developing a Bio-Psychosocial List of Personal Triggers of Depressive Symptoms (exercise 17.1), Examples of Responses to Depressive Symptoms (in module 18), and Personal Action Plan for Depression (exercise 25.4) originally published in Structured Group Psychotherapy for Bipolar Disorders: The Life Goals Program, second edition. Mark S. Bauer and Linda McBride. Copyright 2003. Reproduced with the permission of Springer Publishing Company, LLC, New York, NY 10036.

Bipolar Spectrum Diagnostic Scale, S. Nassir Ghaemi, Christopher J. Miller, Douglas A. Berv, Jeffry Klugman, Klara J. Rosenquist, and Ronald W. Pies. Copyright 2005. Reproduced with the permission of Elsevier.

Robert M. A. Hirschfeld, Mood Disorders Questionnaire Tearsheets, 2000, Jones and Bartlett Publishers: Compact Clinicals, Sudbury, MA.

The depression material in modules 22–24 was developed with support from NIMH grant MH 51338 and has been adapted with permission from Creating a Balance, by G. E. Simon, E. J. Ludman, and S. Tutty. Copyright Group Health Cooperative.

The Sleep-Wake Log is adapted from the Personal Daily Activity and Sleep Routine by permission of Peter C. Whybrow.

This book is dedicated to our patients who over the years have taught us so much, and to our families, who support us in all our endeavors.

Contents

Part III
Working Through Depression

Part IV
Working to Wellness: Physical Health

Part V
Working to Wellness: Your Life Goals

Part VI
Managing Your Care

Overcoming Bipolar Disorder

WHAT IS THIS WORKBOOK, WHO IS IT FOR, AND WHERE DID IT COME FROM?

Welcome to this self-guided workbook, *Overcoming Bipolar Disorder: A Comprehensive Workbook for Managing Your Symptoms and Achieving Your Life Goals.* This book is for individuals who have bipolar disorder (also called manic-depressive disorder). Its purpose is not to cure the disorder, but rather to assist you in living with it, living around it, and living well—in spite of the symptoms of this condition. You have the ability to live well with bipolar disorder, and our aim is to help you to discover and manage your symptoms so that you can achieve what you want from life. Family members and concerned health care providers will also find valuable information and strategies here.

Where did this workbook come from? Our writing team has decades of experience researching, teaching other care providers, and working with people who have bipolar disorder. Much of our work has focused on helping individuals with this condition to help themselves. As care providers, we believe that the individuals with the condition—patients, or clients, in clinical talk—are an incredibly valuable resource. Yet curiously, the client's potential power in combating symptoms of bipolar disorder is often overlooked by care providers … and perhaps sometimes even by you as a client and people important to you as well.

In the busy world of health care, care providers can forget to include the person who has bipolar disorder as a partner in care. But education and skills training can help prepare people with many different types of health conditions to participate fully in their care. Realizing this, two of us, Linda McBride and Mark Bauer, began to develop a program in the early 1990s to help unlock the potential for people with bipolar disorder to be partners in their own care. Others joined us, and we began a series of educational groups called the Life Goals Program. These groups are led by therapists, and the program is now used in the United States and several other countries around the world. The therapist's guide (Bauer and McBride 2003) has been published. But not everyone has access to the therapist-led Life Goals Program since, as we write this, the program is mainly available as part of certain research programs.

So we thought it would be useful to distill the principles of the Life Goals approach into a workbook that could be used by people with bipolar disorder who can't participate in a Life Goals group. This workbook has been written to do something about that "education gap." By "education" here we do not mean just giving out information, but also customizing learning to each individual's personal experience with bipolar disorder … and then helping each person to develop the skills to do something about it. This kind of education is less like a lecture and more like a hands-on workshop—a practical, step-by-step approach by which you develop specific, personalized knowledge and skills to live a more satisfying life with bipolar disorder. This is often referred to as a *self-management* approach, which is an important part of bipolar disorder management. We will outline how this workbook supports this task in a moment. But first, here's a word about the orientation and the assumptions that support this work.

SOME KEY RESEARCH FINDINGS THAT SUPPORT THIS WORKBOOK

Several key research findings, gleaned from a variety of sources and many decades of research, form the foundation on which this workbook is constructed. These research findings derive from many studies, and we will discuss the specifics in more detail later. But for now, think of these as the evidence-based principles that are the basis of this workbook. We briefly list these key findings here and suggest what they might mean to you as an individual as you use this workbook:

▶ *Symptoms in bipolar disorder come and go, but overall, it tends to be a long-term condition.* This means it needs long-term and ongoing management.

▶ *There are biological components to bipolar disorder.* This means that medications are necessary in most cases.

▶ *Bipolar disorder cannot be completely explained by biological factors.* This means that psychological and social factors also need attention.

▶ *Good management can improve outcome.* This includes both good treatment by your care provider and good self-management.

These research findings lead us to two key themes that underlie our work in general and this workbook in particular:

▶ Treating bipolar disorder requires a *bio-psychosocial* (biological, psychological, and social) *approach.* This means that treatment will typically include (1) working with a care provider who prescribes medications *and* (2) using self-management skills to cope with the stress that comes with the condition … and with everyday life. In many cases, formal counseling can help with this second aspect.

▶ *Collaboration* between care providers and the individuals they treat is most likely to be effective in improving outcome. Effective collaboration requires recognizing that each partner has a specific—though different—role to play.

Sometimes we say, "The care provider is the professional expert, and the individual is the values expert." Put another way, we mean, "The care provider is the expert in bipolar disorder in general, and you are the expert in your specific experience with it."

So the goal of this workbook is to help you understand your specific pattern of bipolar disorder from a bio-psychosocial perspective and—most importantly—to help you to develop as an active and effective partner in managing it. Even if you are not currently in treatment—and this is the case for many people with bipolar disorder—this workbook should help you move toward a greater understanding of and more effective coping with the impact of this condition, and it should help you with decisions about whether to seek treatment. The workbook is *not*, however, a substitute for treatment by a clinical expert—rather, it *enhances* clinical treatment.

"Working *through*" is really a key perspective to keep in mind as you read this workbook. True, managing any ongoing condition is work—you already know this well. But the idea is really to work through to "the other side" of bipolar disorder—to your own life's potential. The goal is to get on with your life's work, whatever that life's work may be, despite having this condition. And this workbook aims to help you start getting back to, and keep on working toward, your personal goals, however you define your life's ambitions. Whether we are paid or unpaid, retired, or disabled, we all have lifework to do. Bipolar disorder shouldn't stand in your way.

HOW TO USE THIS WORKBOOK

This workbook is made up of a series of modules. Each module contains information on a specific aspect of bipolar disorder. Most importantly, the modules contain a series of exercises. These exercises take the general information presented, help you apply it to your own situation, and then help you develop or improve skills in managing that aspect of the condition. The pattern looks like this:

General information → Information on your own situation → Skills you can use

If there are people close to you—for example, a friend, family member, or care provider—who you'd like to involve in this learning process in points along the way, feel free to do so. In fact, at certain points in the workbook, we'll suggest you do exactly that. You may learn some surprising things about yourself—and those close to you will certainly learn some valuable things about you.

Each module, or portion of a module, is designed to be read or worked through in manageable time blocks. The full introductory modules (1–7) are about thirty to sixty minutes long and the remaining modules contain exercises for you to work on and may take about fifteen minutes to complete. This means that this workbook can be fit into the spare moments of a busy schedule or used even at times when patience and concentration are at a low point. As you read the modules and complete the exercises, you may develop new insights into signs, symptoms, or issues important to you. We suggest that you update the profiles and lists in the exercises whenever you discover something to add.

The modules are organized into six parts. Modules 1–7 in part I, Bipolar Disorder Basics, are a bit longer on information and shorter on exercises than the other modules. This is because it is helpful to start with some general information about bipolar disorder. We have taken a huge amount of research data in this quickly advancing field and distilled it down to a series of key topics that we present in everyday language. Not everything known about bipolar disorder is covered here, but there are many readily available resources in print and on the Web for more information (see appendix A, Self-Help Resources).

It is important to keep one key perspective in mind as you read the information in these modules. All the research conclusions are *general* conclusions, or conclusions about bipolar disorder *on average*. Some of it may seem familiar to you; some of it will not. None of it necessarily applies to your specific situation. For instance, it is true that sometimes people with bipolar disorder lose jobs or families or have problems with substance use or even attempt suicide. If this sounds familiar to you, we think there is some value in knowing you are not the only one. *But this does not mean that this will happen to you, or if it has happened to you, that you can't deal with it—the fact that you have read this far means that at least part of you believes you can manage this condition and manage your life despite having this condition.*

In part II, modules 8–15 deal with managing—working through—symptoms of mania, and in part III, modules 16–25 deal similarly with depression. What are these symptoms like in general? What are your personal symptoms? Are there stresses—*triggers*—that you can identify and manage? How do you cope with symptoms when they are there? In these modules, we also deal with a variety of "unwanted co-travelers": substance use, psychosis, anger or irritability, anxiety, and suicidality. Somewhat arbitrarily, we chose to deal with the first three co-travelers in the mania modules and the last two in the depression modules. In reality, any of these conditions can occur at any time during the course of bipolar disorder.

In part IV, modules 26–29 focus on physical health and wellness. A healthy lifestyle is critical for all of us. We all know that paying attention to diet, exercise, sleep, and the like can sometimes be a challenge. We also know that having to deal with bipolar disorder can make paying attention to your health even more of a challenge at times—but the payoff can be great in helping you live the life you want.

Module 30 (part V) is a fairly large module designed to help you focus and work on your life's goals and to troubleshoot roadblocks. No one's life goal is to have bipolar disorder, and no one's life goal is to "live with" bipolar disorder. Rather, the condition gets people off track from their real life goals, which, as Freud pointed out long ago, basically come down to "love and work"—whatever loving and working are for you personally.

Finally, module 31 (part VI) recognizes that people with bipolar disorder are typically working with one or more care providers, one of whom usually prescribes medication. This part, Managing Your Care, also recognizes that this relationship with your care provider does not often come naturally and that some pointers can be helpful.

Three appendices provide additional information that may be helpful. Appendix A offers additional Web-based resources about bipolar disorder, ranging from the straightforward to the scientifically technical. Appendix B provides a listing of common medications used for bipolar disorder because wading through the swamp of generic and brand names can be difficult, despite the best efforts of your care provider or pharmacist to explain them to you. Appendix C offers a guide for clinicians that shows how the workbook modules can be adapted for use in individual treatment sessions in Life Goals or other group formats.

We recall the wisdom from several cultural traditions: "Every journey begins with a single step"— or a single module ... We wish you the best on your journey!

## PART I

Bipolar Disorder Basics

Module 1:
What Is Bipolar Disorder?

In this module, you will become familiar with the symptoms and course of bipolar disorder in general and have the opportunity to do a diagnostic screening questionnaire for the condition.

UNDERSTANDING BIPOLAR DISORDER

There are no laboratory tests, no brain scans, and no paper-and-pencil tests that can tell you if you have bipolar disorder. Rather, the diagnosis is made by an experienced clinical provider who takes a careful history and makes interview observations. And it's not just a matter of opinion. The rules of diagnosis are laid out in two manuals, which are in fairly close agreement: the *Diagnostic and Statistical Manual of Mental Disorders* (DSM-IV; American Psychiatric Association 2000) and the *International Classification of Diseases* (ICD; World Health Organization 1994).

Most people have at least a general idea that bipolar disorder has something to do with moods going up and down. But normal moods go up and down in response to the things that happen in everyday life. What is the difference? In bipolar disorder, moods go beyond the ups and downs that come with everyday life.

Depressive Symptoms

The *downs* consist of sad or blue moods, sometimes with a sense that things are bad and will never get better:

▶ Often people stop feeling pleasure in their usual activities; become unrealistically pessimistic, hopeless, or guilty; or even think about ending their lives.

▶ Sometimes there are physical changes as well, including inability to sleep and loss of appetite or eating too much.

Manic and Hypomanic Symptoms

The *ups* are more variable:

▶ Many times the up moods in bipolar disorder are happy and optimistic.

▶ Other times they can make people feel irritable.

▶ Often the main feeling is one of being "speedy" or "racing"—as though a person has too much energy and cannot turn his or her motor off. Some say that it feels like having too much caffeine or taking stimulants.

▶ People's thoughts or words can race so quickly that they can hardly keep up with them.

▶ In some cases, people with manic symptoms will feel they are normal but can't understand why the world around them is going so slowly or why people are constantly telling them to slow down.

▶ Often they have so much energy that they don't need to sleep.

▶ People sometimes become unrealistically confident or optimistic—as some people would say, "too full of themselves."

▶ Being super optimistic and super energetic, or just having energy to burn, they may take on more projects and responsibilities than they can carry off.

▶ Sometimes they spend too much money or get into trouble with risky investments or gambling.

▶ Sometimes they take social risks, like getting involved romantically or sexually when they wouldn't ordinarily.

Note that, while people with depression will almost universally feel that "something is wrong here," this is not always the case when people have manic symptoms. This is not surprising since many of the symptoms above can actually be pleasurable (at least in moderate doses), and people can sometimes be more productive or at least feel that they are. This is what is meant when it is said that sometimes people with manic symptoms lack insight. However, most who are experienced self-managers of their condition know when symptoms are getting out of hand, and part of the focus of modules 8–15 is to work on refining insight into these symptoms.

Mania is diagnosed when these symptoms are so crippling that people can't fulfill almost any of their usual roles in life or if symptoms are so severe as to require hospitalization or, in a small proportion of individuals, if they have what is called *psychosis* (for example, hearing voices, having visions, or holding false beliefs, which will be discussed in modules 6 and 13).

In *hypomania*, the same symptoms can occur as in mania. Hypomania is by definition not as severe as mania but still can cause many difficulties, as we shall see. If manic symptoms require a person to be hospitalized or if they are accompanied by psychosis or have caused very severe problems in someone's life, these periods are considered mania rather than hypomania.

BIPOLAR EPISODES

Periods of manic or depressive symptoms are called *episodes*, and they typically last for several weeks but can sometimes last months or sometimes only a couple of days. According to the *DSM* and *ICD* definitions, depressive episodes have to last for at least two weeks, manic episodes last for at least one week, and hypomanic episodes last for at least four days. However, some manic or depressive episodes last much longer, and some shorter episodes can be crippling as well. Depressive periods tend to be more common, and last longer, than manic or hypomanic episodes.

Historically, it was thought that people with bipolar disorder have manic or depressive episodes that come and go. Those episodes were believed to have beginnings, middles, and endings with essentially normal periods in between episodes (Kraepelin 1899, 1989). We now know that many people with this condition have symptoms that go on for long periods of time.

Heather's Story

Heather had graduated from college and had started working as a financial analyst in a large firm. She was admired for her hard work and long hours, as well as for her ability to get along with others. During her first year at the firm, however, she experienced a severe depressive episode and missed two weeks of work (telling her coworkers and boss that she had an intestinal parasite). She recovered and returned to work without incident but found work a burden for weeks after the episode. Eventually, she returned to her normal mood. However, the next year, while on a business trip, she began to work around the clock in her hotel room. When she didn't emerge for scheduled meetings, her coworkers came to her room and found reams of paper on which she had word processed what seemed to be a very long novel. She was disheveled, with speech so rapid that she was difficult to understand, and jubilant but for reasons no one around her could quite understand. She had great plans, she gushed, to write "a new War and Peace for the twenty-first century" even though she had never written fiction before. After long discussions with her colleagues and friends, she agreed to be hospitalized and received a diagnosis of a manic episode.

As Heather's experience indicates, manic episodes can occur in the lives of high-functioning individuals, sometimes seeming to come on out of the blue. Heather's usual habits and priorities were disrupted by her manic symptoms, which puzzled her colleagues and friends.

Mixed Episodes and Dysphoric Mania

It would be easier if this condition sorted itself neatly into separate, clear manic or hypomanic episodes and depressive episodes (like the name "bipolar" implies). However, manic and depressive symptoms can appear together, and if someone meets criteria for both a depressive and a manic episode at the same time, clinicians will sometimes speak of *mixed episodes*. Researchers and clinicians also speak of *dysphoric* (unhappy or miserable) mania or hypomania, when there is high energy but the mood is not jubilant or optimistic, but rather irritable or even depressed (McElroy et al. 1992). Some research shows that this mixing of symptoms is very common, perhaps more common than pure mania or hypomania (Bauer et al. 2005).

Bipolar Types

There are two types of bipolar disorder. People who have manic periods are considered to have *bipolar disorder type I*. Those who have hypomanic periods, the less severe type of episodes, are considered to have *bipolar disorder type II*. However, in both type I and type II, the periods of depression are equally severe, and people can have as difficult a time with type II as with type I disorder.

IS BIPOLAR DISORDER THE ONLY MOOD DISORDER?

It can help, when trying to understand bipolar disorder, to see how it fits in with the other mood disorders, including major depression, dysthymia, and cyclothymia. In *major depressive disorder* (sometimes called *unipolar depression*), the depressive episodes are indistinguishable from those of bipolar disorder; the difference is that a person with major depressive disorder has never experienced a manic or hypomanic episode. In *dysthymia* (dysthymic disorder), the depression is lower grade but chronic, lasting at least two years. In *cyclothymia* (cyclothymic disorder), the manic and depressive mood swings are typically milder and more brief than in bipolar disorder, but they can still be disabling. In fact, often it's the *inconsistency* rather than the severity of the mood swings that causes the problems in the lives of individuals with cyclothymia.

Occasionally, clinicians and researchers will use the phrase "not otherwise specified," or "NOS," or you will see this on a bill or insurance statement. The phrase "bipolar or depressive disorder NOS" indicates that many of the features of these conditions are present, but a conclusive diagnosis cannot yet be made.

It can sometimes be daunting to keep all these diagnostic terms and conditions straight. We have found it useful to chart these out in a "building blocks" approach: think of the disorder diagnosis as being built out of episode building blocks, almost in arithmetic fashion; we find that this approach helps clinicians and researchers as well (Bauer 2008a).

The Episode "Building Blocks" Approach to Mood Disorder Diagnosis

Episode + episode ...	... = DSM mood disorder diagnosis
Major depressive episode + nothing else	= Major depressive disorder, single episode
Major depressive episode + major depressive episode	= Major depressive disorder, recurrent
Major depressive episode(s) + manic or mixed episode(s)	= Bipolar disorder type I
Manic or mixed episode(s) + nothing else	= Bipolar disorder type I
Major depressive episode(s) + hypomanic episode(s)	= Bipolar disorder type II
Chronic mild depressive symptoms ≥ two years	= Dysthymic disorder
Chronic fluctuations between mild depressive and hypomanic symptoms ≥ two years	= Cyclothymic disorder

EXERCISE 1.1 Self-Screening for Bipolar Disorder

Do the descriptions of depressive or manic episodes seem familiar to you? If you have received a diagnosis of bipolar disorder, chances are they do. If you are wondering whether or not the diagnosis applies to you, you may want to use one of the screening tools that follow. The two screening tools that have received the most scientific testing are the Mood Disorder Questionnaire (Hirschfeld et al. 2000) and the Bipolar Spectrum Diagnostic Scale (Ghaemi et al. 2005).

Before you complete these tests, note this very important point: *a screening tool is not a diagnostic instrument.* It's a shortcut, giving you immediate feedback to address your curiosity about whether your feelings and behaviors could be related to bipolar disorder and answering the question "Should I consult a care provider for a more formal evaluation?" If you have some concern that you might have bipolar disorder, complete the screening tools and take the results to an experienced care provider for further evaluation.

The Mood Disorders Questionnaire (MDQ)

	YES	NO
1. Has there ever been a period of time when you were not your usual self and ...		
... you felt so good or so hyper that other people thought you were not your normal self or you were so hyper that you got into trouble?		
... you were so irritable that you shouted at people or started fights or arguments?		
... you felt much more self-confident than usual?		
... you got much less sleep than usual and found you didn't really miss it?		
... you were much more talkative or spoke much faster than usual?		
... thoughts raced through your head or you couldn't slow your mind down?		
... you were so easily distracted by things around you that you had trouble concentrating or staying on track?		
... you had much more energy than usual?		
... you were much more active or did many more things than usual?		
... you were much more social or outgoing than usual, for example, you telephoned friends in the middle of the night?		
... you were much more interested in sex than usual?		
... you did things that were unusual for you or that other people might have thought were excessive, foolish, or risky?		
... spending money got you or your family into trouble?		
2. If you answered YES to more than one of the above, have several of these ever happened during the same period of time?	YES	NO
3. How much of a problem did any of these cause you—like being unable to work; having family, money, or legal troubles; getting into arguments or fights? *Please circle one response only.*		

No
problem   Minor
problem   Moderate
problem   Serious
problem

	YES	NO
4. Have any of your blood relatives (i.e., children, siblings, parents, grandparents, aunts, and uncles) had manic-depressive illness or bipolar disorder?	YES	NO
5. Has a health professional ever told you that you have manic-depressive illness or bipolar disorder?	YES	NO

SCORING THE MDQ

If you answered yes to seven or more of the thirteen items in question #1; and yes to question #2); and Moderate or Serious to question number #3, then it is worth consulting a clinician regarding a possible diagnosis of bipolar disorder. If you answered yes to either question #4 or #5, it is worth mentioning that to your clinician as well.

The Bipolar Spectrum Diagnostic Scale (BSDS)

Please read through the entire passage before filling in any blanks.

Some individuals notice that their mood and/or energy levels shift drastically from time to time ____. These individuals notice that, at times, their mood and/or energy level is very low, and at other times, very high ____. During their low phases, these individuals often feel a lack of energy; a need to stay in bed or get extra sleep; and little or no motivation to do things they need to do ____. They often put on weight during these periods ____. During their low phases, these individuals often feel "blue," sad all the time, or depressed ____. Sometimes, during these low phases, they feel hopeless or even suicidal ____. Their ability to function at work or socially is impaired ____. Typically, these low phases last for a few weeks, but sometimes they last only a few days ____. Individuals with this type of pattern may experience a period of "normal" mood in between mood swings, during which their mood and energy level feels "right" and their ability to function is not disturbed ____. They may then notice a marked shift or "switch" in the way they feel ____. Their energy increases above what is normal for them, and they often get many things done they would not ordinarily be able to do ____. Sometimes, during these "high" periods, these individuals feel as if they have too much energy or feel "hyper" ____. Some individuals, during these high periods, may feel irritable, "on edge," or aggressive ____. Some individuals, during these high periods, take on too many activities at once ____. During these high periods, some individuals may spend money in ways that cause them trouble ____. They may be more talkative, outgoing, or sexual during these periods ____. Sometimes, their behavior during these high periods seems strange or annoying to others ____. Sometimes, these individuals get into difficulty with coworkers or the police during these high periods ____. Sometimes they increase their alcohol or non-prescription drug use during these high periods ____.

SCORING THE BSDS

Step 1. Now that you have read this passage, please check one of the following four boxes:

- ☐ This story fits me very well, or almost perfectly (6 points)

- ☐ This story fits me fairly well (4 points)

- ☐ This story fits me to some degree, but not in most respects (2 points)

- ☐ This story doesn't really describe me at all (0 points)

Step 2: Now go back and put a check after each sentence that definitely describes you. Each check is worth one point. Then, total the number of check marks.

Step 3: Add your scores from step 1 and step 2. If the total is 13 or more, then it is worth consulting a clinician regarding a possible diagnosis of bipolar disorder.

Helen's Story

From about the time she entered college, Helen had periods of remarkable energy that would each last several weeks. She was upbeat, energetic, needed to sleep only two to three hours per night, and tended to be the life of the party ... even when there was no party; often her friends would have preferred that she slow down a bit. During these periods, she would run up bills on her charge card that she couldn't afford, join campus clubs she couldn't hope to effectively participate in, and even began two clubs on her own. However, she couldn't follow through on all these obligations, and her basic schoolwork began to suffer as well. These periods were distinctly different from her more usual experience and were almost always followed soon after by crashes into depression with restless sleep, poor appetite, poor concentration, self-accusations, and at one point, a suicide attempt. She was seen in student health services and hospitalized for her depression, where she received a diagnosis of major depressive episode and bipolar disorder type II.

Helen's experience illustrates bipolar disorder type II, that is, she experienced recurring episodes of hypomania and recurring episodes of major depression but never had a manic episode. In her case, the disorder diagnosis is based on her recurrent episodes: hypomanic episode(s) + depressive episode(s) = bipolar disorder type II.

In exercise 1.1 you've used two self-evaluation tools to begin to explore the question of whether you might have bipolar disorder. If you screened positive, it is definitely worth consulting a qualified clinician. Even if you didn't screen positive, but have been sufficiently concerned or at least curious enough to read this far, you may want to consider a diagnostic evaluation. Certainly, if you've been bothered by depressive symptoms, it's worth an assessment. Keep in mind also that a diagnosis of bipolar disorder allows you the opportunity to tap into the knowledge of clinically trained health care providers whose sole professional desire is to help you understand, manage, and live with your symptoms.

EXERCISE 1.2 Self-Exploration: A Bipolar Disorder Diagnosis

Making the correct clinical diagnosis is quite important—just as important as with, say, diabetes or high blood pressure. However, making a diagnosis does not mean that you *become* your diagnosis. Our friends and colleagues at the nationwide Depression and Bipolar Support Alliance (DBSA) quite rightly list among their "Seven Dirty Words" for clinicians any reference to, for example, "the manic in room 23" or "the depressive I saw in the office yesterday," because this would unfairly define a person only in terms of their diagnosis (see appendix 1 for contact information or visit www.dbsalliance.org).

It's important not to neglect the diagnosis, but it's also very important not to give up on your hopes and aspirations for life. A constructive follow-up to the question "What is bipolar disorder, and do I have this condition?" is "How does it fit into my life?" We will explore these matters further in modules 3 and 4 and then again in even greater detail in module 30. For now, take a moment to think about what having this diagnosis means to you in positive and negative ways.

What would having a diagnosis of bipolar disorder mean to you? Would it mean something positive? Why or why not, and how?

_____

_____

_____

_____

_____

Would having a diagnosis of bipolar disorder be something negative for you? Why or why not, and how?

_____

_____

_____

_____

In exercise 1.2 you've begun the important task of exploring what having this diagnosis means to your life—neither ignoring the condition nor surrendering your life or sense of self-worth to it.

WHAT *ISN'T* BIPOLAR DISORDER?

There is one more issue concerning diagnosis, and one that may at first seem strange to find in a workbook on bipolar disorder: what *isn't* bipolar disorder? Bipolar disorder gets a great deal of attention and rightly so. It is absolutely certain that bipolar disorder is underdiagnosed and undertreated in the United States, and this is likely in other countries as well (Hirschfeld et al. 2000). However, there is also a lot of attention paid to bipolar disorder in the popular press, and a lot of undesirable behavior gets labeled "bipolar" when it may not be. In some circles, it may even be "in" to think of yourself as having bipolar disorder.

John's Story

On Monday morning, John came into the office for his scheduled appointment. He was a big, hulking young man with ample artistic skill who was enrolled in a local art school. He also had severe bipolar disorder and had been hospitalized several times. His favored artistic medium was oil paint, and his abstract, paint-splashed canvases had received positive reviews at a recent show. But this morning he was furious. "I was at a gallery party on Saturday," he fumed. "And it was full of all these artists yammering on: 'I'm bipolar' or 'I must be manic-depressive' or bipolar this or manic-depressive that. Well, damn it, I really am bipolar!"

John knew what it meant to have bipolar disorder, and he'd paid the price. He didn't appreciate his struggle being trivialized by having the diagnosis applied willy-nilly. This type of fuzzy thinking makes it harder for individuals, and for society, to accept and understand such serious conditions and to focus on the need for their treatment.

Another challenge facing care providers, individuals with this condition, and even those just trying to understand what's written about in the popular press as "bipolar disorder" is that there are some true diagnostic dilemmas that arise when trying to identify bipolar disorder. Here are a few:

> ▶ *Impulsive behavior*, especially if it seems to be a long-term pattern, can be part of many different disorders ranging from attention-deficit/hyperactivity disorder (ADHD) to borderline personality disorder to criminality.

> ▶ *Substance use* can mimic the symptoms of mania, and people can get depressed when they use substances such as alcohol, street drugs, or prescription or over-the-counter medications (there will be more on this issue in module 12).

> ▶ Individuals with bipolar disorder often have other kinds of symptoms as well, such as *anxiety* or *psychosis* (there'll be more on these in module 13 and 21).

> ▶ *High energy* can be a blessing and is not necessarily a problem. The issue is not so much whether this or that symptom is due to mania as much as how it helps or gets in the way of your life's work and goals.

So things can get a bit complicated—and that's why an experienced care provider is needed to make the diagnosis.

WHAT'S NEXT?

Now that you have at least a sense of what is, and isn't, bipolar disorder, we will review in the next module the current scientific understanding of what biological, psychological, and social factors may be responsible for manic and depressive symptoms.

Module 2:
Some Science

In this module, you will become familiar with a bit of the science behind our understanding of bipolar disorder (including biological, psychological, and social factors), as well as why bipolar disorder is a condition that affects our thoughts, feelings, and behaviors.

A BIO-PSYCHOSOCIAL CONDITION

Having some scientific information about bipolar disorder can help you understand the condition and its treatment. It can be particularly helpful when you're trying to figure out why your care provider is recommending something or why this workbook makes some of the suggestions that it does.

As far back as the time of the ancient Greeks, Western civilization has ping-ponged back and forth in its view of mental illnesses. Some scholars were convinced that mental illnesses were purely biological. Others were equally convinced that such illnesses could be understood in purely psychological or social terms. Astute care providers and scientists have come to view bipolar disorder as a complex combination of biological, psychological, and social factors—that is, a *bio-psychosocial* illness.

A Psychoanalyst Speaks

The noted psychoanalyst Otto Fenichel, an astute care provider, wrote at length about mania from a purely psychological—psychoanalytic—point of view. He proposed that in depression, symptoms were caused by a battering superego (like one's conscience) punishing the self, while "the triumphant character of mania arises from the release of energy hitherto bound in the depressive struggle and now seeking discharge" (Fenichel 1945, 408). That's heavy reading, even for psychoanalysts. However, even though he was writing in the 1940s, long before the advent of modern biological studies and treatments, he added, "yet it is impossible to get rid of the impression that additional purely biological factors are involved" (Fenichel 1945, 411).

This module does not provide a comprehensive scientific review, as can be found in some comprehensive references (Goodwin and Jamison 2007; Bauer 2008a). The resources listed in appendix 1 provide a variety of sources at different levels of complexity. But this module should get you started with some basic information to help you, out there where the rubber meets the road.

HOW DOES BIOLOGY HELP US TO UNDERSTAND BIPOLAR DISORDER?

Perhaps the most important event in the study of bipolar disorder was the discovery that a simple chemical compound, lithium, could treat both manic and depressive symptoms in many individuals. This opened the way for an avalanche of biological treatments for the illness. To this day, the study of *psychopharmacological treatment* (that is, medication) for bipolar disorder remains one of the fastest growing areas of psychiatric research.

The discovery of lithium as an effective treatment for bipolar disorder also stimulated tremendous effort in the search for a biological basis of bipolar disorder. The logic was that if chemical compounds could treat bipolar disorder, then the condition must have a biological cause or at least a biological component. And over the past forty years, a massive amount of work has been done searching for the disorder's anatomical, chemical, and genetic basis. As mentioned above, this module cannot, of course, be a comprehensive review of the science of bipolar disorder. Several detailed, comprehensive references are available for more in-depth reading for clinicians and researchers (Akiskal and Tohen 2006; Aubry, Ferrero, and Schaad 2007; Goodwin and Jamison 2007; Bauer 2008a) and for people who have bipolar disorder (e.g., White and Preston 2009). The purpose of this module is to give you a basic overview so that you can more easily understand the types of topics and language that may come up as you talk with your care provider.

Brain Anatomy and Bipolar Disorder

The brain is made up of billions of cells called *neurons*, and each neuron contains chemical substances known as *neurotransmitters*. The brain appears not to be a single organ, like the lung or the liver, but rather a group of interconnected organs working together. Although we do not know the "location" of bipolar disorder—and, in fact, there is likely more than one single location for it in the brain—most of the scientific effort focuses on an area called the *limbic system*, which appears to regulate emotion. The limbic system is just one section of the brain, and it is interconnected with other parts of the brain. Additional research has focused on the *prefrontal cortex*, which is involved in both information processing and regulation of emotion, and on the *hippocampus*, which is involved in learning and memory.

A variety of imaging tools are used for research on these and other areas of the brain; sometimes these are used in clinical care as well. The following box provides a brief summary.

A Field Guide to Brain Imaging: Terms You May Encounter

Structural imaging tools	Functional imaging tools
Purpose: To investigate brain structure	*Purpose:* To investigate brain function
Use: In both clinical care and research	*Use:* Currently, mainly in research
Examples: Computerized axial tomography (CT scan), magnetic resonance imaging (MRI)	*Examples:* Single photon emission tomography (SPECT), positron emission tomography (PET), functional MRI, magnetic resonance spectroscopy (MRS)

Brain Chemistry and Bipolar Disorder

Although no one has yet identified a "home" in the brain for bipolar disorder, we do know that certain chemicals that are found throughout the brain may have something to do with this condition. You may have heard of these chemicals, which, we mentioned above, are called neurotransmitters: norepinephrine, serotonin, dopamine, and the like. These neurotransmitters provide the mechanism by which individual neurons communicate with one another, and research indicates that neuron-to-neuron communication by neurotransmitters is in some way disrupted in bipolar disorder (this is what clinicians and others are typically referring to when they talk about a "chemical imbalance").

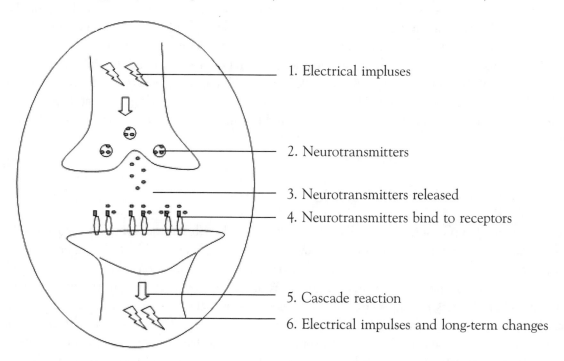

1. Electrical impluses

2. Neurotransmitters

3. Neurotransmitters released
4. Neurotransmitters bind to receptors

5. Cascade reaction

6. Electrical impulses and long-term changes

Figure 2.1: Communication between two neurons (Adam Morganlander. 2008. Reproduced with the permission of Springer Publishing Company, LLC, New York, NY 10036.)

Figure 2.1 provides a schematic of two neurons and how they communicate. Normal neuron communication is fairly well worked out scientifically. The focus in current exploration is on what specific steps in communication are disrupted in bipolar disorder and how the various medications do their work. Here are the steps in neuron-to-neuron communication:

1. Electrical impulses travel down the neuron to trigger neurotransmitter release into the space between nerve cells of the brain (the *synapse*). This then signals the next neuron in a particular pathway. A variety of factors may affect how this electrical impulse travels or how it impacts neurotransmitter release.

2. Neurotransmitters are stored in the nerve cells and may be abnormal in bipolar disorder. These neurotransmitters are actually chemical substances—serotonin, epinephrine, and dopamine. We do know that some medications useful in managing bipolar disorder can affect the level of the supplies of these chemicals.

3. Neurotransmitters are released into the synapse between the neurons. We also know that some medications useful in managing bipolar disorder affect how much neurotransmitter is released by the electrical impulses and how long it stays in the synapse.

4. Neurotransmitters bind to the target neuron on *receptors*. We know that some medications useful in managing bipolar disorder can affect how easily neurotransmitters bind to these receptors.

5. Within the target neuron, when its receptors are stimulated by neurotransmitter binding, a variety of chemical reactions occur involving what are called *second messengers*. These chemical compounds create a *cascade reaction* that then stimulates the production of electrical impulses that carry on the chain of neuron-to-neuron communication. A number of medications useful in managing bipolar disorder affect various steps in the second messenger cascades.

6. In addition, these second messenger cascades cause a variety of long-term changes in the target neuron, such as remodeling of the neuron and synapse by turning on and off genes on the chromosomes (DNA). This area of research, called *molecular neurobiology*, is one of the hottest areas of science and will grow quickly now that all of the human chromosomes have been mapped by the Human Genome Project (http://genomics .energy.gov/).

Genetics and Bipolar Disorder

Genetic research initially focused on identifying a single gene responsible for bipolar disorder, as had been found for other illnesses, like Huntington's disease. More recently, though, researchers began looking for multiple genes with smaller effects that work together and interact with the environment as well. Importantly, though, genetics provides the most powerful information that bipolar disorder is not simply genetic: various studies have shown that among identical twins, who share 100 percent identical genes, only about 60 to 70 percent will match for developing bipolar disorder (Barondes 1998). Thus, genetics is not destiny!

Overall, bipolar disorder does not appear inclined to give up its biological secrets anytime soon. Nonetheless, we know more with each passing month, and most importantly, we continue to develop new treatments.

EXERCISE 2.1 Exploring the Biology of Bipolar Disorder

Even though we don't have a full understanding of the biology of bipolar disorder, it will be helpful for you as an astute participant in your own health care to have a sense of how to sort through the information that is available. For this exercise, close the workbook and go out to find some biological information about bipolar disorder or its treatment. You can "scale up" or "scale down" the complexity of this search depending on your scientific savvy.

So here's the task: You've probably wondered about one or another aspect of the biology of bipolar disorder, maybe because of things you've heard from your care provider, friends, or the news media, or even in this module. Use the outline below to do a bit of research and come up with some questions to ask your care provider. For summaries of recent scientific articles, consult the National Library of Medicine (www.ncbi.nlm.nih.gov/Literature/) or one of the references in the References section. You can search the Web, but beware: not all Web information is accurate! If science is not your thing, try exploring one of the layperson's reputable online resources in appendix A, such as the Depression and Bipolar Support Alliance (www.dbsalliance.org) and the National Institute of Mental Health (NIMH) at http://www.nimh.nih.gov/health/publications/bipolar-disorder/complete-publication.shtml.

What source(s) did you explore?

_____

_____

What did you learn that was new to you?

_____

_____

What was the most striking or puzzling or confusing thing you learned?

_____

_____

Did you find any areas of conflicting information, and if so what were they? (Welcome to the world of science!)

_____

_____

What is one thing you will ask your provider about the next time you see him or her?

_____

_____

After you've asked your care provider about this, try to remember to come back to this page and record his or her response here:

_____

_____

Clinicians and researchers talk about becoming lifelong learners. This should be true of individuals in treatment as well, and you're now on your way! *Note:* If your care provider's response wasn't helpful or wasn't what you wanted, you may be particularly interested in module 31 of this workbook, Managing Your Care.

HOW DOES PSYCHOLOGY HELP US TO UNDERSTAND BIPOLAR DISORDER?

A variety of psychological theories have been advanced to explain bipolar disorder. For instance, you were introduced to a snippet of 1940s psychoanalytic thinking from Dr. Fenichel about the condition. More recent psychological research has focused less on causes of the disorder and more on factors that affect its course.

In addition to psychoanalytic theories, several other approaches to understanding bipolar disorder have been advanced. Most of this theorizing is based on research in depression that has been extended to bipolar disorder. This is because the depressive symptoms in bipolar disorder and unipolar depression are the same. Unfortunately, no clear psychological theory of mania has yet emerged. Nonetheless, each of these theories has contributed a psychological method to the treatment of bipolar disorder. So, not surprisingly, elements of each of these therapies have found their way into this workbook:

> ▶ *Cognitive theory* suggests that people have unrealistically negative beliefs about themselves and their world. These beliefs or thoughts in turn leave them prone to depression (Basco and Rush 2007).

23

▶ *Behavior theory* views depression as a mental giving up when goals cannot be reached (Lewinsohn 1974).

▶ *Interpersonal theory* proposes that depression develops most often in the context of adverse events, particularly loss or conflict related to important relationships (Frank 2007).

As you can probably imagine, no single psychological theory has a lock on bipolar disorder. But if you look at all the medications that work in managing bipolar disorder, you'll find that the same is true for biology as well!

HOW DO SOCIAL FACTORS LIKE STRESS HELP US TO UNDERSTAND BIPOLAR DISORDER?

The research on social factors in bipolar disorder relates mainly to how stresses affect the course of the illness—specifically, the number and severity of episodes (Johnson 2005). It appears that stresses are of two types.

▶ *Physical stress* for some people can trigger or worsen episodes. This can be anything from having the flu to undergoing surgery to sleep deprivation to seasonal changes to medications.

▶ *Social stress* can trigger or worsen episodes for most people. This can mean "good stress" (like getting a new job or taking a trip) as well as "bad stress" (like losing a job or fighting with a significant other). Interestingly, while most people can readily identify negative or threatening stresses, they're not aware that sometimes even positive stresses (successes at work or school or new relationships, for example) can be associated with the onset of symptoms.

EXERCISE 2.2 Stress and Bipolar Symptoms

As with the psychological concerns in exercise 2.2, this exercise is meant just as a teaser for what comes later. You'll work more on the topic of stress and symptoms later, particularly in modules 9 and 17, which work on identifying triggers to mood symptoms.

For now, list at least one physical stressor and one social stressor that seem to have caused a manic or depressive episode. In the first column, write an "M" if the stress caused manic symptoms and a "D" if it caused depressive symptoms. Also, for the social stress, recall that even good things (what we have called positive stress) can cause symptoms. After you describe the social stressor, add a "+" for a positive stress and a "−" for a negative stress. Use a separate piece of paper if necessary.

Physical Stressor	M or D	+ or -	Social Stressor	M or D	+ or -

WHAT'S NEXT?

In this module, we've introduced some of the science of bipolar disorder. It's clear that biological factors are very important, but they are far from the whole story. Psychological and social factors are incredibly important. In fact, one of the foundations of our work, and this workbook, is that bipolar disorder happens to *people*—real and complex people with hopes, dreams, aspirations, skills, priorities, and peculiarities that have nothing to do with this condition that has happened to them, and to those around them. In the next two modules, we'll begin to explore these aspects of bipolar disorder and how they affect you as an individual.

Module 3: Working from Your Core Values

> *In this module, you will explore the difference between self and symptoms, and explore bipolar disorder from the perspective of your life's aims and goals. While most workbooks and treatments focus exclusively on the costs and burdens of the condition, we think the entire story is not told unless you also honestly consider whether bipolar disorder has produced any benefits that might be hard to give up.*

BIPOLAR SYMPTOMS AND YOUR LIFE'S WORK

As we mentioned in the introduction, no one's goal in life is to have bipolar disorder. In the introduction, we also made the more radical suggestion that, no matter how disabled someone is with this condition, their core life goal is not to "live with" bipolar disorder. No one wants, really, to be a patient. People want to live full, happy, independent lives.

Freud once said that living well comes down to two basic things: *"Lieben und Arbeiten,"* love and work. Work is not necessarily something you do for pay, and it's not necessarily even volunteer work. It's what you want to create, what you want to make of your life. Certainly it may be something related to a career, but it may also be something related to making a home, a family, a hobby—something that you *do* that makes your life worth living, that makes you feel productive. Love is more about who you *are* rather than what you do—and who you are is almost always who you are in relation to other people. Usually it's family or friends, but in general terms, it may even be less intimate or not very close relationships—with someone who's important to you and to whom you're important.

There is something very personal and intimate about the symptoms of what we have come to call mental conditions, perhaps especially so with symptoms of bipolar disorder, which has enjoyable highs as well as painful lows. Some feel that they've always sensed something was amiss, typically something on the depressive side, and then along the way, they developed manic symptoms. It can sometimes be difficult to stand aside from and look at these symptoms. It's not like looking at blood sugar levels in diabetes; bipolar symptoms can seem like a part of your very self because, as we mentioned, the symptoms affect thoughts, feelings, and behaviors.

In addition, we have worked with enough people with bipolar disorder to have learned that many people have discovered that mild manic symptoms can be helpful and enjoyable, and in fact sometimes people build their lives not just *around* but also making use of this aspect of bipolar disorder. It is rarer for people to find advantages to having depressive symptoms—although there is evidence from the lives of a number of writers and scientists that depression contributed to their worldview and creativity (Bauer 2008b). Would they have traded their depression and their creativity for more stable mood and worldview? In most cases, we will never know. But clearly bipolar disorder can be intertwined with our sense of self, and for some people, sometimes there may be benefits as well as costs.

So a basic question to be asked early on in this workbook is this: what's wrong with having bipolar disorder? And the answer may be nothing … unless it gets in the way of you living your life, doing your life's work, and reaching your goals.

Jane's Story

Jane was always a kid on the go and a high performer in the classroom and in sports. She had been a national-class skier, and although she was finishing nursing school, she continued to be an avid amateur competitor. She got by on four hours of sleep a night, was passionate about everything she took up, and wherever she went seemed to fill the room with her presence. She worked eighty hours per week, held a variety of supervisory nursing positions, and was a regional ski champ in her age bracket. She experienced several episodes of depression but by and large was a high-energy and somewhat imposing person. She called her care provider after her driver's license was suspended for reckless driving and as her third marriage was dissolving because of an extramarital affair she had impulsively begun. Her care provider suspected bipolar disorder type II, and with information from additional history taking, made the diagnosis. Jane strongly resisted the diagnosis, saying repeatedly, "This is just me. This is just who I am. If it weren't for those depressions, I'd be just fine." The work in treatment revolved around determining which high-energy feelings and behaviors were helpful and which ones were harmful to her overall life goals, values, and priorities. Counseling and medications were geared toward reducing the latter while preserving the former.

For Jane, the first issue at hand, prior to treatment choice, was for both her and her care provider to come to terms with how these symptoms fit into Jane's life and her self-concept. Not unlike some other people with bipolar disorder, Jane hated to give up what seemed to her to be adaptive aspects of the condition even though they often disrupted areas of her life that were important to her.

EXERCISE 3.1 A Quick Profile: Symptoms in Your Life

For some people, bipolar disorder comes out of the blue sometime in their adult life and hits them like a smack in the face. For others, it seems always to have been there. For still others, it seems to have crept into their lives quietly, insidiously, and taken over. Also, for some people, manic and depressive symptoms come and go, while for others the symptoms seem always to be there in the background. It can be helpful to recognize these or other patterns over your lifetime, since this can help you disentangle your symptoms from your sense of self, of yourself as an individual with hopes, dreams, aspirations, skills, priorities, and peculiarities that have nothing to do with this condition.

When did you first notice mood symptoms, and how did you notice them? How about symptoms of bipolar disorder specifically?

_____

_____

_____

What has been the pattern of symptoms over your life? Have they been episodic (coming and going), chronic (always there, at least somewhat), or have they come and gone but left you so devastated that it's been hard to put your life back on track, or has there been some other pattern?

_____

_____

_____

What aspects of the symptoms have bothered you the most?

_____

_____

_____

Were there some symptoms that you enjoyed experiencing?

_____

_____

_____

How has bipolar disorder affected your day-to-day life?

_____

_____

_____

Are there any parts of your life that you have given up on because of having bipolar symptoms? How did it happen that you gave up on them?

_____

_____

_____

In this exercise, you have developed a map of how bipolar disorder has unfolded over the course of your life While most of this workbook is focused on moving forward, this exercise helps to answer the question "How did I end up where I am today?" It helps to have this perspective in mind as we move forward to explore how bipolar disorder affects you in your day-to-day life, and how it affects your family, friends, coworkers—and, not least, your sense of self.

COSTS AND BENEFITS OF BIPOLAR DISORDER

An aspect of how bipolar disorder affects your sense of self is asking, honestly, whether there have been any benefits to having the condition. This may seem strange to you if you have had nothing but trouble from the condition, and certainly examining the problems is the traditional clinical perspective taught in medical school and other clinical training programs. However, for some people we have worked with, there have been benefits, and some will at times find themselves thinking that they really don't want or need treatment. Fair enough: Let's look at this important issue in an evenhanded manner.

The traditional perspective is that care providers are trained to diagnose illness and to "fix" it and that people go to them to get their illnesses "fixed." There's nothing necessarily wrong with that. But it's not the whole story, and sometimes having the mind-set of "the fixer" and "the fixed" can actually get in the way. Specifically, when the going gets tough, and it often does in living with bipolar disorder, you need to come back again and again to why _you_ are running this race in the first place. _You_ have to have a reason to try to manage the condition, and over the long haul, it's got to be more than just "My doctor says I should" or "My family wants me to" or even "It's just the right thing to do." The motivation has to come from you.

Perhaps a tennis match provides the best comparison: You are playing against this condition. Your care provider is like a coach; he or she isn't playing the match but does have professional skills and knowledge that can help you to win the match. This is what we meant when we said in the introduction that the care provider is the professional expert and you are the values expert—the expert in your own personal experience with bipolar disorder.

So, as we said above, managing bipolar disorder comes down to *your* choice, and if it's a real choice, it has to be based on costs and benefits, both. It is not a choice of whether to have bipolar disorder or not. Rather, ask this question: how do the symptoms of bipolar disorder fit into your life? This is the question that we will explore throughout this workbook. The decisions are yours. You are the one who lives with the condition, and you are the one who experiences the treatments. Let's look at how bipolar disorder fits with your life—*your* life in particular.

EXERCISE 3.2 Introducing the Personal Cost-Benefit Analysis

So let's go back and revisit the history described in exercise 3.1 and think of it in a different way. This is the first of several exercises in this workbook that we call a "personal cost-benefit analysis." Almost everything in life has pros and cons, pluses and minuses, advantages and disadvantages, and costs and benefits—and this is certainly true of just about every choice we make. Let's expand on your responses in exercise 3.1 and list the benefits and downsides, if you discovered any. Building on your responses, list some of the pros and cons to having bipolar symptoms. In the first column, please list the benefits to you of having bipolar disorder; list the downsides in the second column.

Bipolar benefits	Bipolar downsides

For most people with bipolar disorder, there are probably some items listed in both columns. What is important at this point is that you assess both the benefits and the costs of bipolar symptoms. Without a *balanced* view of the benefits as well as the costs, an important part of the story of how you make your life choices is missing, and you and your provider need to know and to respect both sides of the coin.

This is not to say you have a choice about whether or not you have bipolar disorder. Rather, the issue is how you decide to manage the condition. For example, you may not have a choice about whether to develop manic symptoms, but once they begin, you have a choice about how to manage them—and this choice is based, consciously or not, on your judgment of the benefits as well as the costs. For Jane, for instance, it was critical to the achievement of her life goals that she and her provider identify what she found beneficial about hypomanic symptoms and determine how to handle these in light of her overall goals. What we are saying is that you have permission to look at both sides and make your life decisions accordingly—after all, these are *your* personal pros and cons, *your* work, *your* love, *your* life. And, more radically, we propose that it is *only* by looking at both sides that you can manage bipolar symptoms over the long haul.

WHAT'S NEXT?

Among the key steps in assessing costs and benefits is looking at the impact of bipolar disorder on all aspects of your life. The next module introduces this process; we will return to how to manage these impacts in some detail in module 30.

Module 4: The Impact of Bipolar Disorder on Your Life

In this module, you will read about the how bipolar disorder can affect the things that make life worth living. First, you will look in some detail at issues of your core values and goals and how they impact your life and your sense of self and self-worth. Then you will switch gears a bit and review how bipolar disorder can affect other aspects that make life worth living: family, friendships, work and school, and hobbies and leisure activities. This more specific look at how bipolar disorder affects those aspects of your life—and what to do about it—is territory that will be covered in later modules.

WHAT MAKES LIFE WORTH LIVING?

In figure 4.1 we list a number of aspects of life that are important to most of us. Think of these as larger and larger circles around you: your family, your friends, work or school, and hobbies or leisure activities.

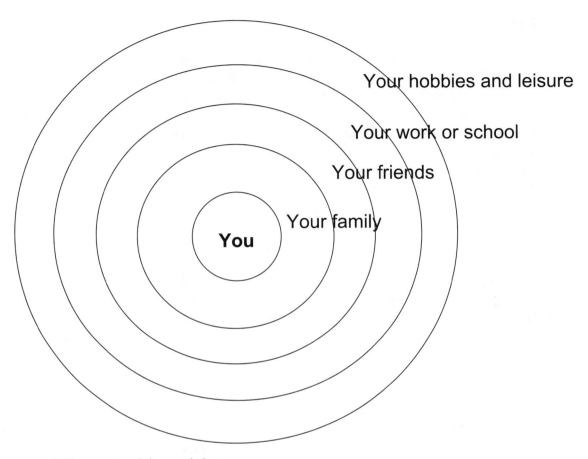

Figure 4.1: What makes life worth living

You may already have found that having bipolar disorder can get in the way of each of these aspects of life, and research on groups of people diagnosed with bipolar disorder certainly shows that's not unusual. However, the research also shows this:

▶ You are not alone in these struggles (though perhaps you've never met anyone else with bipolar disorder).

▶ People with bipolar disorder can live fuller and more gratifying lives by taking care of themselves and by recognizing the impact of their symptoms on relationships with other people. (We will provide a brief overview here and then come back to these areas in later modules of this book.)

A SENSE OF WHO YOU ARE

A sense of who you are, a sense of self, a self-image—all of these things are really at the core of what makes life worth living. When we speak about a sense of self, we mean all those parts of yourself that make you a unique human being: your values, goals, desires, and personal habits. As we mentioned in module 3, having bipolar disorder can scramble your sense of self. If you have difficulty reaching goals because of depression or mania—or for any reason—it is natural to have a tendency to give up. Giving up is different than adjusting your approach or modifying your goals—we all change course all the time in life, sometimes under stress. But giving up on goals—giving up on *having* goals—means cutting off a big part of what makes you who you are.

VALUES AND GOALS

Goals are what make life worth living. These goals are determined by all the things that make us uniquely human—our personalities, our experiences, our inclinations, our desires, and the like. Somewhere along the way, we've developed a set of values and priorities by which we live our lives. We might consider that goals are ends that we strive for (the *what*s in life), while values are the reasons that we have chosen those goals (the *why*s in life).

Sometimes we're consciously aware of these values and goals and sometimes not. But in either case, our sense of who we are and what makes us feel happy is formed by these values and goals. Where these values and goals come from is as unique for each of us as the goals and values themselves. For some of us, values have a spiritual basis. For others, they're rooted in family or culture. Still others seem somehow to have worked out their values with reference to literature or politics or other factors. Sometimes we make a specific choice about goals and values. But often they just kind of sneak up on us, and we find our lives pointed in a particular direction.

In any case, behind it all, our goals and values drive our life choices and make life worth living. But it's easy to get caught up in the day-to-day activities of life and not think about your goals. This is quite relevant to living with bipolar disorder. Your approach to the condition and how you manage it are fundamentally driven by your own specific goals and values—that is, by what you ultimately believe makes your life worth living and makes you a unique human being. And more specifically, when you begin to lose sight of your goals, for whatever reason, you lose sight of your values and your sense of what makes life worth living—that's true of all of us. You can end up feeling something between guilt and emptiness. And this makes it hard to keep on going. This is true for anyone, but for a person living with bipolar disorder, losing sight of goals makes it particularly hard to combat depression and sometimes makes it tough to keep on taking medications day in and day out. What's your reason for getting out of bed in the morning? *Everyone needs a reason.*

EXERCISE 4.1 Goals, Values, and Where They Come From

This exercise will help you begin to explore your goals and values in ways that are relevant to working through bipolar disorder, as we mentioned above. We all have specific goals in life. For some people, it is to make a career, for others, to get through school, to have a happy marriage, to become a champion skateboarder, to paint, or simply to have friends. Goals are your stars to steer by in trying to navigate life with bipolar disorder—in fact, they're both your stars *and* your oars—they give you the willpower to move and they tell you which direction to move in.

Take a moment (or a couple of days) to try to identify some of your major life goals, either now or in the past. What values lie behind them? Where do you think those goals and values came from? When we talk in such general (but important) terms as "goals" and "values," it can be confusing. So it helps to write them down, even in general terms. It is important to bring these things that lurk in the shadows of your daily life out into the spotlight from time to time, to more fully realize what drives your life decisions. Let's consider an example from Jane, whom we met in module 3, and see how her experiences will fit into the table. Then there will be a table for your own work.

So think about your strengths, talents, and deeply rooted interests and look beyond other people's opinions of you (and even your own feelings of doubt) to reach for whatever it is that makes life worth living, that drives your daily decisions. Write down at least one goal you've had—something you've wanted to do in your life. What was the value behind it—the *why*? Why was this goal important? And then ask where this value came from: family, friends, religion, literature, experience, or something else?

Jane's Goals, Values, and Influences

Goal	Value that makes this goal important	What influences in your life shaped this goal and value?
To be an outstanding competitive skier.	*It's important to be the best I can be with the talent I've been given.*	*I suppose a couple influences. I believe God gave me certain talents to use and I'd better use them. And besides, I'm just plain a competitive person!*
To be an excellent nurse.	*Helping people is important to me.*	*Well, I grew up pretty religious and even though I'm not really now, I think still that we're put on this earth to help others. Also, my father was a physical therapist and he liked his job, and I always admired what he did.*

Your Goals, Values, and Influences

Goal	Value that makes this goal important	What influences in your life shaped this goal and value?

So with this exercise you've begun to make explicit some of the most powerful—though subtle—drivers in your life. These will be important to keep in mind as we begin to talk about working through bipolar disorder—that is, as we begin mapping the costs and benefits of the self-management decisions you will make.

Stigma: An Enemy of Values and Goals ... and Self

In the section above, we implied that losing sight of your core values and goals can leave you rudderless, oarless, and without a sense of self or self-worth. This is an appropriate place to introduce another, and sometimes quite subtle, force that sometimes leads people to lose their sense of self, and this is particularly relevant to people living with bipolar disorder: stigma.

Stigma is prejudice, and the type of stigma that we are most concerned with here is prejudice against people with psychiatric symptoms. Stigma is unfortunately still alive even in our modern society.

It makes people want to hide the fact that they have such a condition, even more than they want to hide, say, diabetes or asthma. There's something about bipolar disorder and the like that sometimes seems to frighten people. And if there's something about you that you feel like you have to hide (or maybe *do* have to hide to avoid the stigma), then it's hard to be proud of yourself or even to accept yourself.

To put it briefly and concretely: The stigma of having bipolar disorder leads to rejection by other people because of a group you belong to rather than who you are as an individual; in turn, it can lead to a sense of shame about yourself and often to hurt, depression, and anger. It is a burden that others load onto you. You don't need it, and it doesn't help you live your life according to your own values and goals.

EXERCISE 4.2 Impact of Stigma

Have you experienced stigma from others?

_____

_____

_____

How did it make you feel about yourself and about others? (Describe your thoughts and feelings.)

_____

_____

_____

How did you respond? (Describe your behaviors.)

_____

_____

_____

What, if anything, would you do differently if this came up again?

_____

_____

_____

This exercise may have brought up some painful memories. That's difficult, but that's not the reason to do the exercise: looking forward, you can be more aware of the often subtle encounters you have with stigma and decide how to respond without taking on this burden that you don't need and that isn't yours.

FAMILY MATTERS

Look back at figure 4.1 and its concentric circles. After the self, we come next to family. Perhaps you had bipolar disorder from a very young age. Perhaps you grew up in a family with someone else who had the condition. Perhaps you didn't develop symptoms until adult life, after you already had a spouse or a partner or a family. Whatever your circumstances, bipolar disorder can be hard on families. Some families break up. Although older studies show that more than half of individuals with bipolar disorder have normal family function (Carlson et al. 1974), more recent studies indicate that half to three-quarters of those with the condition have never been married or partnered, or if they have, those marriages or partnerships dissolved (Simon et al. 2004; Bauer et al. 2006). Even in intact marriages and partnerships, there can be daily stress due to manic or depressive symptoms or just due to worrying and waiting for "the other shoe to drop," as spouses of individuals with bipolar disorder sometimes describe it. And sometimes couples end up living in mutual isolation under the same roof. Bipolar disorder can be tough on intimacy.

Remember, though, that we are talking about bipolar disorder on average, and it does not mean that any of this will necessarily happen to you. The point here is that having a family member who has bipolar disorder is difficult for the entire family and this means that it will be important to work on your family and loving relationships.

Jim's Story

Jim and Mary had been married for six years before Jim had his first manic episode, which seemed to come out of the blue. Mary was frightened and then angry. As Jim recovered, more and more of their time together seemed to focus on his bipolar symptoms: Would the symptoms come back? Was he taking his medications? Was this or that great new idea or plan or purchase part of mania or was it the "real" Jim? Jim often felt on the defensive. Weighed down by these preoccupations, their sex life withered away. They underwent a course of family-focused therapy, and both learned more about the disorder. Jim became a better manager of his symptoms, and Mary learned to let her guard down again. At times, they could even joke when Jim came up with one or another of the brainstorms that so attracted Mary to him in the first place: "Lithium level down a bit today, Jim?" Now, nine years after Jim's first episode, they are still married and have three children.

At first their intimacy was threatened by Jim's bipolar symptoms and by Mary's response to them, and by Jim's response to Mary's response (whew!). But with some outside assistance, they were able to better understand bipolar disorder, develop new coping skills, and navigate these challenges to preserve their intimate, loving relationship.

If you're a younger person still living with your family of origin, those relationships are complicated as well—in some ways more complicated. Growing up and growing out into independence takes effort for anyone, and bipolar disorder doesn't make those tasks any easier. We will talk a bit about these issues when we talk about developmental milestones later in this module.

FRIENDS: A CONTINUING SERIES

It is probably no news to you that depression can lead to withdrawal from friends and that mania can cause its own friendship problems. Sometimes in the heat of mania, people will make "friends" they wouldn't ordinarily make. At other times, the drive and expansiveness of mania can put people off. And sometimes it's just the inconsistency that's hard on friendships.

Again, with the warning that this is not necessarily *your* experience or *your* future with bipolar disorder, we know from research studies that the condition can be hard on friendships and social relationships, with somewhat over half of individuals with the condition reporting difficulties in a variety of these aspects of their lives (Goodwin and Jamison 2007).

Maria's Story

Maria was incredibly fun to be around. She was upbeat, cheerful, always interested in her friends and their lives, always committed to this or that project. But Maria also dropped out of sight for long periods of time. Her friends thought they'd offended her or thought she looked down on them because they could never quite keep up with her. Then she'd reappear as if nothing had happened. Some of her friends became wary or dropped away. In fact, Maria was quite ashamed of having bipolar disorder but finally confided in one close friend that she had terribly painful depressive periods and at those times didn't want to see anyone or do anything. Her friend had never suspected this, and Maria's sharing this aspect of her life helped her friend to understand where the inconsistency really came from. They became closer once Maria could safely share this intimate, hidden part of herself, and Maria could begin to call on her friend for support in her difficult depressed periods.

You can see from Maria's experience how bipolar symptoms can subtly drive a wedge between friends and how fear of stigma can play a role in doing this. Sometimes even a single close friend and confidante who knows the real story can be a strong ally and support.

WORKING ON WORKING

Bipolar disorder can be hard on work life. Both depression and manic symptoms can disrupt work relationships and hamper productivity. On the positive side, many people live productive and very accomplished lives despite having bipolar disorder. However, up to three-quarters of individuals with bipolar disorder do not fulfill their work potential, compared to how they were doing prior to the onset of the condition (Harrow et al. 1990; Tohen, Waternaux, and Tsuang 1990).

How, specifically, can bipolar disorder affect work? Figure 4.2 provides a diagram that may help you to recognize patterns in your own experience. Both manic and depressive symptoms present their own, somewhat different challenges.

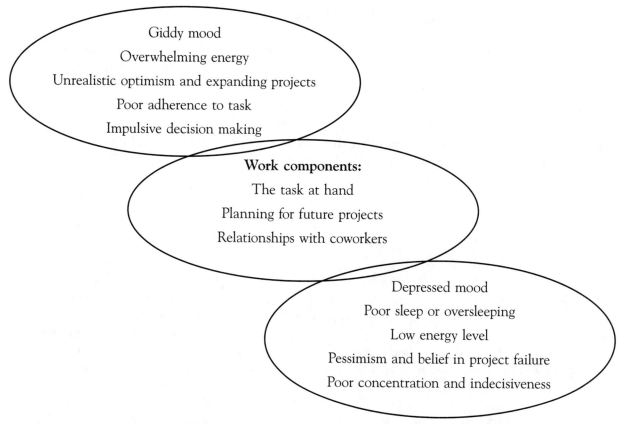

Figure 4.2: Impact of manic and depressive symptoms on work

SCHOOL AND DEVELOPMENTAL MILESTONES

School is considered your work for a particular time in your life (and not necessarily just in youth or young adulthood). Our society is set up to march us through high school and sometimes through college and into a job and a family—those fearsome developmental milestones. Then, life is supposed to calm down (really?). Sometimes people look back at school days and wish for those "easy" times.

But in reality, all the expectations and demands of school can seem like a runaway freight train. And bipolar disorder can sometimes toss sand in the gears, slow things down, and even stop you from heading toward your goals. It's especially important during these dynamic developmental times to keep your goals in mind, even if you have to take a detour or take time out now and then. Both high schools and colleges are beginning to recognize and appreciate the challenges faced by students and families affected by bipolar disorder and are willing to make accommodations. Help is available, and detours don't mean giving up on goals!

> ### *Raul's Story*
>
> Raul was diagnosed with bipolar disorder in his first semester away at college. After a series of incompletes and one failed class, he took the next two semesters off and worked at home. He returned to campus and reenrolled with a reduced course load for his first semester back. He reconnected with some of his old friends and made some new ones. He found himself trying to integrate his own personal experiences with bipolar disorder into his course work and career direction. He decided to major in English and write a thesis on portrayals of mental illness in poetry and began to participate in his college's chapter of Active Minds on Campus, a nationwide association for college students with mental illness, offering support, education, and advocacy (www.activemindsoncampus.org).

HOBBIES, LEISURE, AND RECREATION

A more subtle difficulty that may come with bipolar disorder is that activities that put a little fun in life can fall by the wayside. Maybe depression leads to this. Maybe it's the effort of trying to patch things up after manic episodes. Maybe it's demoralization or financial pressures or just the need to focus exclusively on keeping family and work intact. In any case, somehow hobbies and creative leisure activities can get short shrift, and life's most fun activities can disappear. Life can become narrowly focused and seem like just surviving. But these recreational activities are not fluff—they're just what the word says: re-*creational*. We all need some of these activities to keep our lives well-oiled and to be living at our best.

EXERCISE 4.3 How Does Bipolar Disorder Affect Areas of Your Life?

This is a good point to take a quick census of how bipolar disorder affects your life. This is not meant to be a demoralizing exercise, but rather one that will give you some ideas about where you want to focus your attention as you work through the later modules in this workbook, especially module 30. Skip over the responses that don't apply to you.

Step 1: Using the scale of 0 to 3 listed below, write a number in the first column to indicate the degree to which you feel bipolar disorder affects this aspect of your life.

- ▶ 0 means you're not affected at all.

- ▶ 1 means you're mildly affected.

- ▶ 2 means you're moderately affected.

- ▶ 3 means you're strongly affected.

Step 2: For those marked 1 to 3, write the letters "M" or "D" or both "M" and "D" in the second column to indicate if manic (M) or depressive (D) symptoms cause the impact.

Step 3: In the last column, briefly list the specific impact. You may actually find some positive impacts, and these are worth noting as well.

#	M or D	Life Area	Impact
		Self	
		Loss of sense of purpose or values in life	
		Self-esteem	
		Family	
		Communication at home about duties and responsibilities	
		Communication about how you feel	
		Ability to love family members	
		Ability to feel loved by family	
		Ability to care for your children	
		Ability to care for your older family members	
		Ability to be intimate emotionally with your spouse or partner	
		Friends	
		Ability to trust others	
		Communication about how you feel	
		Ability to be a friend	
		Ability to accept friendship	
		Desire to be with others	

#	M or D	Life Area	Impact
		Work	
		Ability to meet an assigned schedule at work	
		Communication about tasks and projects	
		Communication socially with coworkers	
		On-time completion of specific work assignments or projects	
		Realistic assessment of project quality	
		Realistic project planning	
		Long-range career development	
		School	
		Communication with teachers	
		Communication with fellow students	
		Timely completion of homework assignments or projects	
		Realistic assessment of assignment or project quality	
		Ability to ask for accommodations because of bipolar symptoms if needed	
		Hobbies and leisure	
		"Re-creation" activities	
		Other (specify)	

This exercise gives you a brief introduction to how bipolar disorder has affected your life. It gives you a profile of which areas of your life have been more affected by bipolar disorder and which less so. It can serve as a sort of table of contents for your work in module 30, where you can focus your efforts on managing these aspects of your life.

EXERCISE 4.4 How I Beat the Odds

That last exercise might be a logical end for this module, but let's do one more—a surprisingly useful exercise. In the last exercise, you organized a lot of what has probably already been obvious to you (and maybe even some things you've been mentally beating yourself up for as well!). Well, here is a better final exercise for this module: list examples below of how bipolar disorder *didn't* get in the way of these facets of your life; that is, recall and list times or ways that you, and maybe those around you, coped together to "beat the odds."

Self-image: _____

_____

Family: _____

_____

Friends: _____

_____

Work or school: _____

_____

Hobbies and leisure activities: _____

_____

WHAT'S NEXT?

By working your way through this module, you have gotten some idea of how bipolar disorder can affect your sense of self, as well as many aspects of your social life. It can also impact your physical health. Those important health issues, which are also tied to your sense of self and self-worth, are introduced in the next module.

Module 5: Your Physical Health

> *In this module, you will become familiar with the ways in which bipolar disorder can affect your physical health. We will focus on four issues that are important to everyone: diet, exercise, tobacco use, and sleep.*

BIPOLAR DISORDER AND PHYSICAL HEALTH

Physical health is important to all of us, both for its own sake and for our sense of well-being and self-esteem. There are many aspects of physical health we could focus on, but we have chosen four: diet, exercise, tobacco use, and sleep. Why did we choose these four? Each is important in its own right, but these factors also represent special challenges for people with bipolar disorder. In modules 26–29, we'll explore specific ways to help you to deal with these challenges.

Healthy Diet

A healthy diet is particularly important for people with bipolar disorder because obesity is common in those who have this condition, with up to 50 percent being overweight or obese (Fagiolini et al. 2005). This is probably partly due to depression, which leads some to have binge-eating problems. In addition, several of the medications used to treat bipolar disorder can cause weight gain (Aubry, Ferrero, and Schaad 2007). It is important to note that these factors can lead to other medical conditions, with the most common being high blood pressure, high cholesterol, and type 2 diabetes, which involves problems controlling blood sugar (Aubry, Ferrero, and Schaad 2007; Bauer 2008a). Constructing a healthy diet will be the focus of module 26.

Exercise

Exercise is also critically important. As you may have experienced, depression can lead to reduced physical activity. Lack of exercise can compound the effects of the diet risks mentioned above. In addition, there is evidence that becoming more regularly active may help with the management of depressive symptoms (Frank 2007; Ludman et al. 2003). Feeling like we're in good shape is also a real boost to self-esteem for all of us. Establishing a good exercise routine will be the focus of module 27.

Tobacco Use

Tobacco use may be the furthest thing from your mind if you're already health conscious and have never smoked or used tobacco in other ways. If so, you are in the minority: for reasons we don't understand completely, individuals with depression or bipolar disorder, or a variety of other conditions, become smokers at a much higher rate than other people (Compton, Daumit, and Druss 2006). Perhaps it's because nicotine, the active ingredient in cigarettes and other tobacco products, can sometimes have a calming effect—but then before you know it, you can become addicted. Some studies show that among people with bipolar disorder, a remarkable 30 percent are addicted to tobacco, twice the rate in the general population (Waxmonsky et al. 2005). As you know from many sources of information, like the landmark surgeon general's report *Smoking and Health* (HEW 1964), tobacco use is associated with cancer, heart disease, and a variety of other conditions. It also interferes with getting regular exercise, which is so important for managing bipolar disorder. And quitting smoking will lower your chance of having a stroke, heart attack, or cancer. So it's worth paying special attention to this health risk. Dealing with tobacco use will be the focus of module 28.

Sleep

We all have routines around when we eat, sleep, work, and socialize. Our bodies also have an internal clock. Our clock acts as a cue to help us with our daily routine by telling us when to wake up and go to bed. Keeping a regular schedule and sleep pattern is important for maintaining our internal clock, and keeping our internal clock in sync helps us sleep better and have more energy. However, people with bipolar disorder are often more vulnerable to factors that may change the body's clock. Sleeping and waking patterns especially may be disrupted because of manic or depressive symptoms. In fact, decreased sleep itself can lead to a manic episode. Structuring a routine of daily activities and sleep may help keep your biological clock healthy and on a schedule. More importantly, keeping a regular sleep-wake cycle is a primary step to managing mania and depression. Managing sleep, sometimes called *sleep hygiene*, will be the focus of module 29.

Tom's Story

Tom, age forty-seven, had been diagnosed with bipolar disorder several years previously. Even though he took his medications and his condition was fairly stable, he noticed that he had gained a lot of weight over the years. Tom's primary care provider told him that he had high blood pressure and a cholesterol count over 250, suggesting that he had high cholesterol. She recommended that he eat less fat and get more exercise, but Tom's work schedule was hectic and his medications made him feel tired at the end of the day. He often had little time to eat breakfast before going to work and usually grabbed lunch at the local fast-food place down the street from his work. At dinnertime, Tom was often too tired to drive to the nearest grocery store, which was several miles away. Also, Tom was trying to keep up with mortgage payments and pay off credit card debts, and so he felt that he couldn't afford a membership to the local gym. He tried to go to the gym at one point, using a guest pass, but felt uncomfortable because the gym was near a college and catered to a younger crowd. A coworker convinced him to join the weight-management challenge at work, where they discussed healthy eating habits and had a weigh-in each week. Tom also decided to save money by parking in a lot farther from work and walking to his office. He talked with his care provider, who told Tom that not only did the medication he was taking in the evening cause drowsiness, but it also could cause weight gain. They decided to change his medication to one that reduced these risks. After several months, he was pleased with his ten-pound weight loss and with the fact that his coworkers had begun to notice that he was losing weight.

Tom faced a lot of the health challenges that many people do. In his case, they were compounded by medications used to treat bipolar disorder. His own effort, connection with others, and consultation with his care provider led to improvements in his health—not right away, but with persistence over time.

EXERCISE 5.1 How Does Bipolar Disorder Affect Your Physical Health?

In this exercise, you'll take a census of the ways in which bipolar disorder has affected each of the four key areas of physical health: diet, exercise, tobacco use, and sleep. So, looking at each of these aspects of physical health on the worksheet below, write a number on the line before each response to indicate the degree to which you feel you need to work on it, again using a scale of 0 to 3:

▶ 0 means you're where you should be, and this doesn't need attention.

▶ 1 means this needs a bit of attention but is not a high priority.

▶ 2 means this needs attention and is a high priority.

▶ 3 means this is a really top priority, maybe even a higher priority than getting your bipolar symptoms under control.

After you've chosen a number, briefly describe the specific impact this health aspect has on your life and why you want to work on it.

Effects of Bipolar Disorder on Physical Health

_____ Diet

Note the impact on your life and why you want to work on this:

_____

_____

_____ Exercise

Note the impact on your life and why you want to work on this:

_____

_____

_____ Tobacco

Note the impact on your life and why you want to work on this:

_____

_____

_____ Sleep

Note the impact on your life and why you want to work on this:

_____

_____

The results of this exercise will help you set priorities in working on your life goals, especially when you're considering the strategies provided in modules 26–29. These four health issues—diet, exercise, tobacco use, and sleep—may not necessarily be part of bipolar disorder, but they may require particular attention for people with bipolar disorder who are trying to fulfill their goals in life.

WHAT'S NEXT?

There are several other types of conditions that are not necessarily part of bipolar disorder but can come along with the condition. We call these conditions _unwanted co-travelers_, and the next module deals with them.

Module 6:
Unwanted Co-travelers

In this module, you will learn about some of the other types of symptoms that are not strictly part of bipolar disorder, but that may come along with this condition.

SYMPTOMS ACCOMPANYING BIPOLAR DISORDER

We have talked about bipolar disorder in terms of manic and depressive symptoms, and strictly speaking, those are the core of the condition. But there are other types of symptoms that can come along with mania or depression, and these can be troublesome enough to need some attention in their own right.

Three of these symptoms are irritability, psychosis, and suicidal feelings, and we'll give special attention to these. There are also other types of disorders that tend to occur in people with bipolar disorder more often than in the general public. You'll sometimes hear care providers talk about these as *comorbidities* or *comorbid disorders*. The most common are substance use disorders and anxiety disorders. A few others that also occur from time to time include attention-deficit/hyperactivity disorder (ADHD), borderline personality disorder, and eating disorders.

In module 5, we talked about the increased risk of comorbid medical conditions (such as high blood pressure, high cholesterol, diabetes, or heart disease) that can occur in individuals with bipolar disorder. In this module, we'll introduce other unwanted co-travelers and then discuss some of them in greater detail in subsequent modules. Why bring up these other problems? Isn't life tough enough with bipolar disorder? Well, we hope it's not the case that you have any of these other problems, but you should know what to watch out for. We've seen many situations where a person didn't deal with one or another co-traveler and it made their life much more difficult. In reality, bipolar symptoms and symptoms of these unwanted co-travelers are often intertwined and are best recognized and dealt with together.

Irritability in Mania and Depression

Irritability is often present in mania, sometimes coming and going with the flow of events, sometimes there with a life of its own. Often it is the face of mania that others first see—and are most affected by. However, irritability can also be a part of depression. It is not uncommon for people to get snappy when they are depressed, and often men in particular will cover up depressed or anxious feelings with irritability. Identifying and handling anger and irritability is covered in more detail in module 14.

Psychosis Can Complicate the Situation

Psychosis is usually defined as having delusions or hallucinations. *Delusions* are fixed, false beliefs; they are stronger than suppositions or hunches—they are conclusions that are falsely held more than they are opinions. For instance, if you believed you were President Millard Fillmore's brother or sister, that would be a delusion. If you were absolutely convinced that Fillmore was the greatest president the United States ever had, however unusual that belief might be, it would not be a delusion, but rather, a strongly held opinion.

Hallucinations are false sensations, usually sounds or visions but also sometimes smells or tastes or feelings on the skin. Clinical assessment is usually helpful in telling whether certain experiences are delusions or hallucinations, or are something else. Regardless, they can be quite frightening, though sometimes a particular hallucination can be a calming or supportive voice and can be soothing. Regardless, they can be part of either mania or depression, and are dealt with in more detail in module 13.

Harriet's Story

"Signs and clues" brought Harriet to the hospital. She was convinced from "reading the pattern of the traffic lights" for the prior week that her daughter was in grave danger. In particular, she was afraid that her daughter was going to be molested, as Harriet herself had been as a young woman. She was so concerned that she was up three nights straight, traveling the city looking at traffic lights, and far from being tired, she was energized the following days and spent hundreds of dollars on a variety of security systems as well as DVDs of movies that would give her "clues" to the identity of her daughter's future assailant. When she arrived at the hospital looking for help, she was talking rapidly and was very easily irritated. She had been treated at the hospital clinic for several years for post-traumatic stress disorder (PTSD) and insisted that this was all that was wrong with her. Eventually she agreed to come in to the hospital and to take medications, and her mania and psychosis lessened.

As Harriet and her care providers discussed the events of the prior week, it became clear that this month was the anniversary of her rape. She had begun to have nightmares and flashbacks again and had stopped sleeping, initially by her own willpower, to avoid the nightmares. The sleep deprivation had then taken on a life of its own and, coupled with the daytime stress of her PTSD symptoms, apparently led to her first manic episode, which included psychotic features (delusions).

Suicidality Can Occur at Times

Suicide is a risk in a variety of conditions, and bipolar disorder is no exception. Self-endangering behavior can occur during depression but can also occur during mania. Often people who have tried to end their lives report that the mental pain was too much to endure and that they thought it would never end—they saw no way out. Sometimes the main feeling that drives suicidal thoughts is depression; other times it's anger. Regardless, to the person who feels suicidal, there seems at the time to be no better alternative. The key terms here are "no way out" and "no better alternative" to ending one's life. Is that really so? It is not. People who are suicidal often isolate themselves and are unable to explore options, to see solutions to resolve their problems, or to be hopeful and optimistic about the future. *Note that it's vitally important that you talk with someone right away if you have these feelings.* Suicidality is dealt with in more detail in module 20.

COMORBID DISORDERS

Since people with bipolar disorder tend to experience problems with substance use and anxiety more often than the general public, we'll discuss these issues in more detail.

Substance Use Problems Are Common in Bipolar Disorder

Many studies have shown that at some time in their lives, two out of three people with bipolar disorder will have a problem with substance use, and one out of three people with bipolar disorder will have an *active* substance abuse problem at any one point in time (Bauer 2008a). Most commonly the drug of choice is alcohol, but cocaine and marijuana, among others, are also frequently used. In addition to these *illicit* (illegal) drugs, certain prescribed drugs known in medical-legal terms as "controlled substances" can be abused by overusing them, selling them, or trying to get duplicate prescriptions.

All the difficulties that come along with bipolar disorder can be compounded by substance use. Then, why is there a connection? Each person's answer to this question is different. But each person's main question should be the one we implied in module 3: does it help or hurt my life's work?

Might Substance Use Be a Problem?

Have you ever wondered whether your own use of alcohol or drugs (prescription, nonprescription, or illegal) might be a bit heavy or even out of control? Here's a way to explore this. The CAGE (Ewing 1984) and the AUDIT-C (Bush et al. 1998) are two screening tests for alcohol problems (you can substitute a drug of choice for alcohol if that is more relevant for the CAGE test). Again, as with the MDQ and BSDS screening tools from module 1, these are *screening* tools. *They don't make a diagnosis.* They only suggest whether you might do well to have a conversation with a care provider about substance use. Take a moment to take these two brief screening tests and see what you think.

EXERCISE 6.1 Screening Tool for Alcohol (Substance Use) Dependence: The CAGE Questionnaire

Please note: This test will only be scored correctly if you answer each one of the questions. Please circle the one response to each item that best describes how you have felt and behaved over your whole life.

Have you ever felt you should **C**ut down on your drinking (or substance use)?

     Yes   No

Do people ever **A**nnoy you by criticizing your drinking (or substance use)?

     Yes   No

Do you ever feel bad or **G**uilty about your drinking (or substance use)?

     Yes   No

Do you ever need an **E**ye-opener in the morning to steady your nerves or get rid of a hangover? (Or did you ever need to use substances the next day to keep from getting withdrawal symptoms?)

     Yes   No

SCORING THE CAGE

Two or more yes answers suggest that you may have a problem with alcohol or other substances.

EXERCISE 6.2 Screening Tool: The Alcohol Use Disorders Identification Test (AUDIT-C)

Please circle the one response to each item that best describes how you have felt and behaved during the past year.

1. How often did you have a drink containing alcohol in the past year?

    Never   (0 points)

    Monthly or less   (1 point)

    2–4 times a month   (2 points)

    2–3 times a week   (3 points)

    4 or more times a week   (4 points)

2. How many drinks containing alcohol did you have on a typical day when you were drinking in the past year?

1–2 drinks on a typical day	(0 points)
3–4 drinks on a typical day	(1 point)
5–6 drinks on a typical day	(2 points)
7–9 drinks on a typical day	(3 points)
10 or more drinks on a typical day	(4 points)

3. How often did you have six or more drinks on one occasion in the past year?

Never	(0 points)
Less than once a month	(1 point)
Monthly	(2 points)
Weekly	(3 points)
Daily or almost daily	(4 points)

SCORING THE AUDIT-C

Total the number of points for all three responses (12 points maximum).

Score of 4 or more:	Concern of hazardous drinking
Score of 8 or more:	Concern of alcohol dependence

Based on your scores in these exercises, you may have a better idea of whether your alcohol or substance use is out of control. Following up with trained clinical providers who specialize in working every day with people who have recognized their alcohol or substance use problems is the key to becoming healthier. You will also be working through substance use issues in depth in module 12.

Anxiety Disorders Are Surprisingly Common in Bipolar Disorder

At any one point in time, one out of three people with bipolar disorder will also have an anxiety disorder (Bauer 2008a)—anxiety disorders are as common as substance use disorders among people with bipolar disorder. Anxiety disorders are of several different types. The main symptoms can be mental anxiety, as in what is called generalized anxiety disorder, or physical anxiety, as in what is called panic disorder. Post-traumatic stress disorder (PTSD), as in Harriet's case, is also somewhat common. You will read in more detail about these conditions and learn more about managing anxiety in module 21. Modules 22–24 deal with anxiety and depression together, but anxiety can present difficulties during mania too, as well as when your mood is stable.

Other Co-travelers You Should Be Aware Of

Because they aren't experienced as frequently as substance use or anxiety disorder, we won't deal in detail with many other co-travelers. You might want to be aware, though, that several other conditions can occur along with bipolar disorder, including attention-deficit/hyperactivity disorder (ADHD), borderline personality disorder, and eating disorders such as anorexia and bulimia. Some resources in appendix A will help you find more information about these conditions.

WHAT'S NEXT?

By this point in the workbook, you have received a pretty good introduction to what bipolar disorder, in general, is like; how it fits into your life specifically; and some of the unwanted co-travelers, physical and mental, that may come along with it. In the next module, you'll find an outline of what treatments are available.

Module 7: The Clinical Side of Treatment for Bipolar Disorder

In this module, you will review the treatments for bipolar disorders and create a log of your personal experiences with medications or therapies—a written account you can share with your care providers to help improve your treatment.

TREATMENTS FOR A BIO-PSYCHOSOCIAL CONDITION

As we mentioned in the introduction and in module 2, understanding and treating bipolar disorder requires tuning in to biological, psychological, and social aspects—it is a bio-psychosocial condition. Typically, bipolar disorder is treated with one or more medications plus some type of counseling or psychotherapy. The counseling may be very structured—even guided by a step-by-step manual—or educational and with a more informal kind of support. This module will briefly outline some of the types of medications and therapies that are available.

COLLABORATIVE CARE AND JOINT DECISION MAKING

Please note this most important aspect—there is no single "best" treatment for everyone with bipolar disorder; treating the condition is a joint exploration between you and your care provider.

A Field Guide to Care Providers

We've tended to use the term "care provider"; another general term is "clinician." These are professionals who work with individuals with bipolar disorder or other related health conditions. But who, exactly, are these providers? What is their training and what do they do? The following table is by no means exhaustive but will give you an idea of the types of clinicians most often involved with treating bipolar disorder or related conditions.

Provider type (educational degree)	Description
Psychiatrists (MD, DO)	Psychiatrists are medical doctors, like surgeons or internists. They can prescribe medications or conduct psychotherapy.
Psychologists (PhD, PsyD, MA)	Psychologists receive masters or doctoral degrees in graduate school. They are not trained to prescribe medications, but do conduct psychotherapy and may do other types of specialized treatments such as hypnosis.
Advanced practice nurses (MSN, RNPC, NP, RNCS, RNC)	Advanced practice nurses go by several names, such as "clinical specialist" or, for medical fields, "nurse-practitioner." They have advanced nursing training, often work in primary care, can prescribe some medications, and may conduct psychotherapy.
Other mental health clinicians (LSW, MSW, LICSW, LMHC)	Clinical social workers and other mental health clinicians offer counseling or help with life problems relating to the illness. They have various backgrounds and usually specialize in a specific area.
Primary care physician (MD, DO)	Primary care physicians are medical doctors, as are psychiatrists. They both take care of a wide variety of medical problems and also prescribe medications for a wide variety of mental conditions. More straightforward mental conditions can be treated in primary care, but more complex situations require assessment by a psychiatrist—just as more complex heart conditions require consultation by a specialist, a cardiologist.

Options, Options, Options

Despite the decades of research and clinical experience, no one single treatment has turned out to be the cure-all. Is this bad news? We think not: this means that there are a number of options that are potentially equally good.

In the real world of treatment, providers are guided to a series of possible treatment options, usually summarized in *clinical practice guidelines,* which are based on research data and clinical experience. These may be large books or one-page diagrams, depending on the type of guideline and the particular condition.

The provider usually comes up with several options that should be equally effective. Sometimes the provider will present only one option that he or she believes will work best for you, having thought through the relative advantages and disadvantages of several treatments.

Key note: It's always appropriate to ask, "Well, what are my options?" After all, you're the one taking the medication or going through the therapy. If you went to a car dealer and the salesman chose a model for you based on what he thought you said that you wanted, wouldn't you ask the same thing before signing the contract? For example, you don't need to know how a turbocharger for the engine works, but you should at least know what happens if you have it and what happens if you don't. Since there are options, decision making becomes a partnership.

CONSIDERING INNOVATIVE TREATMENTS

One of the treatment options you may discuss with your provider is medication. Maybe you have already had this discussion or are already taking medication. In this module, we'll mention different types of medicines most often prescribed for bipolar disorder. We'll discuss strategies to help you to be confident and knowledgeable when you make treatment decisions with your provider about such medications or other alternatives you may hear about.

The media is constantly full of information about new treatments, medications, nutritional supplements, and alternative therapies for a variety of problems. Whether you're listening to an advertisement or discussing traditional medications with your prescriber, it is important to make informed decisions, be able to evaluate what you hear, and weigh the personal costs and benefits.

It can be easy to believe advertisements, especially when they promise breakthrough results. The weight-loss industry is a multibillion-dollar industry based on the promise of easy miracle cures. Herbal and "natural" treatments for many conditions are well publicized. A huge proportion of the U.S. population uses one or more so-called natural remedies. Please note that just because something is called "natural" or "herbal" doesn't mean it is safe or better than traditional medicine. In fact, as of this writing, there are no restrictions from the U.S. Food and Drug Administration (FDA) that ensure quality control with regard to these products. That means we cannot rely on the label to tell us that what is advertised is actually in the product or present in the amount described. It's left up to the manufacturer to police how closely the contents match the label. Many of these over-the-counter products have side effects and can have interactions with other medicines that can be dangerous, so it's important to check with your care provider before taking any of these types of remedies—even if they are "natural."

PLAYING AN ACTIVE ROLE IN TREATMENT

Outcome improves when a person with bipolar disorder plays an active role in his or her own treatment (Bauer, McBride, et al. 2006a, 2006b; Simon et al. 2006). You provide valuable information. You express your priorities and limitations when it comes to making decisions about treatment options. You provide feedback on what's working and what's not. The care provider is the professional expert, and you are the values expert.

Consider this scenario: You have two options. Some medications that treat bipolar disorder may carry the risk of causing tremors, but wouldn't have any effect on your weight; another equally effective medication may have a risk of causing weight gain but not tremors. Which treatment is right for you? The care provider can't make that decision alone—he or she can provide information to help you with your decision and may even have some strong recommendation based on your history; the reasoning behind the recommendation may be based on new research about the effectiveness of medications in treating people with bipolar disorder, or it may be based on your personal history of how similar medications affected you in the past. Ultimately, though, the choice is yours. You will find more discussion of these topics and some hints for managing your care in module 31.

EXERCISE 7.1 Informed Decision Making Around Medications

This exercise provides some practice in identifying situations where you could make a choice about your treatment. This helps to prepare you for the next opportunity. Recall a time when your care provider prescribed a new medication or therapy for you.

Did your care provider answer all of your questions in the past? Were there other things you wanted to know but didn't ask? What were your concerns about getting this new treatment? Were you able to discuss these?

_____

_____

_____

Now, looking forward, what questions will you have to be sure you get answered with the next treatment decision? What seems to be hardest to ask about, and why? Jot down your thoughts on the lines below.

_____

_____

_____

Now write some of the general questions you have about the current treatment you are receiving on an index card and tuck it away to take with you to your next appointment.

In the future, when your care provider suggests a new medication, therapy, or treatment, you will have a chance to ask questions about the reason that option is the best one for you. Writing down the usage instructions is important. Detail the symptom or issue that it is addressing: how to tell if the medication is working, the side effects, and what to watch for if it isn't working. It is often difficult to tease out if any problems are due to how your body is reacting to the new medication or due to the medical condition itself. Consulting your care provider will make this clear.

OVERVIEW: MEDICATIONS

This workbook will not provide a summary of medication types, actions, side effects, and so on. We certainly won't weigh in with opinions about whether this or that medication is better than another. Rather, the purpose of this section is to help you to get to know some names that you might come across in treatment. Appendix A lists some resources for learning more, and appendix B provides a list of some common medications in each of the classes discussed below.

Mood Stabilizers: Lithium Plus

The term "mood stabilizer" is widely used but doesn't have an official definition. The ideal mood stabilizer is a single agent that does just that: stabilizes mood so that manic or depressive symptoms don't occur, or at least aren't so severe as to disrupt your life's work and your relationships. Thus far, the medication that comes closest to this ideal is lithium. It is effective for both mania and depression over the short and long term. It is likely that, in the future, certain neuroleptic and anticonvulsant medications (see below) will also receive that informal name—"mood stabilizer"—as research evidence accumulates.

Antidepressants

Antidepressants are, not surprisingly, medications that treat depression. Major classes include the following:

▶ Tricyclic antidepressants (TCAs), for instance, desipramine (e.g., Norpramine), doxepin (e.g., Sinequan)

▶ Selective serotonin reuptake inhibitors (SSRIs or SRIs), for instance, fluoxetine (e.g., Prozac), escitalopram (e.g., Lexapro)

▶ Serotonin-norepinephrine reuptake inhibitors (SNRIs), for instance, venlafaxine (Effexor), mirtazapine (Remeron)

▶ Heterocyclic antidepressants, for instance, bupropion (Wellbutrin, Zyban), nefazodone (Serzone)

Sometimes other medications or devices are used for depression, including lithium (e.g., Lithobid, Eskalith); stimulants, for instance, methylphenidate (e.g., Ritalin); thyroid hormones, for instance, tri-iodothyronine (e.g., Cytomel); electroconvulsive therapy (ECT, or in layperson's terms, shock therapy); bright visible-spectrum light (via light boxes); reverse transcranial magnetic stimulation (rTMS); and surgery to implant a vagal nerve stimulator (VNS). *Note:* One tricky aspect of treating bipolar depression is that most antidepressants (excluding lithium, ECT, and certain anticonvulsants) may also cause mania.

Antimanics

The major antimanic agents include the following:

▶   Lithium

▶   Anticonvulsants (see below)

▶   Neuroleptics (see below)

▶   ECT is sometimes used, as are a variety of other medications, including some antianxiety agents

Anticonvulsants

It was discovered by accident that certain *anticonvulsants* (antiseizure medications) were helpful in calming agitated behavior. It is interesting that not all anticonvulsants share this effect. The major anticonvulsants used in bipolar disorder are divalproex or valproic acid (Depakote), carbamazepine (e.g., Tegretol), and lamotrigine (Lamictal). Oxcarbazepine (e.g., Trileptal) and gabapentin (Neurontin) are also occasionally used. These are best known for their antimanic effects, though lamotrigine may be an antidepressant as well.

Neuroleptics

These are also called *antipsychotics*, or, in the old days, *major tranquilizers*. They were developed for schizophrenia but have been shown in general to be effective for mania as well. They are sometimes also used as add-on treatments for depression, for example, for insomnia or anxiety. There are two major classes of neuroleptics. The most commonly used these days are the *atypical antipsychotics*, or *second-generation antipsychotics* (SGAs), such as olanzapine (e.g., Zyprexa) and risperidone (Risperdal). Additionally there are *typical neuroleptics*, or *first-generation antipsychotics* (FGAs), including the older agents, such as haloperidol (e.g., Haldol), perphenazine (e.g., Trilafon), and chlorpromazine (e.g., Thorazine).

Antianxiety Agents

As we mentioned in module 6, anxiety can be a common co-traveler in bipolar disorder. The oldest and most widely used group of antianxiety agents is the *benzodiazepine* group, which also used to be called *minor tranquilizers*; these include such medications as diazepam (Valium), lorazepam (e.g., Ativan), and alprazolam (e.g., Xanax). This group of medications is often used for sleep as well, particularly temazepam (e.g., Restoril) and triazolam (e.g., Halcion). Benzodiazepines are used carefully in bipolar disorder since they may be addictive, and as we will discuss further in module 12, substance abuse can be a difficult co-traveler to deal with. Neuroleptics are also used for anxiety, as is another agent, buspirone (e.g., BuSpar). Insomnia is also sometimes treated with neuroleptics, the antidepressant trazodone (e.g., Desyrel), or other sleep medications such as zolpidem (e.g., Ambien).

EXERCISE 7.2 Let Your Fingers Do the Walking

Chances are you are taking one or more medications, or have in the past. Go to one of your sources of reliable information (recall exercise 2.1) and do some research about the effects of a medication you have taken, including its side effects and dosage range. Does your experience with the medication seem "typical"? Has it had the desired effect? Have you experienced any of the listed side effects? Or is your experience different? For instance, is the medication being used for a different purpose? Are you taking an unusual dosage? Are you having a side effect that is not listed?

_____

_____

_____

Now that you've jotted down the specifics, take your observations in to your next appointment and ask your care provider some questions!

TRACKING TREATMENT OVER TIME: MEDICATIONS

Treating bipolar disorder symptoms takes time. Even if you live in the same town throughout your treatment, fill your prescriptions at only one pharmacy, and see one care provider for check-ups, a notebook or logbook that lists your medical history and your experiences with each medication will provide valuable information in your treatment planning process. True, your care provider and pharmacist can note any severe reactions or allergies to medications. But your logbook serves a different purpose. Rather than just listing your medical reactions (allergies, hives, being more thirsty or hungry) to a particular medication, you can write down how the medication made you feel (focused, jittery, content, tearful, or something else). By working closely with your care provider and writing in a notebook, you become keenly aware of your personal experiences, which, in turn, can influence your treatment decisions, improving your treatment over time. You can also refer to your notes to explain to your care providers about your reactions.

Bill's Story

When Bill came to his evaluation with a new psychiatrist, he was taking an antidepressant, two antipsychotics, an anticonvulsant, and a sleep medication. He was tired all the time and had gained thirty pounds over the previous year. These side effects were becoming intolerable for him because he was someone who really enjoyed being active with his kids. His psychiatrist consulted clinical practice guidelines and presented Bill with a series of options, describing the potential effects and side effects of each. They jointly made some treatment decisions, and over six months, she gradually changed Bill's medication to include lithium, a new antidepressant, and a single neuroleptic. She provided psychoeducation and referred Bill for a course of twelve sessions of cognitive behavioral therapy, which included a wellness and weight-loss component. Bill lost only a few pounds but overall was pleased with his increased physical activity and has plans to keep working on his weight. In social situations he found himself able to keep his self-defeating thoughts in check and was pleased that he was dating again.

As we said, there are always options, options, and more options ... Sometimes it just takes time to find the right one.

EXERCISE 7.3 Writing Your Experiences with Medications in a Logbook

This exercise will assist you in becoming a manager of your medication experiences, a coinvestigator with your provider into what treatments work best for you. To get started, find a notebook, or staple or clip a few pieces of paper together. Or, better yet, make some copies of the following logsheet. Start your logbook entries by describing the medications and treatments you currently take. Add any information you can recall about past treatments that you would like to tell your provider about. Use a new page for each medication.

Medication Logsheet

MEDICATION NAME: _____

Start date: _____ End date: _____

Dose: _____ Number of times per day and hour taken: _____

What it's for:

_____

_____

_____

Occasions when dose was increased or decreased and why:

_____

_____

_____

How well it's working on a scale of 1 to 10 (circle one number):

1	2	3	4	5	6	7	8	9	10

1 = Poor
not working

10 = Great
working well

How you know it's helping:

_____

_____

_____

Any side effects on a scale of 1 to 10 (circle one number):

1	2	3	4	5	6	7	8	9	10

1 = None
no side
effects

10 = Intolerable
many side
effectsl

If you stopped taking this medication, the reason why:

_____ Not working

_____ Side effects hard to deal with

_____ Different medicine was better and replaced this one

_____ Expense

_____ Other reason (please describe): _____

Any tricks to reduce side effects (e.g., when to take, to take with food, etc.):

_____

_____

_____

Questions for provider:

_____

_____

_____

Trying to complete all sections of this exercise will give you clues about how well you understand your medication treatment—for each medication you're taking. Take a look at the blanks. If you don't know why your providers are prescribing a certain medication, simply ask them. If you can't identify what's working or what's causing side effects, ask your provider for the information and request changes if necessary. You're actively taking medication every day, so you should be actively reviewing each medication to ensure that it's the best possible treatment, tailored for you.

OVERVIEW: PSYCHOTHERAPY

Psychotherapy is almost always used as an add-on to medications rather than instead of medications. Formal, structured psychotherapies are time limited, with a beginning, middle, and end; many have refresher sessions thereafter. Supportive or general psychotherapy may be time limited or ongoing. Research evidence indicates that any of a variety of psychotherapies may be helpful in bipolar disorder, and no one type is any better than others (Miklowitz et al. 2007). We'll describe psychoeducation, cognitive and behavioral therapy, family therapy, and interpersonal and social rhythms therapy in more detail.

Psychoeducation

A variety of specific types of *psychoeducation* (psychological education) are available for bipolar disorder (Colom et al. 2003). Some types are one-to-one with a care provider; others use groups (like the Life

Goals Program; Bauer and McBride 2003). Individual forms allow more private attention, while groups allow mutual learning and support. Education is part of all of the other therapies listed here. Recall that the most effective forms of education are less like a lecture and more oriented to hands-on activities.

Cognitive and Behavioral Therapy

Cognitive and behavioral therapy tend to be combined to one degree or another. *Cognitive therapy* works on thought patterns that are disabling. *Behavior therapy* works on behavior patterns that cause problems in life. Some of these techniques have been incorporated into this workbook in the sections on anger and panic, and you will learn more about them in modules 14 and 21.

Family Therapies

Family therapies include *family-focused therapy* and individual or multifamily therapies (Miklowitz et al. 2007). They have been useful both for individuals with the illness and for their families. Some types of family therapy focus on educating the family, and others emphasize smoothing out relationship issues.

Interpersonal and Social Rhythms Therapy

Interpersonal and social rhythms therapy is based on the observation that some people with bipolar disorder often end up living isolated lives and that both their social and their physical routines get disorganized, making the depression or even manic symptoms worse. Addressing social and relationship issues (interpersonal) and regularizing sleep-wake routines (rhythms) in order to stabilize mood are the foci of this approach (Frank 2007). Module 29 will explore sleep patterns in further depth.

TRACKING PSYCHOTHERAPY OVER TIME

If you are in therapy, perhaps you are writing your feelings and actions in a notebook to help you recall how things are going between therapy sessions. The following exercise provides a method to increase your awareness of the usefulness of therapy for you.

EXERCISE 7.4 Writing Your Experience with Psychotherapy in a Logbook

As was suggested in exercise 7.3, make some copies of the following logsheet, or make up your own sheet. Start your logbook entries by describing the psychotherapy you are currently involved in. Add any information about your past treatments that you'd like to tell your provider about. Use a new page for each type of psychotherapy if you have participated in more than one.

Therapy Logsheet

THERAPY NAME: _____

Start date: _____ End date: _____

How often (number of times per week or month): _____

Times you've increased or decreased frequency or duration of therapy (please describe situation):

_____

_____

How well it's working on a scale of 1 to 10 (circle one number):

1	2	3	4	5	6	7	8	9	10

1 = Poorly   10 = Great

How you know it's helping:

_____

_____

Any side effects (even psychotherapy can have side effects!) on a scale of 1 to 10 (circle one number):

1	2	3	4	5	6	7	8	9	10

1 = None   10 = Intolerable

If you stopped therapy, the reason why:

_____ Not working

_____ Negative effects hard to deal with

_____ Different therapy or medicine was better and replaced this one

_____ Expense

_____ Other reason (please describe): _____

Questions for provider:

_____

_____

With the two logbook exercises in this module, you should have the basis for tracking your bio-psychosocial treatment over time; this will help you identify what's working and how, and what's not working so well. This will allow you and your care provider to jointly manage your treatment.

WHAT'S NEXT?

So, there you have the basics of bipolar disorder and its treatment, in seven easy modules. Let's now move on to the details of your own specific experience of the condition and to developing specific strategies that will help you to manage it!

## PART II

Working Through Mania

Module 8: Constructing a Personal Mania Profile

This module is designed to help you develop awareness of your personal signs and symptoms of mania, including early warning signs of impending episodes.

MANIC SYMPTOMS: WHAT'S YOUR EXPERIENCE?

Like all medical illnesses, bipolar disorder has a variety of symptoms that are "typical" or "average" or "characteristic" for the condition. However, also as with all medical illnesses, each person's specific pattern is different. Recognizing your own specific, current personal profile of symptoms will empower you and support your efforts to manage this condition.

You will spend the next two modules exploring this profile of manic symptoms. In this module you will construct your own profile of symptoms, and in module 9 you will identify triggers for your manic symptoms.

Recall that working *through* bipolar disorder is a process, and a key first step to effectively managing mania is to learn how to recognize your personal symptoms. Note that, for simplicity, we'll use the terms "mania" and "manic episode" from here on—but the management tools apply to hypomania as well.

As discussed in module 2, mania can affect thoughts, feelings, and behaviors, and we find it useful to keep these three dimensions in mind. As you construct your Personal Mania Profile, remember that sometimes during mania people do things that they later regret. Recalling your manic episodes may bring up upsetting or embarrassing experiences, such as the loss of important relationships, jobs, and other things related to a sense of personal value and worth. These losses are painful. So if you're a person with such memories, take your time with this. Remember, you're not alone in trying to understand these feelings, and describing your own personal experience of manic symptoms is the first step to controlling them.

EXERCISE 8.1 Some Background for Your Personal Mania Profile

This exercise will ask you to describe some basic qualities of your experience of mania. This will help get you in the mind-set for the more specific work to be done in exercise 8.2, "Constructing Your Personal Mania Profile."

There are many words people use to refer to mania besides "high." Some call it "charged up"; others, "racing," "excited," or "hyperactive." What words do you use to describe these feelings to yourself or to others?

_____

_____

_____

Is there a typical length for your manic episodes? If so, it may be days, weeks, or even months. Give an approximation. If there is no typical length, what's been the range in length that you've experienced, and how variable are the lengths of these episodes?

_____

_____

_____

Describe how the onset of mania has been for you. A manic episode can develop in a variety of ways. For instance, it can come on slowly and then gradually increase in severity over time. Or it can come on quickly, and you can abruptly switch from one mood state to another. It's not unusual to experience more than one pattern. Again, how variable has your experience been?

_____

_____

_____

Now list some of the thoughts, feelings, and behaviors that are typical of your manic periods, or that have tended to occur on more than one occasion. For instance, with regard to feelings, some people feel good when they have mania; others feel racing, irritable, and depressed rather than good. How would you describe your personal experiences?

Thoughts:

_____

_____

_____

Feelings:

_____

_____

_____

Behaviors:

_____

_____

_____

With this exercise, you've written out some of the qualities you've experienced in a manic episode. In exercise 8.2, you will distill these into more of a checklist format that will be a shorthand record for you and will also be helpful for your care provider to see.

EXERCISE 8.2 Constructing Your Personal Mania Profile

The profile is organized around thoughts, feelings, and behaviors. In the table below, place a check in the "√" column next to each symptom you've experienced during mania (we'll come back to the other columns later). Recall that the list should represent *your* experience with mania, not what you've read is supposedly typical—this is about your personal experience, even if it's different from anything you've ever heard of anyone else experiencing. In fact, blank spaces are provided at the bottom of the table so you can fill in personal symptoms that are not already listed.

Now, among these thoughts, feelings, and behaviors, there may be some that come on *so rapidly* that you hardly know they're beginning and—*wham!*—they're already overwhelming. Identify these experiences with an "X" in the "X" column.

Personal Mania Profile

√	X	F	E	Thoughts
				Difficulty with concentration and memory
				More religious thoughts
				Thoughts about having special abilities or powers
				Racing or sped-up thoughts
				The rest of the world is in slow motion
				Thoughts jumping from one idea to another quickly
				Paranoia or other concerns that people are plotting against you
				Hallucinations: unreal voices or visions
				Thoughts of suicide
				Other thoughts (describe)

√	X	F	E	Feelings
				Feeling high, completely optimistic, or euphoric
				Feeling depressed
				Feeling more energetic
				Feelings change quickly
				Feeling impatient or irritable
				Feeling unusually cheerful and happy
				Feeling unusually self-confident or invulnerable
				Having a know-it-all attitude
				Other feelings (describe)

√	X	F	E	Behavior
				Loud, rapid, and raging speech
				Less need for sleep
				Overly sociable; giving more advice
				More or less sex drive
				Doing multiple projects, more than are practical
				Spending more money impulsively; going on shopping sprees
				Involvement in dangerous or risky activities
				Other behaviors (describe)

You now have a shorthand version of your typical manic episodes. In addition, you've identified those symptoms that take you by surprise. In the next section, you'll update this form by marking symptoms noticed by friends or family members in the "F" column. Later in this module, you'll mark the "E" column to denote early warning signs you may experience during a manic episode.

FAMILY, FRIENDS, AND YOUR PERSONAL MANIA PROFILE

Sometimes with mania (or depression) you yourself may not be aware of certain thoughts, feelings, or behaviors. But others close to you may see changes that can help you identify—and therefore manage—your manic symptoms.

EXERCISE 8.3 Team Building with Your Personal Mania Profile

If there is a close friend or family member you trust enough to share your Personal Mania Profile with, and who knows you well enough to be aware of your manic symptoms, please do so. In exercise 8.2, add any symptoms that person identifies by placing a mark in the "F" (for "friend" or "family") column. All of you may be aware of the identical symptoms. For other symptoms, others' insight may add new information that will be helpful to your management of these periods. In addition, if you show them the Personal Mania Profile worksheet, they may learn more about your experience of this condition, and this may help them better understand what happens when you have manic symptoms (remember Maria's story in module 4, about selectively sharing her experience of depression with a friend).

HOW DO MANIC EPISODES BEGIN?

An alarm is a warning that something is beginning to go wrong. For example, if a smoke alarm goes off, people typically look to find out where the smoke is and to confirm there's a fire. Some manic symptoms tend to come on early. We can think of the early warning signs and triggers of mania as alarms. When one of these alarms goes off, it's time to take action to snuff out an episode—in other words, find the smoke and put out the fire before it gets out of hand.

These early warning signs are symptoms that are particularly important to identify, since they can help you to respond early, before things get out of hand. And being able to respond early will give you more control over your manic symptoms—and your life.

EXERCISE 8.4 Identifying Your Personal Early Warning Signs of Mania

Go back to your Personal Mania Profile and look at the column marked "E" (for "early"). Put an "E" in this column for those symptoms that come on particularly early in mania. These will be the ones that sound an alarm and tell you, "Hey, I ought to do something now, before things get out of hand." What that "something" is will be the subject of modules 10–12. But to start this process, let's just identify your alarms, your early warning signs.

If you can't readily identify any immediately and you have the type of episode that you seem to find yourself in the middle of all of a sudden, that's okay. As you think more extensively about your profile and you think back over prior episodes (and maybe discuss these with family or friends), it is likely that some early warning signs will disclose themselves.

Now that you have completed your Personal Mania Profile, you have at your fingertips an outline of your typical or frequent manic symptoms, including those symptoms that come on particularly quickly. You also have a sense of the symptoms that others recognize but you may not. You've also identified those early warning signs that set off alarms that can get you into action before mania becomes severe. Of course, you can update your Personal Mania Profile as you think more about your manic symptom pattern.

Lou's Story

Lou, age thirty-five, had been married for six years and had two children in elementary school. He had a job working as a teacher in the high school in a nearby town. He'd been in the hospital for mania four times. His first episode occurred when he was twenty and attending the university. He didn't really understand much about his manic episodes—he just seemed to find himself in the middle of these overwhelming thoughts, feelings, and behaviors, and often ended up in the hospital because of them. On the advice of his psychiatrist, he began listing his symptoms and how they came on. He realized that he'd typically awaken after about three hours of sleep, somewhere around 3:00 A.M., and have a lot of thoughts going through his mind. Subsequently, he'd have extremely high energy and feel great for a few days, making lots of purchases for projects he'd start but unfortunately leaving many incomplete because he'd change his mind midstream and go from one project to another. His spending led to a strain on his budget. Soon after, he'd begin to have problems at home and at work and, though still having racing thoughts and many plans, he'd feel quite depressed and would occasionally contemplate suicide.

He constructed his Personal Mania Profile and discussed it with his wife and his psychiatrist. To his surprise, they each identified irritability as a typical and early symptom. To their surprise, they learned that depression and even suicidal thoughts could be part of Lou's experience of mania.

When Lou realized that he could understand and deal with mania, his wife and psychiatrist became more effective and empathetic allies. He now works collaboratively with his care provider if he has a decrease in sleep or lots of overly ambitious ideas, and they meet to plan his treatment to prevent a full manic episode from occurring.

WHAT'S NEXT?

Now you've developed your own specific Personal Mania Profile. The next task is to identify events or other factors that have triggered, or started, a manic episode. So the next antimanic skill to work on is identifying those triggers, and that is the focus of module 9.

Module 9: Identifying Mania Triggers

In this module, you will learn about stress and related factors that may trigger a manic episode. You will then develop a list of your own personal triggers for manic episodes so that you will know what to be particularly careful of and what to avoid, if possible.

TRIGGERS FOR MANIC SYMPTOMS

Research indicates that a variety of factors can be associated with the onset of manic symptoms (Johnson 2005; Goodwin and Jamison 2007; Bauer 2008a). It is important to recognize such potential triggers because avoiding or reducing exposure to them can reduce the likelihood that manic symptoms will occur, or can reduce their severity. Such triggers can be of two types: psychosocial and physical or biological. Remember the bio-psychosocial approach from module 2? It comes in handy in thinking about triggers. We will review each type of trigger in turn.

Psychosocial Stress and Manic Symptoms

When you look back over manic episodes you have had, you may be able to identify an event or factor that had some impact on you psychologically or socially and that may have triggered a manic episode. Although most of the research is on stresses that may trigger depression, stress may also trigger mania (Johnson 2005). Obvious examples are job loss or divorce or another significant loss that has some sort of psychological or social impact.

Although we tend to think of stress as being due to something bad or difficult, stress can be brought on by many changes, good or bad, in the regular routine of your life. So good things like getting married or getting a promotion can sometimes be as stressful as difficult things like getting a divorce or losing a job. Stress is part of life for everyone. But a person with bipolar disorder, faced with the same stress as someone else, may be less able to cope with or shrug off that stress, which can then sometimes trigger manic or depressive episodes. Some common psychosocial stressors, positive and negative, are listed in the following table.

Some Psychosocial Events That May Trigger Mania

Some generally negative or difficult events

▶ Divorce

▶ Death of loved one

▶ Job loss

▶ Financial stress

▶ Forced job change or new work assignment

▶ Traumatic event

▶ Anniversary date for a traumatic life event

▶ Having an unwanted visit from family or friends

▶ Young adult child leaving home abruptly

Some generally positive events that are often not thought to be stressful

▶ Moving

▶ Job promotion

▶ Vacation

▶ Holidays

▶ Retirement

▶ Having a desired visit from family or friends

▶ Getting married

▶ Having a baby

▶ Young adult child leaving home as their next developmental stage

Physical or Biological Factors and Manic Symptoms

A variety of physical or biological stresses can cause manic symptoms (Bauer 2003, 2008a). The most prominent of these factors is abuse of drugs like cocaine or amphetamines. However, alcohol and a variety of other drugs can also be potent triggers for mania. Even caffeine and certain prescribed medications can have this effect. Examples of prescribed medications that might be triggers include antidepressants, as we mentioned in module 7, and corticosteroids. You can check with your care provider and even the pharmacist to see whether any over-the-counter medications you are taking may also affect your moods. Sometimes medical conditions themselves can trigger manic symptoms.

In addition, other physical factors can trigger manic symptoms. For instance, sleep loss, either purposeful or accidental, can trigger mania. It is not uncommon, for example, for students with bipolar disorder to study all night for exams and end up, unfortunately, becoming manic prior to the test.

For some people there can also be a seasonal component to mania. Research indicates that some are more likely to become manic in the spring or fall, when day length is changing rapidly, while others may have a very regular seasonal pattern, with depression in the winter and mania in the summer (Goodwin and Jamison 2007). If either of these is the case for you, you may have little control over these triggers, but identifying them means that increased watchfulness, and sometimes treatment change, as directed by your provider, may be helpful.

Some of these common physical or biological triggers are listed in the following table. Note also that there are some stresses that don't fit into a single category and may truly be bio-psychosocial. For instance, moving to a new place may be a good or bad psychosocial stress, but may also involve long days of packing and moving and accidental sleep loss. Having a new baby is another obvious example where emotional reactions (psychosocial) and sleep loss (physical or biological) may both cause stress.

Examples of Physical or Biological Factors That May Trigger Manic Symptoms

Drugs of abuse

▶ Alcohol

▶ Cocaine

▶ Hallucinogens

▶ Caffeine

▶ Withdrawal from sedatives or alcohol

▶ Change in nicotine use

Other medical or physical conditions and factors

▶ Certain hormonal imbalances (e.g., Cushing's disease)

▶ Infections

▶ Sleep loss

▶ Menstrual cycle

▶ Seasonal cycle

Neurological conditions

▶ Dementia

▶ Head trauma

▶ Delirium

▶ Stroke

▶ Multiple sclerosis

Prescribed medications

▶ Antidepressants

▶ Decongestants

▶ Inhalers for asthma

▶ Stimulants

▶ Levodopa for Parkinson's disease

▶ Corticosteroids

▶ Anabolic steroids

▶ Disulfiram (Antabuse)

WHAT ARE *YOUR* TRIGGERS?

As with other modules in this workbook, we have begun by listing some examples that describe bipolar disorder *in general*. However, the key next step is to explore the issue of what *your own specific* experience of this condition is. This then allows you to manage your own pattern of symptoms more effectively and to work through the condition to reach your life goals.

Learning your personal triggers for a manic episode will help you to develop prevention strategies to cope with, limit, or prevent a full manic episode from occurring. Perhaps you can't remember what was going on before your manic episodes occurred. That's okay; sometimes the episode starts so quickly that it's hard to pinpoint what could have triggered it. And sometimes it can feel as though mania occurs spontaneously with no apparent cause, even when you've been following your plan of care. With time, you may be able to recognize the triggers. You can ask the trusted friends or family members who helped you to complete the Personal Mania Profile if they recall any clues. You may not recognize the triggers right away, but you might just surprise yourself one day and see a pattern that will help you to manage the next episode.

EXERCISE 9.1 Developing a Bio-psychosocial List of Personal Triggers of Manic Symptoms

In this exercise you will begin the task of identifying psychosocial and physical or biological triggers for your manic symptoms. In the list below, fill in details about the specific factors in your daily life that have triggered manic symptoms for you. And, of course, come back and update the list frequently as you become aware of other triggers.

Take another look at the lists of personal triggers above. For each factor that has triggered manic symptoms for you in the past, score it by writing a number in the space at the far left using the following scale:

- ▶ 3 = Always a trigger
- ▶ 2 = Sometimes a trigger
- ▶ 1 = May have triggered me once, or not sure
- ▶ 0 = Not a trigger

#	Psychosocial triggers	Description of events
	"Bad" life events	
	"Good" life events	
	Other stressful events (involving work or family)	
	Other personal or social factors	

#	Physical or biological triggers	Description of events
	Change in medication (psychiatric or medical, prescription or over-the-counter)	Which medications?
	Alcohol or drug use, or withdrawal.	Which substances?
	Physical illness	Which illness?
	Cyclic change (seasons, menstrual cycle)	Which seasons or cycles?
	Other changes in daily routine	What changes?
	Other physical or biological factors	

Now you have constructed a fairly specific list of factors that you'll want to pay attention to in your life. Avoiding or minimizing these triggers can help you avoid or minimize manic symptoms. For some triggers that are unavoidable (for example, medical conditions or needed medications), identifying these factors can help your care providers work more closely with you to monitor for manic symptoms in high-risk situations or to change treatment strategies. Some of these triggers may have been apparent to you previously, and some may surprise you. As you develop the habit of thinking of bipolar disorder as a bio-psychosocial condition, add other triggers that you identify to this list.

Joe's Story

Joe hadn't had a manic episode for years. He was taking his medications and keeping up with his appointments with his therapist and psychiatrist. He had a routine of sleeping about six to seven hours a night and working full-time as an architect. His aging mother, who had memory loss, lived nearby. As her ability to function diminished, he and his sister took turns spending nights sleeping at her home to be available should she need help. He became more and more concerned about her declining health, often finding himself worrying about her while he was trying to work. After doing this for a few months, Joe was awakened by his mother several nights in a row. During the following few nights he lay in bed awake worrying about her. Soon he noticed that he did not feel tired during the day, even though he had only slept a few hours. He also noticed he was beginning to have problems sleeping and would frequently wake up during the nights he spent at home. Joe recalled that in the past when he'd worked late on a deadline for his firm, his decreasing sleep routine had eventually triggered mania. He valued his mood stability and chose to use his knowledge about his personal triggers and symptoms to prevent a manic episode. Joe called his sister and told her he planned to hire a home health aid to spend the night with his mother. He also decided, with the help of his psychiatrist, to take a short-term course of medication to restore his sleep pattern. Within a few days, Joe was again back to sleeping six to seven hours a night, and his energy level and mood become stable. By recognizing the potential triggers, Joe had managed to avoid a full-blown manic episode.

Joe was a highly accomplished professional and, like many of us, lived a highly complicated life. Triggers for Joe were indeed bio-psychosocial, including both his worry about his mother's declining health and his own sleep loss in trying to care for her.

WHAT'S NEXT?

At this point, you've developed a fairly specific Personal Mania Profile, including typical symptoms and rapidly occurring symptoms. You've also identified those alarms, your early warning signs, that tell you that it's time to take action to prevent mania. And now you've also identified a series of psychosocial and biological or physical triggers that should be avoided or minimized; for those triggers that are unavoidable, you know that you may be at increased risk for mania when they occur. Recognizing early symptoms and triggers allows you to talk with your care provider about them and to respond in other ways to minimize their impact.

But what do you do when you find yourself having to deal with manic symptoms that you haven't been able to prevent? These tactics are the subject of modules 10–12.

Module 10: Cataloguing Coping Responses to Manic Symptoms

In modules 8 and 9 you drew up a profile of what your manic periods are like—the symptoms, the early warning signs, and the triggers. Now in this module, you will identify your responses to those symptoms—how you handle them, what you do with them, and what they seem to do to you.

WORKING THROUGH BIPOLAR DISORDER BY RESPONDING TO MANIC SYMPTOMS

In your Personal Mania Profile, you have painted a picture of how manic symptoms change the way you think, feel, and act—not what the psychiatric textbooks or diagnostic guides like the *DSM* or *ICD* say, or what science says manic symptoms are like in general, but your own *personal* profile. You have listed the typical symptoms and figured out which ones are early warning signs (module 8) and have also identified physical and psychosocial triggers (module 9).

Now we'll expand our view and look carefully at how you act, the choices you make, and how you find yourself behaving when you have manic symptoms. We call these *responses* to manic symptoms. We purposely separate them from the manic symptoms themselves, because the focus of managing your life with manic symptoms is to identify those actions over which you have some control—or could have some control. For instance, racing thoughts or lack of sleep may not be experiences you have control over, and you couldn't be expected to. On the other hand, spending money, starting projects, and the like may be actions you have more control over—or could have. The crux of managing mania, and the other symptoms that come along with bipolar disorder, is to enlarge your sphere of control over your life—to become less a passive conduit for manic symptoms and more an active manager of your symptoms and your life.

RESPONSES TO MANIC SYMPTOMS: COPING OR OTHERWISE

Many people feel like manic symptoms hit them like a tidal wave. They seem to be something coming from outside of them that sweeps them off their feet. The truth is that symptoms can hit like a tidal wave, but it's a wave that comes from inside. At the beach when a wave rolls into you, what do you do? You push back to keep your balance. Or you go with it and glide along for the ride—hopefully on the crest, head above water, enjoying the view and the wind on your face … and not tumbling, headfirst, underwater, and into the sand.

Responses or reactions to mania are like what we do when we're hit by that wave. Sometimes maybe you try to right yourself, keep your balance, and stand your ground with as much stability as possible. Other times maybe you float along and enjoy the ride. And still other times, maybe it's a little bit of both. The key to managing your life goals with mania cropping up from time to time is to figure out how to respond. So the next step in this process is to identify and list your specific responses to mania.

We use the term *coping responses* to describe dealing with situations by trying to keep your balance. But it's very important to identify all kinds of responses. We want to make sure you are with us on one critical point: *there are no predetermined right answers, and there are no "good" responses, and we don't*

Dropping In on a Life Goals Session

In a Life Goals Program group session, the therapist asked members to share stories of how they have responded to having manic symptoms—what they thought, did, and felt. The variety of the responses around the table amazed everyone. Jim said, "When I start to feel racing or my sleep dips down to less than four hours per night, I take an extra risperidone." Pete offered, "I find myself pulling out the credit cards more often, and to be honest, I go with it for a while. Then I realize how pissed off my wife will be when the next statement comes in, and I try to remember to leave my credit cards in my dresser drawer." Jeannie was saying, "I usually have a bourbon or two to slow things down and try to get to sleep and—" when Harry cut in and said, "Heck, I have a bourbon or two too—but it's to keep me going, and boy does it!" Pam had been quiet for most of this discussion, and when the therapist noticed this and asked her, she shook her head and said, "You know, I can't say as I 'cope' at all—I just find myself whirling away doing this or that, sometimes cleaning, sometimes cooking all night long and freezing things for weeks in advance, and sometimes—and I don't like to admit this—going out after my boyfriend is in bed, uh, looking for, shall we say, trouble."

So you can see that there are remarkable differences in how people respond to manic symptoms. For example, Jeannie planned her use of alcohol, Harry was fairly exuberant about his use of alcohol, and Pam was clearly uncomfortable—a little ashamed, perhaps—about some of the ways she responded to her manic symptoms.

give out gold stars when it comes to identifying better responses to mania. You're going to come up with some responses to manic symptoms in your life about which any care provider, family member, or other person with the condition would say, "That's a good way to try to manage things, to keep your balance, to snuff out the mania." You'll likely also come up with responses that any of these people would say, "Hmm, that wasn't the best idea in the world—look what trouble came from that." This is completely normal. If living with bipolar disorder was all about easy or "proper" responses, there'd be no need for this workbook. So let's dig in.

CONSTRUCTING A CATALOGUE OF RESPONSES

There can be great variability in the way people respond to manic symptoms—as great as the variability of the symptoms themselves and the people who experience them. Some responses are planned out and helpful in the long run, for example, taking an extra dose of prescribed medication as directed by your provider or leaving the credit cards at home in the day if spending impulses are getting stronger. As mentioned, we tend to call these coping responses. Other responses may be planned but not something most people would recommend, for instance, drinking alcohol or beginning business ventures that are fueled by an unrealistic sense of optimism. Still other responses hardly seem to be thought out at all—they are more reactive, for example, being in an exuberant manic high at a party and taking a hit off a crack pipe that's being passed around to accentuate the good feelings or "just because." Regardless of being planned or unplanned, "good" or "bad," we find it useful to think of all these reactions as responses to manic symptoms.

The following table contains some examples people have given us of how they've responded to manic symptoms. Some may strike you as good responses, others as bad responses, some as familiar, and still others as strange.

Examples of Responses to Manic Symptoms

▶ Worry about a deadline at work and stay up all night trying to meet it

▶ Give things away

▶ Write in a notebook

▶ Listen to soft music, dim the lights, and take a warm bath

▶ Try to keep my sleep cycle on track

▶ Call my care provider to set up an appointment to solve a problem

▶ Pray

▶ Get as far away from people as possible

▶ Call people in the middle of the night

▶ Tell myself it feels too good to let it stop

▶ Stay away from people who stress me out

▶ Ride my bicycle all night

▶ Leave the area until it all passes

▶ Eat large quantities of high-calorie food

▶ Shop till I drop

▶ Finally tell people off who bug me

▶ Drink alcohol to try to sleep

▶ Take my medication as prescribed

▶ Talk with friends

▶ Shop with a credit card

This list is incomplete, of course. More to the point, it's not necessarily a list of responses that *you* have experienced. So now the job is to make a list, a catalogue, of how you respond when you have manic symptoms—whether or not those responses are good for you in the long run. Then in the next module, we'll look at the pros and cons, the pluses and minuses, of these responses.

One thing is particularly important in this next exercise: don't be critical of yourself and don't put down only what you think is a "good" or "proper" response—write down *all* the responses you can think of, good or bad, proper or otherwise. Be like a scientist, like a naturalist, observing nature. The question at this point is what you do, not what you *think* of what you do.

EXERCISE 10.1 Cataloguing Responses to Manic Symptoms, Coping or Otherwise

In this exercise, you will construct a list of the ways you've responded to manic symptoms. Simply list the ways you've responded when you realized you were having manic symptoms. Include ways you tried to ease the pain that you were experiencing, ways you may have tried to preserve or increase the good feelings, and any other response you may have had during times of mania. If you didn't realize until later that you were having manic symptoms, what did you do then? List those responses too. And remember: *just list; don't evaluate or judge yourself.*

1. _____

2. _____

3. _____

4. _____

5. _____

How does the list look? How do you feel when you read over it? Some items in this list may have brought up painful memories; others, a sense of relief or pride; and still others, a chuckle. The point of this exercise, though, has been simply to identify and list the responses you've had. This is a critical step to keeping your life moving in the direction you want, even if you have manic symptoms.

WHAT'S NEXT?

Now you have a catalogue of the ways you've responded to manic symptoms. It's no more than a catalogue, or a list. We hope you didn't make too many value judgments or dwell on the impact of less helpful responses, and hopefully if you did, you didn't beat yourself up too much for the problems those responses may have caused. In module 11, you'll begin to look at the impact of these responses—but not in a judgmental way. Rather, you'll look at the pros and cons, the costs and benefits, of responses. You won't judge against some external standard of good or bad or right or wrong—rather, you'll ask yourself in what ways these responses helped you in your life's work and in what ways they got you off track. This is the essence of what we call the personal cost-benefit analysis.

Module 11: Introducing the Personal Cost-Benefit Analysis for Responses to Mania

> *In this module, you will use your catalogue of responses to manic symptoms from module 10 and evaluate how these responses have worked for or against you in pursuing your life goals. This will help you to increase your awareness of this aspect of your life and help you to increase control over your life even if manic symptoms are present.*

THE PERSONAL COST-BENEFIT ANALYSIS: A KEY TECHNIQUE

There are upsides and downsides to just about everything in life. If you buy a four-wheel-drive vehicle instead of a two-wheel-drive vehicle, you'll be able to go off-roading and be more secure on slick roads, but you'll burn more gas. If you order lasagna for dinner at your favorite Italian restaurant, you'll have a great meal, but you probably won't lose any weight. If you go to the gym in the evening tomorrow, you'll be in better shape (and able to work off that lasagna), but you'll miss your favorite TV show. And even if you marry the guy or gal of your dreams, you give up the hunt for someone even more perfect.

So why should responses to manic symptoms be any different? All choices are trade-offs, and all choices have costs and benefits. Care providers spend a lot of time and energy pointing out the downsides of certain "bad" or "unhealthy" responses to mania (or you might hear "maladaptive," "harmful," or "suboptimal")—responses like stopping medications, using drugs or alcohol, and the like. And care providers also spend a lot of effort reminding people of the upsides of "good" or "healthy" (or "beneficial," "appropriate," "proper," or "adaptive") responses like increasing medications, putting away the charge cards, or going to the emergency room when necessary. But if life were that simple, everyone would do the best thing and do so without effort.

A key step to making sure you're managing bipolar disorder in a way that supports your own life goals and values is to see how the way you deal with manic symptoms lines up with these goals and values. This, really, is what makes a response to mania "good" (helps you pursue your values and goals) or "bad" (gets in the way of living your values and reaching your goals).

Good Effects of "Bad" Responses

It's not difficult to find good effects of "good" responses. If someone has manic symptoms that lead to loss of sleep, which in turn leads to worse mania, a good response of taking more medication to go to sleep (under a clinician's guidance) should bring sleep patterns back to normal and reduce manic symptoms. It's also not difficult to find bad effects of "bad" responses. If someone drinks alcohol to heighten the effects of mania or as a "social lubricant" and increases their spending, projects, and sexual encounters, it's likely to make matters worse on several fronts.

But "bad" responses can have upsides, too. Let's look at an example and consider why someone might let themselves drift into what seem like bad responses—they see a benefit somewhere.

Harry's Story

Harry (from module 10) had been a combat fighter pilot, and was proud of it. He lived for many years among hard-driving, hard-drinking, risk-taking fellow pilots, and he thrived. After twenty years in the service, he had his first manic episode and was retired on disability. He made the transition to civilian work fairly well, taking a job in sales. He continued to drink heavily, though he never got into legal trouble, because of it. In fact, the three-martini lunch was the norm in his job, and that was just fine by him. Harry found that alcohol made him even more sociable and confident, and meeting with clients over lunch or dinner and a couple (or a couple more) drinks seemed to help in closing the deals he was trying to make. A few drinks before bed also helped Harry unwind and fall asleep, though he seldom slept soundly and woke up most mornings with a hangover. He tended to forget his medications on particularly heavy drinking days and on those days felt little need for them. His care provider was concerned about Harry's alcohol use, and this led to more than a few tense sessions between them.

Harry saw only the beneficial sides of alcohol, while his care provider was concerned about both current and future risks. But meeting Harry where he was in life required understanding the benefits that Harry perceived he was getting from drinking: increased sociability, apparent help at work, a feeling of solidarity with others, and help sleeping.

Bad Effects of "Good" Responses

Just as "bad" responses can have upsides, "good" responses can have downsides. For example, if your medications weren't working for manic symptoms, it would probably be "good" for you to check in with your care provider. What could be more sensible, especially if you have an empathetic, skilled care provider? Well, there can actually be costs here as well: sometimes people feel guilty about "bothering" their clinicians, or they feel they need to be stoic (to put up with it). You need to give feedback to your care provider about your responses and work together to achieve the best outcome. In module 31, you'll learn ways to improve your partnership with your care provider.

Pam's Story

Pam's manic symptoms seemed to her to come out of the blue and come on quickly. Eventually, though, she learned to recognize her early warning signs before things got out of hand. In Pam's case, it was usually taking an excessive interest in cooking, sometimes cooking late into the night, and sometimes buying cookbooks or subscribing to cooking magazines that she had little need for. When she would catch herself in "front-burner mode," as she came to call it, she knew to contact her care provider, who was more than willing to make medication adjustments in the office or over the phone. Pam, however, was hesitant to call her care provider. "She must be so busy, and I feel like a bother.... It makes me feel bad to think about starting yet another medication because I think 'Here we go again, I'm starting all over again.' ... And my boyfriend doesn't really understand and he'll give me a hard time if I go to the appointment and there's no dinner on the table when he gets home."

Pam knew what she had to do, and she had a receptive and understanding care provider. Yet there were still costs that she found hard to accept if she was to make the step to contact her care provider. Some of these costs are internal, like her guilt about bothering her care provider and her pessimism that came from having to admit to and not minimize the symptoms that had come back. Some of these costs were external, like risking conflict with her boyfriend. Clearly, there were downsides even to her doing the "right" thing.

EXERCISE 11.1 Personal Cost-Benefit Analysis of the Effects of Your Manic Symptoms

For each of your responses to manic symptoms, you'll describe briefly how the upsides and downsides help or hinder your striving toward your life goals and toward living out your core values. Pam's example, in the table below, will give you an idea of how this might look. To complete this exercise, refer to your personal responses to your manic symptoms (module 10) and to your previously identified core values (module 4). If the previous exercises are incomplete, feel free to add extra detail here. Keep in mind that these exercises may help you to focus on issues in a new way, and this may generate fresh ideas too.

Choose one or two responses to manic symptoms from module 10 and exercise 10.1. Try to pick one response that most people would consider healthy and one response that most people would consider not so healthy. Write them in the first column of the table after Pam's example. Write the positive effects (upsides) and the negative effects (downsides) of each response in the middle two columns. Fill in the last column by referring to exercise 4.1, where you identified several core values and life goals. Copy the blank form before filling it out so that you can come back and do the exercise with other responses.

Pam's Personal Cost-Benefit Analysis of the Effects of Her Manic Symptoms

Response to manic symptoms	Positive effects (upsides)	Negative effects (downsides)	Impact on life goals and core values
A "healthy" response: *I call my care provider when manic early warning signs appear.*	*I will get some support, encouragement, and some good advice. My care provider usually finds a helpful medication for me.*	*I feel bad about myself because I am bothering her. I feel hopeless, frustrated, and bad about myself because I have to admit to myself that it's happening again. I really don't have the time. My boyfriend will be mad at me.*	*I really want to make my relationship with my boyfriend work. He's a good guy even though he doesn't understand "this bipolar stuff," as he likes to say. I can't really be myself with him unless he accepts this part of me, and if I keep denying it, I'll never really be close to him.*
A "not-so-healthy" response: *I buy more cookbooks and subscribe to more magazines that I don't need.*	*I cook delicious meals and desserts that my boyfriend tends to like.*	*I spend too much money on cookbooks and magazines. They just sit in piles and remind me that I lapsed again. I stay up too late cooking and feel so tired the following day.*	*When I cook these nice dinners to share with my boyfriend, we have a great time together. Spending money on cookbooks that we don't need causes arguments between us.*

Personal Cost-Benefit Analysis of the Effects of Your Manic Symptoms

Response to manic symptoms	Positive effects (upsides)	Negative effects (downsides)	Impact on life goals and core values
A "healthy" response:			
A "not so healthy" response:			

Now that you've given yourself a couple of examples, let's review how a personal cost-benefit analysis works:

▶ Step 1: Identify your responses to manic symptoms. Honesty time: *Give equal time to the "bad" as well as the "good."*

▶ Step 2: What are the costs and the benefits of each? Honesty time: *Don't forget the upsides of the "bad" responses as well as the downsides of the "good" responses.*

▶ Step 3: How does each of these responses work for or against your core values and life goals?

Continue this exercise for all of the manic symptoms that you can identify. Looking at how you respond in healthy and unhealthy ways to your manic symptoms increases your awareness of how you make choices when manic symptoms occur. As you practice and become more experienced in identifying these responses to manic symptoms (step 1) and doing a personal cost-benefit analysis on them (step 2), you will gradually be able to choose purposefully—to *act* rather than to *react*—and to choose in ways that are consistent with your life's goals and values (step 3).

WHAT'S NEXT?

In the next three modules you will address in more detail three of the unwanted co-travelers that we introduced in module 6: substance abuse (module 12), psychosis (module 13), and anger and irritability (module 14). We will pay particular attention to personal cost-benefit decisions around substance use, since substance abuse is so common among people with bipolar disorder. Then you will learn more about psychosis and irritability, and how to manage these troublesome symptoms should they occur. Finally, in module 15, the last module on mania, you will pull together the information you have learned in modules 8–14 to construct a Personal Action Plan for Mania.

Module 12: Applying the Personal Cost-Benefit Analysis to Substance Use

In this module, you will apply personal cost-benefit analysis to the use of substances (whether or not you have a substance problem) and assess how alcohol or drugs have helped or hurt you in pursuing your life goals.

THE SPECIAL CASE OF SUBSTANCE USE

Forgive us if we seem a bit preachy here, but it's especially important to spend some time on the special situation of substance use. Why? Well, we don't have any crusade against, for example, alcohol. But recall from module 6 that substance *abuse* is a frequent co-traveler with bipolar disorder. The reasons are not entirely clear, but as we said, about two out of three people with bipolar disorder will have substance problems at some time in their lives and, remarkably, about one out of three will have an active substance problem at any given time (Goodwin and Jamison 2007; Bauer 2008a). That doesn't mean you necessarily have a problem, but it *does* mean that you're at higher risk to develop this problem than the average American—about six times higher (Goodwin and Jamison 2007). We've been talking, in the last four modules specifically, about manic symptoms and responses to them. But substance use can be an issue in any mood state—manic, depressed, or normal mood.

So this module would be worthy of your attention even if you've never had a problem with alcohol or drugs and did not screen positive in the CAGE or AUDIT screeners in module 6. Whatever your alcohol or drug use might be like, problematic or not, do walk through this module with us.

SOME FACTS ABOUT ALCOHOL AND DRUG USE

Many, many studies have documented the problems that can come along with substance use (summarized in Bauer 2003). We find it useful to divide these into physical and social problems. Let's run through the list.

Physical Problems That Can Come from Excessive Alcohol or Drug Use

Drinking alcohol excessively and using drugs exacts a physical toll on the body, including the following problems:

Alcohol

▶ *Medical neurological problems:* sedation, seizures during withdrawal, delirium when intoxicated or withdrawing, head trauma from falls or fights, dementia, balance problems, permanent numbness or tingling in the hands or feet

▶ *Skin:* easy bruising, varicose veins all over your body

▶ *Hormones:*

    ▶ Men: shrunken testicles, breast enlargement

    ▶ Women: decreased fertility, menstrual problems

▶ *Metabolism:* vitamin deficiencies, diabetes, obesity

▶ *Ears/nose/throat:* cancers

▶ *Lungs:* pneumonia from swallowing vomit during intoxication

▶ *Heart:* heart rhythm problems, permanent heart failure

▶ *Stomach and bowels:* internal varicose veins, ulcers, liver failure, cancers

▶ *Blood:* anemia, blood-clotting problems

▶ *Muscles and bones:* trauma during intoxication, weakness

Any intravenous drugs

▶ Serious heart infections

▶ HIV/AIDS

▶ Hepatitis B and C

▶ Tuberculosis

▶ Serious skin infections

▶ Track marks

Any inhaled or smoked drugs

▶ Nasal irritation and perforated septum

▶ Asthma, chronic lung disease

Marijuana

▶ Sedation

▶ Poor concentration

▶ Cancer risk similar to tobacco

Sedatives (e.g., benzodiazepines, barbiturates)

▶ Sedation

▶ Seizures during withdrawal

▶ Delirium when intoxicated or withdrawing

▶ Head trauma from falls

Stimulants (e.g., cocaine, amphetamines, ecstasy)

▶ Seizures

▶ Heart rhythm problems

Opiates (e.g., heroin, prescription drugs)

▶ Decreased sex drive and performance

▶ Menstrual irregularities

Hallucinogens (e.g., LSD, ketamine)

▶ Loss of control, panic

▶ Flashbacks

Social Problems That Can Come from Excessive Alcohol or Drug Use

Drinking alcohol excessively or using drugs can also result in the following social problems:

▶ *Work problems:* problems with boss and coworkers, decreased productivity, decreased pay, job loss

▶ *Housing:* loss of housing, substandard housing

▶ *Family:* conflict with spouse and children, divorce

▶ *Legal:* tickets or arrests for driving while intoxicated, disorderly conduct, assaults, or drug possession and dealing; disruptive pending court dates; probation; prison time

▶ *Social activities:* time spent using, instead of engaging in other activities to further life goals and core values loss of "clean and sober" friends

▶ *Religious or spiritual:* loss of contact with faith community, loss of spiritual center

And So the Question Is …

If all this is wrong with alcohol or drugs, why use them? And especially, why use them to excess? Well, as you've probably already guessed, of course there must be upsides. The upsides are unique to each person. And, as described in module 11, it's important to figure out how both the upsides and the downsides fit into your life goals and core values. So let's do a cost-benefit analysis similar to the one in exercise 11.1, this time focusing on your own specific pattern of substance use.

EXERCISE 12.1 Costs and Benefits of Substance Use

As we mentioned above, substance use can be an issue in any mood state—manic, depressed, or normal mood. The reasons to use substances, and the impact of using them, may be different across the various moods.

Take a moment to think about how you use substances during mania, how you use them during depression, and how you use them when your mood is normal. Describe the costs and benefits for you of substance use in each of the three mood states. List the upsides and downsides (benefits and costs). Then, describe the impact of these benefits and costs on your life goals and core values.

We separate substance use costs and benefits according to their use in mania, depression, and normal mood because their impact—their costs and benefits—in each mood state may differ. This added perspective will give you further insight regarding how substance use works for or against you in the pursuit of your life goals.

Costs and Benefits of Substance Use

Substance(s) used:	Positive effects (upsides)	Negative effects (downsides)	Impact on life goals and core values
Substance use pattern during mania:			
Substance use pattern during depression:			
Substance use pattern in normal mood:			

Now that you have a sense of the costs and benefits of substance use in each of the three mood states, you are prepared to think about the optimal pattern of substance use for you, again, in the context of your life goals.

EXERCISE 12.2 Specify Your Optimal Pattern of Substance Use

In this exercise, you will use the information from exercise 12.1 to determine your optimal pattern of substance use. Keep in mind that your use of substances should be driven by your life's goals and values—not the reverse.

The tricky issue, of course, is to figure out what is "optimal," or "most healthy," in terms of substance use. Look hard and honestly at your responses to exercise 12.1. Where does your pattern of substance use *get in the way* of your life's goals and values, rather than enhance them? What changes would need to be made in your pattern of substance use to make certain that using substances, even "a little bit" or "recreationally," does not hinder you on your way to your life's goals?

Be brutally honest with yourself—in fact, some people find it easiest to be honest doing this exercise by pretending they are their own best friend or counselor or guardian angel. With this type of "honesty check" approach, outline what you think truly would be optimal for you—*from the perspective of your overall, long-term, most important life's goals.*

Identify your optimal pattern and decide on limits

Amount and type of alcohol: _____

    Frequency: _____

Amount and type of other substances: _____

    Frequency: _____

Under what circumstances should you *absolutely not* use substances and why?

Alcohol: _____

_____

Other substances: _____

_____

It may take a bit of time and some trial and error to find a usage pattern that fits your lifestyle and doesn't cause problems. You may have to change your upper limits a few times. The best way to find a good pattern is to set your limits at the start of each week. Use the following Substance Use Logsheet to record your usuage each week. And how do you set limits? As always, the key is to ask, honestly, "Is this pattern of use interfering with my life's goals?"

Substance Use Logsheet

Dates	M	Tu	W	Th	F	Sa	Su
Alcohol type 1:							
Alcohol type 2:							
Total number of drinks							
Substance type 1:							
Substance type 2:							
Total amount of substances							

EXERCISE 12.3 Tempting Situations

Did you find yourself in any risky situations in regard to substance use this week?

_____ Yes   _____ No

If you answered yes, please describe what you were doing at the time (for example, walking past a hotel bar, being with friends who were using, etc.).

Situation 1: _____

Situation 2: _____

Please rate the level of urgency you felt to drink alcohol or use substances during these situations this week (circle one number).

1	2	3	4	5	6	7	8	9	10

1 =
Light urge

10 = Very
strong urge

Please rate your level of satisfaction with how you dealt with the situation by choosing to participate or not to participate (circle one number).

1	2	3	4	5	6	7	8	9	10

1 =
Very satisfied

10 = Very
dissatisfied

Try to be aware of each tempting situation you encounter in the future, assess your level of urgency to participate, and evaluate your response to the situation. Then, use this information to help you to make better decisions when new situations arise.

WHAT'S NEXT?

Substance use is just one of bipolar disorder's co-travelers. In module 13, you'll explore psychosis, and in module 14 you'll learn ways to manage anger and irritability. As with substance use, each of these may occur in either mania or depression. We will deal with the depressive symptoms in some detail in later modules.

Module 13: Working Through Psychosis

In this module, you will review the meaning of the term "psychosis" and learn several strategies for managing psychotic symptoms.

AN ADDITIONAL CHALLENGE IN BIPOLAR DISORDER: PSYCHOSIS

Not everyone who has bipolar disorder has psychosis. Not everyone who has psychosis has bipolar disorder. Rather, as you may recall from module 6, the term "psychosis" is used when a person has delusions or hallucinations. Delusions are fixed, false beliefs, and hallucinations are sensory experiences that are not grounded in reality (e.g., voices or visions). We consider psychosis to be one of the unwanted co-travelers that might come along with bipolar disorder because, while psychotic symptoms are not formally part of mania or depression, they can occur during some manic or depressive periods for some people. About one-third of people who have bipolar disorder severe enough to require hospitalization have psychotic symptoms (Bauer, McBride et al. 2006a).

Typically, psychotic symptoms in bipolar disorder are limited to periods of mania or depression and do not occur at other times. The people with manic or depressive symptoms who have psychotic symptoms at times of normal mood are given the diagnosis of *schizoaffective disorder, bipolar subtype*. This is because there are some similarities with the disorder called *schizophrenia*, which typically is characterized by delusions or hallucinations that are ongoing over months or years.

COMMON PSYCHOTIC SYMPTOMS

As introduced in module 6, there are two main hallmarks of psychosis: delusions and hallucinations. If a person has either of these, they are considered to have psychosis.

It is important to note two issues here. First, if you experience psychosis, it does not necessarily mean that you are severely ill—though it is advisable to consult with your care provider if you suspect that you are having delusions or hallucinations. Second, even if you do have psychotic symptoms, they are treatable and don't necessarily mean that you won't do well in the future. Again, consultation with a good clinician is very important.

NONPSYCHOTIC EXPERIENCES

Also, be aware that there are a couple of situations in which people say they are hearing voices but this is not a psychotic symptom. It is important to give an accurate description of your symptoms so that your care provider can make an accurate diagnosis and prescribe the best treatment.

Voices Inside the Head

These are thoughts that are foreign, external, and usually disturbing. They seem to come from nowhere and implant themselves in one's mind. Sometimes they seem to be coming from a particular person or being—almost like a voice. But if you can't hear them *outside* your head, like a person's real voice coming in through your ears, the more proper term for these is usually "intrusive thoughts" or sometimes "obsessions." An example that happens to almost everyone from time to time is when you make a mistake and a thought intrudes like "Oh, you're such an idiot" or "You never do anything right." Sometimes these voices inside the head can be quite persistent and severe and seem very much to come from something outside of us—but it's not the same as truly hearing an external voice, which is what we call a hallucination.

Hallucinations While Falling Asleep or Waking Up

It is not uncommon for people with or without bipolar disorder to have seemingly real experiences when falling asleep or waking up. This kind of "waking dream" is caused by one part of the brain falling asleep or waking up before another; sometimes sedating medications can make this happen. These experiences are called *hypnogogic* (when falling asleep) and *hypnopompic* (when waking up) hallucinations. These aren't considered to be psychotic. Rather, psychotic hallucinations occur when a person is fully awake and not intoxicated or withdrawing from substances.

> ### *Harriet's Story Revisited*
>
> Recall Harriet's story from module 6. During her manic period, she had delusional symptoms. She was convinced that she was getting messages from traffic signals that were critical for her daughter's well-being. These thoughts were more than a hunch or a guess or a hypothesis for her. During this time-limited period, she was certain of the special meaning that traffic lights held for her and her daughter. As typically happens with psychosis in bipolar disorder, when her mood symptoms (mania) remitted, so did her psychotic symptoms (fixed false beliefs—delusions—regarding messages from the traffic lights).

CAUSES AND TREATMENT OF PSYCHOSIS

Not surprisingly, we don't know exactly what causes delusions or hallucinations. However, many studies provide good evidence that an excess of the neurotransmitter dopamine in one part of the brain may be involved (see the discussion about chemicals in brain cells in module 2 for details). The main treatment for psychosis is medication, particularly neuroleptics or antipsychotics (see module 7 for details).

Managing Psychotic Symptoms

There is a great deal that you can do for yourself to manage psychotic symptoms, and that is what this module is about. One of the keys to managing psychotic symptoms is to recognize that while they may be dramatic to other people, they may not necessarily seem unusual to you at first. This is because our beliefs and our sensory perceptions are part of our very being—the lenses through which we see the world. If the lens is a bit out of focus, how would we really know?

Watching Closely to Recognize Psychosis

A critical step in recognizing psychosis is to develop what we call an *observing self*. Using your observing self is not something specific to psychosis—it's a normal part of life; we do it all the time. Let's say, for instance, that someone cuts you off in traffic. Your first response, impulsively, might be to catch up to them and run them off the road, or at least shout at them. Sometimes you might do exactly that, right away and without thinking twice. Other times you might get flushed, tense every muscle in your body, swallow hard, and curse under your breath, but also think about what would happen if you cut the person off in retaliation or challenged them, and then resist the urge to go after them. You go on your way—and eventually (often slowly!) the anger drains away. In this second instance, we'd say that your observing self kicked in and helped you to do a very quick—even unconscious—cost-benefit analysis.

Similarly, with psychosis it is helpful to have an observing self kick in to help you sort through what is real and what is not and what is somewhere in between. Try the brief experiment in exercise 13.1 to get a feel for this.

EXERCISE 13.1 The Television Experiment

Turn on the television and sit with your nose about two inches from the screen. Turn up the volume. It's overwhelming! You can't really see the images clearly, you can't concentrate because the noise is too distracting, and it can even be difficult to think about changing the channel or turning the TV off.

Now back it up a bit—flop down on the couch or in your favorite chair. Now you can see more clearly, you can hear better when the noise isn't so overwhelming, and you can plan to change the channel, lower the volume, or turn it off. You may want to continue to listen to the same channel, even at that loud volume, but now the choice is *yours*. Having an observing self kick in is like giving yourself some distance between your self and your perceptions and beliefs of the moment.

THREE STRATEGIES TO DEAL WITH PSYCHOSIS

Let's consider three types of strategies for putting your observing self into gear around delusions or hallucinations. Each of these strategies focuses on strengthening your mind either to cross-check the believability of a delusion or hallucination or to get on with life despite them. You will notice that these three strategies are very different in approach. One we call "Being a Scientist," and another, "Being a Zen Monk." The third strategy is an exercise "For the (Very) Active Mind." These are very different kinds of roles to take, and some people find one works better than another. But the strategies can be complementary, and you may get benefit from each of them at different times. Each can strengthen that observing self and help you to see what's going on in a particular situation.

Debbie's Story

Debbie went in for an evaluation and during the interview told the psychiatrist about the voices she heard and how it was sometimes hard to get stuck in traffic because she began to have thoughts that this was all planned by some invisible power out to get her. "How long ago did you stop working?" asked the psychiatrist. Debbie indignantly replied, "Stop working? I could never stop working. My office needs a good manager, and my family needs the income, and I'm not about to stop because of some voices and scary thoughts!"

Debbie's story illustrates two points. First, she was clearly experiencing psychosis. Second, despite her psychotic symptoms she was remarkably resilient and didn't let even the voices get in the way of her life goals of working and providing for her family.

If Debbie completed the "Being a Scientist" exercise (13.2), she might come up with additional reasons to explain the behaviors of other drivers.

EXERCISE 13.2 Being a Scientist

One way to think about psychosis is that it is a problem with being *overly certain* about something, say, a belief or a perception. This leads to inflexibility in thought, feeling, and behavior, and in many ways, flexibility is a hallmark of being healthy. We sometimes say that one key to dealing with psychosis is to turn a *certainty* into a *question*—or a *hypothesis*, as a scientist might say. We're not saying to turn a certainty into an out-and-out "No." Rather it can become a supposition, a conjecture, a guess, a "perhaps," or a "maybe." When you think about it, most occurrences in life have more than one possible interpretation, and the same is true with delusional beliefs.

To begin, in the following worksheet write in the first column a current or recent event about which you have a very strongly held belief (delusional or not). Fill in the middle column by writing what you were convinced was the cause of, source for, or interpretation of this situation. List *all* the other possible explanations that you can think of in the last column. Return to the list and add more over the next few days.

Examining Debbie's Beliefs Scientifically

The event or situation	Belief about the cause, source, or interpretation	Alternate explanations
When I was stuck in traffic, the guy in the car next to me turned and snarled at me. His face turned red, and then he laughed at me.	I went through a red light last week in my neighborhood. I cut off a guy in a gray Chrysler just like that, and I am sure that's him. I've seen him on this freeway all week. I know he's getting back at me, torturing me until he moves in for the kill.	It's possible that's not the same guy—a lot of guys drive gray Chryslers. It's possible that it is the same guy—after all, if you commute to downtown from my neighborhood, you're likely to be on this freeway. But maybe he's as frustrated as I am being stuck in traffic and that's why he looks so mad. And maybe he was listening to the radio and heard something funny and laughed. In fact, I've caught myself being absentminded and staring at people in other cars stuck in traffic and not thinking a thing about them. Maybe it is the same guy and he's giving me what for for cutting him off, but that's far different than following me or being out to kill me.

Examining Your Beliefs Scientifically

The event or situation	Belief about the cause, source, or interpretation	Alternate explanations

Taking a step back and acting like a scientist, then, helps you to realize that there are explanations you could consider other than the one that comes immediately to mind. Giving these other alternative explanations real consideration doesn't necessarily mean saying no to the original one. It's just about spending some time thinking about the other possibilities as well. This develops your observing self, like the way you gave yourself some distance from that TV set in exercise 13.1.

EXERCISE 13.3 Being a Zen Monk

This exercise taps into a very different strength of your observing self, and to do this we'll think in terms of being a Zen monk rather than a scientist. Zen meditation has been practiced for over 2,500 years by millions of people. We're not suggesting that you become a Zen practitioner, or even meditate, but there is one core aspect to that kind of practice that is very relevant to managing psychosis—it's so relevant, in fact, that it's been incorporated in a variety of psychotherapies to treat a variety of mental conditions. It's called *detachment*.

Everyone has tried at one time or another *not* to think about something. For instance, we now ask you for the rest of the day *not* to think about a green lollipop. Chances are, by tomorrow morning you'll have an image of a green lollipop well fixed in your mind! The same is true for a variety of bothersome thoughts, whether they are delusions, obsessions, or various impulses—if you set out to try not to think about them, you end up thinking about them all the more! Plus, you're exhausted by the end of the day and typically down on yourself as well for failing at your task.

The Zen monk ("mindfulness") approach is simply to let the thoughts in, as if they are coming in one ear, and then let them out again, as if they are going out the other ear. Sure, they'll rattle around in your head for a while, but the harder you try to push them out, the more they'll rattle around in there. As Zen practitioners would say, "Don't *attach* to the thought." This can work for delusions, and for hallucinations as well, when you take the attitude, "Well, there's nothing new here—I've heard or seen this all before." The important thing is not to fight with these thoughts and not to buy into them. Rather, treat them as if this, too, shall pass—and it will. Give it time. This gives your observing self additional distance (like with that TV set in exercise 13.1) and additional strength. Sometimes we say, "You will be thinking your thoughts, instead of them thinking you."

So the crux of this exercise is simply to sit and let the thoughts flow in … and flow out again. Sit in a comfortable chair, loosen your clothing, and put your feet flat on floor. Breathe from your belly, letting the air flow in through your nose and out through your mouth, allowing yourself to inflate your relaxed belly (this is different from more typical Western, chest-inflation breathing), and then letting it out again. Some people like to count slowly: "1–2–3" on the in-breaths and "1–2–3–4–5" on the out-breaths.

The thoughts will still come—no one can stop their mind from thinking! Sometimes the thoughts will be psychotic, anxious, depressed, racing, or otherwise. Whatever they happen to be, let them flow in … and then flow out again. No one can control their *first* thought—the idea is not to allow a *second* thought to follow the first: stick with your counting.

Try this for no more than ten breaths at first—just ten. Like all of us, you'll find that it doesn't come naturally at first. No one is perfect. Even people who practice this type of meditation daily for years get sidetracked. Random (and usually negative) thoughts will still sidetrack you at times—but don't worry (worry only gives you more negative thoughts!). When you realize that you're sidetracked by a stream of thoughts, just return to your counting.

Gradually, you can work your way up, using a timer, to one, five, fifteen, and thirty minutes, as much time as you feel would be helpful (and do use a timer so that you don't have to keep checking your watch to see how much time has passed). Try this practice in free moments, or distressed moments—whenever you like.

EXERCISE 13.4 Reflections on Being a Zen Monk

Now, a true Zen-like exercise would have no lists to complete, no workbook spaces to fill in, and, in fact, no thoughts that stayed long enough to be written down. We do find it helpful to do a little writing, though. Simply fill in a few notes below about your experience:

Date: _____   How long or how many breaths: _____

What kinds of thoughts were most persistent? _____

_____

_____

How did you manage to get back on track with your counting? _____

_____

_____

How did this exercise affect your handling of your symptoms? _____

_____

_____

Come back to this exercise after you have been practicing meditation for a couple of months and see how your experience has changed. Also, consider meditating in response to other symptoms such as anxious and depressive thoughts, since it may be useful with these as well.

EXERCISE 13.5 For the (Very) Active Mind

Sometimes being like a Zen monk—using the mindfulness strategies—can be frustrating. At times, it can be as if there is just too much rattling around in your head to let go of it all. At those times, it helps to have some alternate strategies, including some distractions, some physical activity, a companion to talk with, or some medications to take. So remember this perspective, and to support the process, fill in the following table with some aids that will help.

Let's use Debbie's example to get started.

Debbie's Alternative Strategies

Distractions	Physical activities	Companion to talk with	Medications to take
When I'm stuck in traffic, I play the radio, either news with a story line I can follow or music that I can sing along with.	*Not much I can do stuck in a traffic jam, but I do have some neck and back exercises that I can do, and I focus on the muscles and the joints instead of those scary thoughts.*	*Again, there's not much I can do in traffic, and I try never to use my cell phone while driving. But I do go over the last conversation I had with my son that morning and I try to reconstruct it word for word to keep my mind engaged with someone else.*	*If I'm still feeling shaken and obsessed when I get to my desk at the office, I'll follow my care provider's treatment plan and take an extra perphenazine.*

Your Alternative Strategies

Distractions	Physical activities	Companion to talk with	Medications to take

WHAT'S NEXT?

We have one more co-traveler, anger and irritability, to work on in the next module, and then we'll pull all this work together in your Personal Action Plan for Maria in module 15.

Module 14: Anger and Irritability

In this module, you will learn about feelings of anger and irritability and how they are experienced by people with bipolar disorder. You will develop a list of your own personal triggers for getting angry so that you will know what to be particularly careful of and how to avoid, if possible, unhealthy consequences of anger. Then you will choose personal coping strategies that will help you manage potential conflicts.

ANGER AND IRRITABILITY IN BIPOLAR DISORDER

Everyone experiences feelings of anger or irritability, but people with bipolar disorder are especially prone to these feelings and the adverse effects of anger. In fact, sudden feelings of anger or irritability are key symptoms of mania. Inappropriate anger attacks occur in up to 60 percent of people with bipolar disorder (Mammen et al. 2004). Moreover, up to 40 percent of people with bipolar disorder reported feelings of abnormal irritability, which is defined as feelings of excitability or annoyance (Deckersbach et al. 2004). However, anger and irritability can also be part of depression, and sometimes the most prominent aspect of depression, at least as experienced by the people around someone with bipolar disorder.

When you live with bipolar disorder yourself, you know the experience when your mood shifts and disrupts your normal life activities. These swings may be mild or severe, but for many people, the symptoms of mania may include excessive irritation or aggressive behavior, and depressive symptoms can include irritability, agitation, and anger. Also, during manic or depressive episodes, you may have developed negative thought patterns and beliefs that everything is bad. This habit of viewing things negatively may predispose you to becoming angry more easily than at times when you can see the world from a positive perspective.

WHAT IS ANGER?

Anger is natural and even a necessary emotion for survival, but it can be destructive when expressed inappropriately. Like an alarm, anger tells you something is wrong with a situation. In general, what causes anger?

▶ *Stress*—when faced with health, money, work, or personal problems

▶ *Life events*—when remembering bad things that have happened to you

▶ *Frustration*—when not in control of a situation or when overwhelmed by tasks

▶ *Fear*—when feeling that a relationship or a job may not work out

▶ *Resentment*—when feeling hurt, rejected, or oppressed

▶ *Disappointment*—when expectations aren't met

Anger has three components that can be described as psychological, biological or physiological, and cognitive (Mayo Clinic 2007):

▶ Psychological anger refers to your feelings, which can vary in intensity from mild frustration and disappointment to sadness to intense rage.

▶ Biological or physiological anger refers to the body's responses, when your heart rate or blood pressure rises or your muscles tense.

▶ Cognitive anger refers to your thoughts while you're angry, such as believing that you're justified to be angry or thinking that no one listens to you.

ANGER TRIGGERS

It is important to be aware of your feelings of anger and to identify when expressions of anger are unhealthy. Have you ever slammed your office door when you were frustrated at work? Have you ever yelled at the clerk in a store or a pharmacist on the phone when the person couldn't help you fast enough? These ways of managing anger are not only ineffective, but may also lead to personal or legal problems. Anyone's past life history can contribute to the way they react or overreact to situations. For instance, people who have been ridiculed, neglected, or victimized in the past may have built up negative feelings over time based on these events. Sometimes it is not the person or the event in the present that makes you feel angry, but it's your way of thinking—based on your past personal experiences—that creates these angry feelings. By becoming aware of and avoiding potential triggers, you are less likely to experience the intensity of the conflict.

Personal Triggers

In module 9 you identified triggers that automatically spark certain symptoms of mania. Triggers also exist for anger and irritability, whether or not you have manic symptoms. Triggers for anger can lead to anger, and an angry response can lead to the other person's angry response, which can itself be a new trigger and can escalate a situation quickly. Often this scenario involves circumstances where you believe you've been treated unfairly or your expectations have not been met.

EXERCISE 14.1 Identifying Your Personal Triggers of Anger

Think about things or events that might trigger feelings of anger for you. Try to think of situations in which you got very angry and describe them in the spaces below.

Conflicts with friends or family:

_____

_____

Problems at your job or school:

_____

_____

Other (specify):

_____

_____

When you recognize what events are triggers for you, you can prepare yourself to cope with the sudden onset of feelings and potentially avoid the situation.

WHAT IS YOUR ANGER PATTERN?

Some people can tolerate more stress, frustration, and disappointment than others. The same situations, conflicts, or events may trigger anger for you and not for someone else. There are many different ways to express anger when you feel the intensity of the emotion. By reflecting on how you express your anger, you can determine whether you need to learn new skills to respond in healthier ways.

EXERCISE 14.2 Your Personal Blueprint of Anger

In the space provided below, note those characteristics that describe your experience with anger. Use "M" to describe anger during mania, "D" to indicate anger that occurs during depression, and "M" and "D" for those feelings that happen during both mania or depression or at any time. Just leave the space blank if the description doesn't apply to you at all.

Your angry feelings

_____ Experience physical symptoms, like headaches, muscle tension, or a racing heart

_____ Experience intense feelings and scream loudly at others for an extended period of time

_____ Subject yourself to angry feelings for hours or days

_____ Hide or hold back angry feelings from others

_____ Feel angry more often than most people you know

_____ Other (please describe): _____

Your angry behavior

_____ Use body language that is threatening

_____ Lash out with anger by hitting, throwing, kicking, or hurting things or people

_____ Calm yourself down by drinking alcohol, taking sedatives, or using other drugs

_____ Surprise other people at how intense your anger becomes

_____ Other (please describe):_____

If you marked several of these items, you could benefit from consciously working on how you experience and express anger. Realizing how your anger pattern differs depending on your mood can clue you in to your pattern and help you manage your anger better. Keep in mind that you can learn to change your reactions and responses, and even reduce your physical symptoms.

Alternatively, you may have developed positive strategies like those mentioned in the list below to cope with angry feelings. Place a check in the space if you get relief by employing these strategies.

Your angry feelings

_____ Become aware of intense feeling, yell briefly, and return to normal mood

_____ Other (please describe):_____

Your angry responses

____ Exercise intensely to deal with anger and feel relief

____ Discuss issues with a trusted friend

____ Write in a journal

____ Use relaxation techniques (yoga, meditation, breathing exercises, etc.)

____ Other (please describe):_____

The techniques in this module will help you to create new positive habits that can replace unhealthy ones.

CONSTRUCTIVE EXPRESSIONS OF ANGER

If you have been wronged, it is natural to feel angry. But how you express these feelings through words, gestures, or actions can be problematic due to the intensity of the anger emotion. It's important to manage your reaction in a constructive, controlled way.

There are three basic ways to handle anger: controlled expression, suppression, and calming strategies (Mayo Clinic 2007).

Expressing Anger in a Controlled Manner

Verbalizing feelings using an assertive, reasonable tone of voice is, in the long run, typically more helpful to your efforts to achieve your life goals than outbursts or violence (though outbursts may feel better at the time!). Being assertive means that you clearly state your needs without hurting or overpowering others.

Suppressing Anger

Holding in your anger or stopping yourself from thinking about it can be a healthy reaction when you convert the energy to a positive, constructive behavior. The key is to make sure that you find a way to calm yourself or a healthy way to express your feelings that doesn't lead to just suppressing the anger you have. It is also important to be careful not to turn the anger inward or plot schemes to retaliate. The danger is that anger turned inward can lead to sleep problems, high blood pressure, tension headaches, and increased depression.

Calming Strategies

Controlling your outward behavior and your internal responses to the anger can allow you to calm yourself and let the angry feelings fade away. Relaxation or visualization techniques such as counting to ten, meditation, breathing exercises, or even exercising can help ease your physical responses and help you focus on something positive.

EXERCISE 14.3 Describing Current Conflicts

In this exercise, take an honest look at your current conflicts. In the first column, identify people, places, and other factors involved. Be specific. In the middle column, describe any verbal outbursts or violence as well as the strategies you used, including expressing or suppressing your anger or trying to calm yourself. In the last column, describe events, including things that have occurred in the past that aren't related to this specific situation but may affect the current conflict. After completing the worksheet, see whether your responses form a pattern.

Here's an example (see Jerry's Story, later in this module).

Describing Jerry's Current Conflicts

Situation that causes anger	Your response to the conflict	Unrelated life events
Coworker telling me to shut up	Becoming angry and yelling at coworker that he has no right to talk to me in that manner and that my opinions are important	When I was a child, my father would tell me to shut up and that I was just a kid who didn't know anything.

Describing Current Conflicts

Situation that causes anger	Your response to the conflict	Unrelated life events

It may be helpful to review your responses to this exercise in light of the following questions:

What are the patterns of your anger?

_____

_____

_____

Are there patterns to your responses, like outbursts or suppression strategies?

_____

_____

Is anything from your past a specific trigger for anger?

_____

_____

_____

MANAGING ANGER

In managing anger, the goal is to develop and strengthen your observing self, which allows you to make choices in your own long-term best interest, like you did in module 13 on psychosis. When thinking about managing anger, there are several approaches that can assist you. Here are the three Rs of anger control: retreat, rethink, and respond (Jacobs 1994).

Retreat

Step back from a heated discussion and take a break, a time-out, or a breather, rather than jumping in and expressing the first thing that pops into your head. Learning skills to relax, such as meditation, breathing exercises, or exercise, and scheduling personal retreats, even during your lunch break, may help you control your temper.

Rethink

Slow down and calm your racing thoughts and take your time to think about what's happening before you respond. You will be more effective in resolving the conflict if you get in touch with your feelings, listen carefully to what others are saying, and try to brainstorm possible solutions to the issues.

Respond

When you're feeling calmer, concentrate on using slower speech and a calm tone of voice that is not defensive or judgmental or insulting. Using silly humor, not sarcasm, can defuse the tension. Some people find it's helpful to write a script and rehearse it in private in order to stick to the main concerns. Remember to use "I" statements when describing the problem to avoid criticizing or placing blame. For instance, say, "I'm unhappy that you didn't come home earlier," rather than, "You should have been home earlier." Talking to a person you can trust with your feelings, a friend or a therapist, can help you express your anger, especially when you cannot feel calm enough to talk directly to the person who angered you.

OTHER APPROACHES FOR ANGER MANAGEMENT

So often our bodies hold the tension that anger produces. You can convert the energy and release the tension through physical activity. Taking a walk or playing any sport (hitting a ball, shooting baskets, throwing a Frisbee) can redirect the energy in a healthy way. If you are in a location where you don't have this opportunity, you could write your feelings in a journal, listen to music, or focus your thoughts on calmer, more positive times. This is also a good opportunity to use some of your "Zen monk" techniques (exercises 13.3 and 13.4).

It may seem the most difficult idea to accept, but forgiving the person you're angry with and not holding a grudge against him or her for words or actions will help you to heal. This allows you to take control of the issue at hand for the long run and not have it control and consume you.

EXERCISE 14.4 Coping Strategies to Deal with Anger

Now you're going to exercise your observing self a bit by using the retreat-rethink-respond model. Hopefully you're not seething with anger right now (but it's okay if you are—we didn't mean to offend you, honest!). So think back to a past situation when you were angry. Maybe, in fact, you can look back at some of the situations you described in exercise 14.3. In the left-hand column, describe the situation specifically, identifying people, places, and other factors involved. Were there times when you used all three of the three Rs, or any of them? They work best when you use them together because they end up leading you to act to change the situation.

Strategies to Deal with Anger

Situation that causes anger	Retreat-rethink-respond strategies you used	Effect on outcome

Did you recall using these tactics, even if you didn't recognize them as such? How did they work? Did you have any victories, partial victories, or total failures? The important thing going forward in your life from here is to practice and to strengthen that observing self so you can get what you want ... even if it means giving up the satisfaction of the well-placed zinger or the gratification from an outburst in that particular moment.

Jerry's Story

Jerry had bipolar disorder for many years and was effectively managing it with medications. Recently, Jerry had gotten a new job in a larger company that seemed like a great career move. However, his new boss was a stickler for detail and had been pressuring the employees to become more efficient in productivity. This boss was very demanding of Jerry in particular. Jerry was spending longer hours on the job and also had a longer commute to a different part of the city, which involved more rush hour traffic. One day on his way to work, Jerry was cut off by another driver on the highway. He ended up speeding to catch up with the other driver to yell at him, and he got a speeding ticket. Because of this incident, Jerry was late for work. Later that day, Jerry's boss called a meeting with the employees to get an update on their sales. When Jerry's boss started asking pointed questions regarding his work, Jerry suddenly lost his temper and yelled at his boss during the meeting. Jerry was reprimanded for this incident and later apologized to his boss. While Jerry felt lucky that he did not lose his job, he felt frustrated with his new position. His wife also told him that she'd noticed that he had been getting angry a lot more quickly. At that point, Jerry realized that he was working longer hours and losing sleep, which in the past had been a trigger for his manic episodes. Jerry decided that he needed to see his provider to help him assess his anger and implement coping strategies that could work for him.

Jerry's reactions to the pressures of his new job, demanding boss, and congested commute triggered his anger. It's completely understandable and without any relevance to bipolar disorder. However, in people with this condition, the stress—and the anger itself—can be a trigger for even bigger problems (mania) that can make the anger worse … and so begins the spiral. Jerry recognized that losing control and yelling at another driver and his boss were warning signs that he was headed for trouble, and in addition, he realized that he might be heading for mania. We often don't know which comes first, the chicken or the egg (the anger or the mania), but he was wise to know he needed to contact his provider, both to develop a short-term strategy to alleviate stress regarding his work situation and to develop a long-term strategy to deal with the intensity of emotions that might occur—as well as to keep a watchful eye out for mania.

ADDRESSING SPECIFIC TRIGGERS

As with mania and depression, it helps to directly address triggers of anger. Let's start with Jerry's example and then see if you can develop a sense of your own anger triggers and how to deal with them.

EXERCISE 14.5 Preventing Negative Consequences of Anger

Writing down your anger triggers and possible coping strategies for preventing the negative consequences of anger can often be helpful. For example, such an exercise might help Jerry cope with the stress of his new position and his rising anger.

Preventing Negative Consequences of Anger: Jerry's Experience

Identify trigger	Identify possible coping strategies
Stress of new position	*1. Review performance expectations with new boss.* *2. Review work hours required.* *3. Define personal retreat during the day by specifying break time and location.*
Traffic congestion in morning commute	*1. Map alternative route.* *2. Leave earlier in morning to avoid crowded time.*

Preventing Negative Consequences of Anger: Your Experience

Identify trigger	Identify possible solutions
	1. 2. 3.
	1. 2. 3.
	1. 2. 3.

WHAT'S NEXT?

At this point, you've worked through mania, including developing your own profiles of manic symptoms, early warning signs, and triggers. You've identified and assessed the costs and benefits of your coping responses and addressed the unwanted co-travelers of substance abuse, psychosis, and anger. In module 15, you will pull all of this together by creating a Personal Action Plan for Mania that will help you to work through mania.

Module 15: Personal Action Plan for Mania

> *In this module, you will pull together what you've learned to avoid, minimize, and cope with manic symptoms. You will use this information to develop a Personal Action Plan for Mania.*

WHAT IS A PERSONAL ACTION PLAN FOR MANIA?

A Personal Action Plan for Mania is an outline of personal coping strategies to prevent or limit a manic episode. You'll write your plan on a worksheet and on a card that you can keep with you for when times get tough. We've learned that it is most effective to anticipate difficulties and to plan how you'll respond, so having your Personal Action Plan for Mania ready before you'll need to put it into action is a good strategy.

CAN YOU REALLY HALT A MANIC EPISODE?

As for other jobs, you'll basically need knowledge and tools to complete the work successfully. We can think about stopping a manic episode in the same way we think about what it takes to keep a car running well. A car that runs well requires scheduled maintenance and repairs. Sometimes, even if you keep up with the service on your car, there will be times when it will need a tune-up. You'll notice the brakes are slow to grip or the ride isn't as smooth as before or you'll hear a noise. If you have the knowledge and resources, maintaining and keeping your car running will probably go pretty well. But like most things, you can expect to run into a few rough spots. Keeping things going well when you have bipolar disorder includes maintenance and sometimes a tune-up. It means you'll be using the tools you're learning in this workbook to attend to your symptoms and checking in with your care provider when needed. It also means having the reasonable expectation that you can accomplish changes over time that will allow you to feel more in control.

WHAT TOOLS ARE NEEDED TO HALT A MANIC EPISODE?

One of the core tools needed to halt or control manic symptoms is believing that you can actually do it. It's paradoxical, isn't it? You need to be optimistic, but not overoptimistic. It's being in tune with how you're feeling and behaving and feeling positive that you can manage an episode. At any rate, you have to believe in yourself. You also have to commit—you have to make mood stability your top priority so that you can continue your life's work. It's important to know and respond to your personal early warning signs and personal triggers for mania. You also have to have ready a number of coping strategies—that work for you—to manage symptoms. And you can bring this all together in an action plan.

Believing in Yourself

You may be feeling upbeat and confident that you're learning and understanding more about bipolar disorder. That's our goal. But learning to manage mania can be challenging on several fronts. Looking back at the problems mania has caused in the past can be discouraging. If you've tried hard to keep things going well and things have fallen apart from time to time, you're not alone. It takes practice and patience, and sometimes self-forgiveness, to live well with bipolar disorder.

Valuing Mood Stability

Choosing to be mindful of a manic episode and applying prevention strategies for managing one can be challenging. It's possible that, in some way, you've found mania to have benefits as well as costs and disadvantages. Recently, several celebrities have shared how bipolar disorder has created problems in their lives. In your life, you may recall that mild manic symptoms were helpful in some way … but they also signaled that there was trouble around the corner. In module 11, you spent time analyzing your responses to coping with manic symptoms and also learned that every decision has trade-offs. Take a moment to review exercise 11.1, "Personal Cost-Benefit Analysis of the Effects of Your Manic Symptoms." Keep in mind that a key step to managing mania is to see how it fits into your core values and life goals. Having stable moods will allow you to accomplish the things you want.

DEVELOPING A PERSONAL ACTION PLAN FOR MANIA

Now we're going to dig in and develop your Personal Action Plan for Mania. This means pulling together and extending work you've done in previous modules and distilling it down to what amounts to a very specific, concrete list of pointers and tactics—small enough to fit in your wallet. Is this all there is to managing mania? Of course it isn't. But the personal action plan is like a medical-alert bracelet you can check to give you the basics and remind you of all the work you've done in this section of the workbook—wherever you happen to be. So the next few exercises will help you to pull together your work in prior modules and will distill the information down into your Personal Action Plan for Mania.

Personal Early Warning Signs of a Manic Episode

Look back to module 8, where you constructed your Personal Mania Profile, a list of signs and symptoms of mania. These thoughts, feelings, and behaviors are your core symptoms. You learned that the signs and symptoms of mania are expressed differently by everyone. You also learned that understanding how your thoughts, feelings, and behaviors change when you're having mania takes time and practice.

EXERCISE 15.1 Identifying Your Personal Early Warning Signs of Mania

Take a moment to review your Personal Mania Profile in exercise 8.2, where you placed an "E" (for "early") in the column next to the symptoms you identified as your early warning signs. List them again here and add any other early signs you've noticed to this list:

1. _____

2. _____

3. _____

4. _____

Triggers of a Manic Episode

When you recognize your early warning signs of a manic episode, you tune in to the thoughts, feelings, and behaviors that develop in the beginning of the episode. If you think back to the discussion in module 9 about triggers, you'll recall that something happens, either external to you (in terms of a stressful situation) or internal to you (in terms of your reaction to this stress), that may cause these signs and symptoms to emerge. Biological triggers include sleep loss, seasonal changes, and reactions to drugs (prescription or illegal), alcohol, or caffeine. Psychosocial triggers include life events, such as promotions, job loss, or vacations. Becoming aware of and responding to these triggers is the next step in managing mania.

EXERCISE 15.2 Identifying Your Triggers of Mania

Turn back to module 9, where you constructed your list of personal triggers of a manic episode. Update that list of triggers in exercise 9.1, if you have anything to add, and then write down the most common triggers for your manic periods below:

1. _____

2. _____

3. _____

4. _____

Laura's Story

Laura had a seasonal pattern of recurring mania. She was most vulnerable during the month of May. Laura managed her bipolar disorder with medications, routine appointments with her care provider, and a structured routine to get plenty of rest, nutritious meals, and daily activities. As May approached, Laura was feeling well but began having difficulty sleeping. On May 20, she woke up after only three hours of sleep and spent the remainder of the night tossing and turning. Within a few days, Laura was pacing a lot in her apartment and feeling very anxious. At her job, she thought she was disappointing her supervisor by not keeping up with her work, though she felt great at times and took on more assignments than she could handle. She had "a lot of thoughts," felt angry with herself, and started getting irritated with her friends. Laura noticed that something was wrong and decided to check her list of early warning signs to see if she was headed for a manic episode. Her list included decreased sleep, pacing, anxiety and worry, having lots of thoughts, and feeling alternately great and angry. Laura realized it was time to call her care provider to prevent a full manic episode from occurring and to select a treatment based on her preferences and past experience as well as her provider's knowledge about treatment approaches to help stabilize manic symptoms. Her care provider gave her support, helped her make sense out of how things were going at home and work, and helped her track how her symptoms of mania were responding to her medications.

Responses to Mania: Beneficial and Not So Beneficial

This is "where the rubber meets the road" in working through bipolar disorder to achieve your life goals: when you're in the midst of a manic episode, or when you're in the upswing, what do you do?

EXERCISE 15.3 Focusing on Your Beneficial Responses to Mania

Turn back now to module 10 and read over your typical coping responses in exercise 10.1. What worked for you and what didn't? Remember to think from the long-term point of view: what helps you reach your own life goals, and what gets you sidetracked or heading backward?

List specific responses to emphasize:

1. _____

2. _____

3. _____

4. _____

List specific responses *not* to do:

1. _____

2. _____

3. _____

4. _____

CONSTRUCTING A PERSONAL ACTION PLAN FOR MANIA

The next step will be to get even more concise and put together a wallet-sized "crib sheet" to keep with you as a memory jog, to keep you focused on your life goals despite manic symptoms. This doesn't mean that living your life with bipolar disorder reduces to a wallet-sized card, or that that's all you need to manage the disorder. Instead, as we suggested earlier, it's like having a medical-alert bracelet for diabetes, which is a signal to others in an emergency to activate a medical care system geared toward managing diabetes. It's the same for this wallet-sized action plan—only it's a signal to you, and the care system is within *you*: it's your management plan. Just write the key strategies on this card and don't forget to add your support person—your family member, friend, neighbor, or coworker, or even a health care professional—who you would call to assist you in an urgent or emergent situation.

EXERCISE 15.4 Personal Action Plan for Mania

Let's distill this information now. Fill out the wallet card below. Later you'll do another one for depression, and the cards can be photocopied and kept together.

Action Plan for Mania

Key early warning signs:	Responses *not* to do:
1. _____	1. _____
2. _____	2. _____
Triggers to avoid or manage, and how:	Contact provider: _____
1. _____	Phone: _____
2 _____	Contact support person: _____
Responses to do:	Phone: _____
1. _____	
2. _____	

WHAT'S NEXT?

You're now more familiar with your early signs and triggers of mania, the stressors that may lead to the initiation of a manic episode. This information helped you to develop an action plan and will make it possible for you to better manage your condition and to prevent or limit future manic episodes. Remember to give yourself a break and accept that setbacks happen in life, but they need not stop your progress toward wellness. With time, you'll find the coping plans that work best for you and do not have bad effects. Even though you have good days and bad days, you've come a long way in improving your mental health.

In part III, we'll apply the techniques you've learned in part II to recognizing and coping with symptoms of depression and to working through depression.

PART III

Working Through Depression

Module 16: Constructing a Personal Depression Profile

This module is designed to help you develop an awareness of your personal signs and symptoms of depression, including early warning signs of impending episodes.

DEPRESSIVE SYMPTOMS: WHAT'S YOUR EXPERIENCE?

Like all medical conditions, bipolar disorder has a variety of symptoms that are "typical" or "average" or "characteristic" for the condition. However, also as with all medical conditions, each person's specific pattern is unique. Recognizing your own specific, current personal profile of symptoms will empower you and support your efforts to manage this condition.

You will spend modules 16 and 17 fleshing out this profile of depressive symptoms, as you did for manic symptoms. In this module you will construct your own profile of symptoms, and in module 17 you will identify triggers for your depressive symptoms.

Recall that working *through* bipolar disorder is a process, and a key first step to effectively managing depression is to learn how to recognize your personal symptoms. As discussed in module 1, depression, like mania, can affect thoughts, feelings, and behaviors, and we find it useful to keep these three dimensions in mind. As you construct your Personal Depression Profile, remember that depression can be painful. Recalling your depressive episodes may bring up difficult memories. If this is the case, take your time with this. Remember, you're not alone in trying to understand these feelings, and describing your own personal experience of depressive symptoms is the first step to controlling them.

EXERCISE 16.1 Some Background for Your Personal Depression Profile

In this exercise, you'll describe some basic qualities of your experience of depression. This will help you get into the mind-set for the more specific work to be done in exercise 16.2, "Constructing Your Personal Depression Profile."

People use many words to refer to depression besides "down." Some call it "feeling low" or "the blues." What words do you use to describe these feelings to yourself or to others?

_____

_____

_____

Is there a typical length for your depressive episodes? If so, it may be days, weeks, or even months. Give an approximation. If there is no typical length, what's been the range in length that you've experienced and how much does the length vary?

_____

_____

_____

As with a manic episode, a depressive episode can develop in a variety of ways. For instance, it can come on slowly and then gradually increase in severity over time. Or it can come on quickly, and you can abruptly switch from one mood state to another. Describe how the onset of depression has been for you. It's not unusual to have experienced more than one pattern. Again, how variable has your experience been?

_____

_____

_____

Now list some of the thoughts, feelings, and behaviors that are typical of your depressive periods, or that have tended to occur on more than one occasion. For instance, with regard to feelings, some people feel down or sad when they are depressed, others feel anxious or irritable, and still others just feel numb. How would you describe your personal experiences?

Thoughts:

_____

_____

_____

Feelings:

_____

_____

_____

Behaviors:

_____

_____

_____

So in this exercise you've written down some of the qualities that describe your experience of depression and have gotten a sense of the length of time and the variability of a typical depressive episode. In exercise 16.2, you will distill these into more of a checklist format that will be a shorthand record for you and will also be helpful for your provider to see.

EXERCISE 16.2 Constructing Your Personal Depression Profile

The profile is organized around thoughts, feelings, and behaviors. In the table below, place a check in the "√" column next to the symptoms you've experienced during depression (we'll come back to the other columns later). Recall that the list should represent *your* experience with depression, not what you've read is supposedly typical—this is about your personal experience, even if it's different from anything you've ever heard of anyone else experiencing. In fact, blank spaces are provided in the column at the far right so you can fill in personal symptoms that are not already listed.

Now, among these thoughts, feelings, and behaviors, there may be some that come on rapidly and quickly feel overwhelming. If so, mark these with an "X" in the "X" column.

Personal Depression Profile

√	X	F	E	Thoughts
				Difficulty with concentration and memory
				Thinking things are bad and are not going to get better
				Difficulty making decisions
				Thinking that others don't care when they really might
				Frequent thoughts about dying or suicide
				Paranoia or concerns that people are plotting against you
				Unreal concerns that you are worthless or evil
				Hallucinations: unreal voices or visions
				Dwelling on past problems or failures
				Other thoughts (describe)

√	X	F	E	Feelings
				Worthlessness
				Numbness
				Feeling depressed, down, or blue
				Lack of energy
				Impatience or irritability
				Feeling helpless or overwhelmed
				Pessimism about the future
				Feeling panicky or anxious
				Loss of appetite
				Increased appetite
				Loss of sex drive
				Other feelings (describe)

√	X	F	E	Behavior
				Restlessness or pacing
				Inability to sleep
				Sleeping too much
				Trouble starting or finishing projects
				Keeping away from people
				Stopping work
				Stopping usual recreational activities
				Fighting without good reason
				Frequent crying with little or no reason
				Preparing a suicide plan
				Other behaviors (describe)

You now have a shorthand version of your typical depressive episodes. In the next sections, you'll update this form by marking the symptoms noticed by friends or family members in the "F" column and marking the "E" column to denote early warning signs you may experience during a depression episode.

FAMILY, FRIENDS, AND YOUR PERSONAL DEPRESSION PROFILE

Sometimes with depression (or mania) you yourself may not be aware of certain thoughts, feelings, or behaviors. But others close to you may see changes that can help you identify—and therefore manage—your depressive symptoms.

EXERCISE 16.3 Team Building Around Your Personal Depression Profile

As you know from developing your Personal Mania Profile in module 8, involving friends, family, or other "team members" can help to you to develop an accurate and complete Personal Depression Profile.

In exercise 16.2, add any symptoms those close to you might have identified by placing a mark in the "F" column (for "friend" or "family"). You can ask for this input now, and/or you can mark symptoms family or friends have noted in the past.

EARLY WARNING SIGNS FOR A DEPRESSIVE EPISODE

As with mania, in depression some symptoms tend to come on early. These early warning signs are particularly important symptoms to identify since they can help you to respond early, before things get out of hand, and take more control over your depressive symptoms.

EXERCISE 16.4 Identifying Your Personal Early Warning Signs of Depression

Go back to your Personal Depression Profile to the column labeled "E" (for "early"). Put an "E" in this column for those symptoms that come on particularly early in depression. These will be the ones that sound an alarm and tell you, "Hey, I ought to do something now, before things get out of hand." You'll begin to deal with them in modules 17–19, so to start this process, let's just identify your early warning signs.

Now that you have completed your Personal Depression Profile, you have an outline of your typical or frequent depressive symptoms, including those symptoms that come on particularly quickly and those that others recognize but you may not. You've also identified those early warning signs that alert you to take action before depression symptoms become severe. Of course, you can update your Personal Depression Profile as you think more about your pattern of depressive symptoms.

WHAT'S NEXT?

Now you've developed your Personal Depression Profile based on your own experiences. The focus of module 17 is to identify events or other factors that have triggered a depressive episode.

Scott's Story

Scott, age forty-five, had been married for nineteen years and had two boys in elementary school. He and his wife decided to move to a new house in a better school district and closer to his work. Scott began to sleep later in the mornings because his commute was shorter, but then sometimes he just continued to sleep and skipped work altogether. He began to worry, snacked all day long, and gained weight. When the boys would come home after school, Scott didn't take his usual active interest in their day and did very little to help them with their homework or to play with them. He noticed he felt draggy, irritable, and down, and he believed that his negative thoughts were related to his job difficulties, which were increasing. He didn't really understand why his life seemed to be falling apart, though he vaguely remembered a similar period while he was a senior in high school. He found that he just wanted to sleep all the time. He would get to school late then, and now he would arrive late for work, if at all. His wife was losing patience and reminded him that oversleeping was an early warning sign, characteristic of depressive moods. A coworker and his wife encouraged him to arrange a psychiatric consultation. The psychiatrist worked with Scott to develop his Personal Depression Profile. After listing his thoughts, feelings, and behaviors, Scott realized that he was depressed, as he realized he had also been in adolescence. Together, Scott and his psychiatrist developed a plan to address his symptoms and treat his depression.

The first step in Scott's case, as in the case of most people, was to recognize and describe the pattern of depression in order to begin to map a treatment approach.

Module 17: Identifying Depression Triggers

In this module, you will learn about stress and related factors that may trigger a depressive episode. You will then develop a list of your own personal triggers for depressive episodes so that you will know what to be particularly careful of and what to avoid if possible.

TRIGGERS FOR DEPRESSIVE SYMPTOMS

Research indicates that a variety of factors can be associated with the onset of depressive symptoms for people with bipolar disorder. It is important to recognize such potential triggers, because avoiding or reducing exposure to them can reduce the likelihood that depressive symptoms will occur, or can reduce their severity if they do occur. As with mania, such triggers can be of two types: psychosocial and physical or biological. Recall again the bio-psychosocial approach, which will come in handy in thinking about triggers. We will review each type of trigger in turn.

Psychosocial Stress and Depressive Symptoms

When you look back over depressive episodes you've had, you may be able to identify an event or factor that had some impact on you psychologically or socially and that may have triggered a depressive episode. Recall that stress can be brought on by many changes, good or bad, in the regular routine of your life. So good things like getting married or getting a promotion can sometimes be as stressful as difficult things like divorce or losing a job. Stress is part of life for everyone. But a person with bipolar disorder, faced with the same stress as someone else, may be less able to cope with or shrug off that stress, which can then sometimes trigger depression or depressive episodes. Turn back to module 9 to review the types of good and bad stresses people have said may trigger a mood episode.

Physical or Biological Factors and Depressive Symptoms

It is well established that a variety of physical or biological stresses can cause depressive symptoms, and the evidence is even stronger than the evidence for stress triggering mania (Bauer 2008a). The most prominent of these factors is abuse of drugs like cocaine or amphetamines. However, alcohol can also be a potent trigger for depression. Even caffeine or certain prescribed medications can have this effect. Examples of prescribed medications that might be triggers include antidepressants, as we mentioned in module 7, and corticosteroids. Sometimes medical conditions themselves, and the pain that accompanies them, can trigger depressive symptoms. As with mania, for some people there can also be a seasonal component to depression, with a very regular seasonal pattern of depression occurring in the winter (Goodwin and Jamison 2007). Although you can't stop the seasons (except maybe by moving to the tropics), identifying seasonal changes as triggers allows you to increase your watchfulness and, if necessary, seek a change in treatment with your provider during those times. Take a moment to flip back to module 9 to review the physical or biological stressors that can cause a mood episode.

The following table lists a number of medications that may trigger a depressive episode. *Note:* this list differs from the list of mania-triggering medications in module 9.

Medications and Drugs That May Trigger Depression

High blood pressure medications

▶ Alphamethyldopa (e.g., Aldomet)

▶ Clonidine (e.g., Catapres)

Ulcer medications

▶ Cimetidine (Tagamet)

▶ Ranitidine (e.g., Zantac)

Psychotropic agents

▶ Benzodiazepines

▶ Neuroleptics

Drugs of abuse

▶ Alcohol

▶ Sedatives

▶ Amphetamines (withdrawal)

▶ Cocaine (withdrawal)

▶ Nicotine (withdrawal)

Hormones

▶ Corticosteroids

▶ Oral contraceptives

▶ Anabolic steroids

WHAT ARE *YOUR* TRIGGERS?

As with other modules in this workbook, we have begun by listing some examples relevant to bipolar disorder *in general*. The key next step is to explore your own specific experience of depression triggers. This will then allow you to manage your own pattern of symptoms more effectively and to work through the condition to reach your life goals.

Although depression may occur spontaneously with no apparent cause even when you've been following your plan of care, learning your personal triggers for a depressive episode will help you develop prevention strategies to cope with, limit, or prevent a full depressive episode from occurring. You can ask the trusted friends or family members who helped you to complete the Personal Depression Profile if they recall any clues. You may not recognize the triggers right away, but you might just surprise yourself one day and see a pattern that will help you to manage the next episode.

EXERCISE 17.1 Developing a Bio-psychosocial List of Personal Triggers of Depressive Symptoms

In this exercise you'll begin the task of identifying psychosocial and physical or biological triggers for your depressive symptoms. In the list below, fill in details about the specific factors in your daily life that have triggered depressive symptoms for you. And, of course, come back and update the list frequently as you become aware of other triggers. Once you've filled in this list, come back to each factor that has triggered depressive symptoms for you in the past and rate how often it has bothered you by writing a number in the first column using the following scale:

▶   3 = Always a trigger

▶   2 = Sometimes a trigger

▶   1 = May have triggered me once, or not sure

▶   0 = Not a trigger

#	Psychosocial triggers	Description of events
	"Bad" life events	
	"Good" life events	
	Other stressful events (involving work or family)	
	Other personal or social factors	

#	Physical or biological triggers	Description of events
	Change in medication (psychiatric or medical, prescription or over-the-counter)	Which medications?
	Alcohol or drug use, or withdrawal.	Which substances?
	Physical illness	Which illness?
	Cyclic change (seasons, menstrual cycle)	Which seasons or cycles?
	Other physical or biological factors	What changes?

Now you have constructed a specific list of factors that you'll want to pay attention to in your life. Avoiding or minimizing these triggers can help you avoid or minimize depressive symptoms. For some triggers that are unavoidable (for example, medical conditions or needed medications), identifying these factors can help your care providers work more closely with you around monitoring depressive symptoms in high-risk situations and/or to change treatment strategies. Some of these triggers may have been apparent to you previously and some may surprise you. As you develop the habit of thinking of bipolar disorder as a bio-psychosocial condition, add additional triggers that you identify to this list.

WHAT'S NEXT?

At this point, you've developed a fairly specific Personal Depression Profile, including typical symptoms and early occurring symptoms. You've identified those alarms, your early warning signs, that tell you that it's time to take action to prevent depression. And now you've also identified a series of psychosocial and biological or physical triggers that should be avoided or minimized. For those triggers that are unavoidable, you know that you may be at increased risk for depression when they occur. Recognizing early symptoms and triggers allows you to talk with your care provider about them and to respond in other ways to minimize their impact.

But what do you do when you find yourself having to deal with depressive symptoms that you haven't been able to prevent? These tactics are the subject of modules 18 and 19.

José's Story

José was pumped. Here he was, a twenty-two-year-old single guy, just graduated from a hot-shot liberal arts college, and he had landed a job with a big bank in Manhattan. He would have a salary that was nearly what he and his parents had shelled out each year for his college education, he had found an apartment with a friend of a friend that fit within his budget, and he was finally on his own. His first week at work went incredibly well—he was in high spirits and called his folks on a regular basis to tell them how happy he was with his new life; though he didn't tell them this—he was ecstatic to be out of the house and on his own and away from their sometimes overprotective and meddling ways. Work was fast paced, but José always had enough energy to make deadlines and do a top-notch job; in fact, it was reminiscent of his days in college: José had what he considered his "energy gift," the ability to get by on four hours of sleep a night. He made a number of friends at work and had an active social life. Curiously, though, over the first couple of months in the job, José became less energetic. The work didn't flow quite as easily, he was having problems with concentration and task completion, and, overall, he was not quite "on his game" in meetings with his boss and coworkers. He became more and more worried about his ability to perform at work and dwelled more and more on his shortcomings and imperfections. He found that he couldn't fall asleep at night and much of the day he felt keyed up and nervous and, unusual for him, more introspective and self-accusatory. He stopped going out with his coworkers after work and spent most weekends and evenings alone at home. He called his parents less frequently, and when they did talk, his parents knew that something was amiss. They suggested that he might see a counselor, but José responded, "It's all right, I'm just going through a tough time at work."

José had life by the tail. He was finally where he wanted to be in life … and yet something was going wrong. José didn't understand what was happening—he just knew that something was not right. José was beginning to experience his first episode of major depression, and curiously, it appears to have been brought on by some aspect of his new job, his new life, and perhaps even his leaving home and becoming more independent.

Module 18: Cataloguing Coping Responses to Depression

> *In the last two modules, you have constructed a profile of what your depressive periods are like—the symptoms, the early warning signs, and the triggers. Now in this module, you will identify your responses to those symptoms—how you handle them, what you do with them, and what they seem to do to you.*

WORKING THROUGH BIPOLAR DISORDER BY RESPONDING TO DEPRESSIVE SYMPTOMS

As with mania, by expanding your view, you can look carefully at how you act, the choices you make, and how you find yourself behaving when you have depressive symptoms. These are *responses* to depressive symptoms and are distinct from the depressive symptoms themselves. The focus of managing your life with depressive symptoms is to identify those actions over which you have some control—or could have some control. For instance, poor concentration or unrealistic guilt may not be experiences you have control over, and you couldn't be expected to. On the other hand, withdrawing from people and stopping your usual recreational activities may be actions you have more control over—or could have. The key for depression management is to gain control over your responses to depression—to become less a passive conduit for depressive symptoms and more an active manager of your life.

RESPONSES TO DEPRESSIVE SYMPTOMS: COPING OR OTHERWISE

Many people feel like symptoms of depression (and mania) hit them like a tidal wave. When that wave of depressive symptoms hits them, they respond in a variety of ways while trying to stabilize themselves. So the issues become, first, to identify those responses you choose when depression sets in and, second, to try to strengthen the responses that serve your long-term life goals and values. But for now you'll begin, as you did when exploring mania, by simply cataloguing your responses—*without judging them*. As sergeant Joe Friday said on *Dragnet*, "All we want are the facts, ma'am."

Dropping In on a Life Goals Session

When Kristie, the Life Goals therapist, walked into the room for the week's session, she felt something was different. There was a palpable heaviness in the room. The group members were not chatting as they usually did before the session. In fact, everyone seemed to be looking at their laps. No one was even shifting around in their chairs—all seemed leaden. It seemed, she thought, as though someone had died. "Either that," she thought, "or maybe I've just walked into a grade school classroom where someone's done something wrong and the students are waiting for me to find out what and punish them all." Kristie had been through this kind of session before, and she knew better than to be a cheerleader or to pour energy into the room in hopes of lifting the mood. Instead, she simply remarked on what she perceived: "I don't know about you, but I feel a real heaviness in the room, as if everyone is depressed," she said. Predictably, there was little response at first. She waited. Virginia admitted that that was indeed the case—she'd been hypomanic for a few weeks, but that mood had broken a few days before, and she said she couldn't keep her mind off of all the foolish things she thought she'd done. Michael chimed in that at least she'd had a few good weeks—he felt like he'd been depressed for years and there was no end in sight. Carl sat silently, as did the others.

Sometimes, groups can reflect what's happening within people. Kristie saw and felt the heaviness, and trying to engage the group brought out more depressive comments—or no response at all. The response of the group members was, not surprisingly, to hunker down in the face of depression; all that came to the surface were depressive thoughts—in this case self-criticism and hopelessness.

CONSTRUCTING A CATALOGUE OF RESPONSES

Some of the ways people respond to depressive symptoms are listed in the following table. As with mania, some responses may strike you as good responses and others as bad ones. See if some responses are familiar to you.

Examples of Responses to Depressive Symptoms

▶ Avoid friends.

▶ Stop recreational activities and exercising.

▶ Try to maintain the daily routine and pretend everything is fine.

▶ Seek out a trusted friend.

▶ Pray.

▶ Drop out of treatment.

▶ Get your hair done.

▶ Stop work.

▶ Keep appointment with your clinician.

▶ Ask family or friends to help with some responsibilities that you can't handle for now.

▶ Stop medications.

▶ Use alcohol and drugs.

▶ Plan suicide.

▶ Shop ("retail therapy").

In the next exercise, you'll have the opportunity to list how *you* respond when you have depressive symptoms—whether or not those responses are good for you in the long run. Then in the next module, we'll look at the advantages and disadvantages of these responses.

As we discussed in detail, when talking about responses to mania, remember not to judge your responses as "good" or "proper" responses—write down *all* the responses you can think of, good or bad, proper or otherwise. Just observe your thoughts and record them like a scientist would. The question at this point is what you do, not what you *think* of what you do.

EXERCISE 18.1 Cataloguing Responses to Depressive Symptoms, Coping or Otherwise

In this exercise, you'll construct a list of the ways you've responded to depressive symptoms. Simply list the ways you've responded when you realized you were having depressive symptoms. Include ways you tried to ease the pain that you were experiencing, ways you may have tried to preserve or increase good feelings, and any other response you may have had during times of depression. If you didn't realize until later that you were having depressive symptoms, what did you do when you did realize? List those responses too. And remember: *just list; don't evaluate or judge yourself.*

1. _____

2. _____

3. _____

4. _____

5. _____

6. _____

7. _____

8. _____

Reading over the list now, how do you feel? Some items on this list may have brought up painful memories; and others, a sense of relief or pride. The point of this exercise has been simply to identify and list the responses you've had, even though you may recall painful times. This is a critical step to keeping your life moving in the direction you want, even if you have depressive symptoms.

WHAT'S NEXT?

Now you have a catalogue of the ways you've responded to depressive symptoms. Hopefully you didn't beat yourself up too much for the less-than-helpful responses you may have made. You'll begin to look at the impact of these responses—the positive and the negative impact—through exercises in module 19. You may view these responses as pros and cons, or costs and benefits. You won't be asked to make judgments using some external standard of good or bad or right or wrong; rather, you'll ask yourself in what ways these responses helped you in your life's work and in what ways they got you off track—just as you did when exploring mania.

Module 19: Applying the Personal Cost-Benefit Analysis to Responses to Depression

In this module, you will take the catalogue of responses to depressive symptoms you developed in module 18 and evaluate how these responses have worked for or against you in pursuing your life goals. By doing this, you'll increase your awareness of this aspect of your life and increase control over your life, even if depressive symptoms are present.

THE PERSONAL COST-BENEFIT ANALYSIS: A KEY TECHNIQUE

At this point, it will help you to review the specifics of the personal cost-benefit analysis techniques you learned for responses to mania (see module 11). Recall that all responses to symptoms—*all* responses—have a positive side and a negative side. You might refer to these in your own words as pros and cons, costs and benefits, or pluses and minuses. Your job is not to judge the "goodness" or "badness" of your responses. Rather, you will simply be identifying the benefits and the costs of how you respond—that is, you will be asking the question "How does this response help me live according to my values and pursue my life's goals, and how does it get in the way?"

Carl's Story

Carl was diagnosed with bipolar disorder when he was in his midtwenties. He had finished college and most of graduate school in physiology when he had his first manic episode and was hospitalized for mania with psychotic features. Although he hadn't had such a serious episode nor been hospitalized since that first time, he had periodic hypomanic episodes and several long bouts of depression that included two suicide attempts. Despite these symptoms, Carl had built a solid career as a research physiologist for the pharmaceutical industry and had raised three children, the last of whom had just graduated from college. He and his wife had a stable and intimate marital relationship, and from all external appearances, Carl was a successful worker and family man. However, he constantly battled low-level depression and found it quite difficult to function when his depressive symptoms became severe. He had been in ongoing treatment with the same psychiatrist for twenty years, and two years prior, at his psychiatrist's suggestion, he had enrolled in a Life Goals Program group. On this particular day, Carl was very depressed and he was anxious as well. He had little to say during the Life Goals session and at home was withdrawn from his wife though still civil in his interactions with her. He struggled to get his work done during the workweek and had little to say to his coworkers beyond what was necessary. After his third silent Life Goals session, he spoke up in response to the therapist Kristie's query about stresses that could trigger depression. "I'm worried sick about my son, José. He's just left home and has a great job in Manhattan, but for the past month or so, when we talk to him on the phone, he sounds like he's depressed. I'm so afraid he's getting what I have. I can't stop thinking about it, and it's really killing me at home and at work." The group and Kristie spent some time discussing Carl's concerns and providing support and encouragement. Kristie, in particular, focused less on the stress itself— which was certainly significant and something that Carl could not control—and more on how Carl was responding. There were some very useful aspects to his response, most notably his continuing to work and his trying to stay engaged with his wife. She also explored the degree to which withdrawing from others at work was adaptive and how it was not—that is, the costs and benefits of withdrawal.

Clearly, Carl was working hard to keep his life on track in the face of both a significant stress that would worry any caring parent—concern that a child is not doing well—and a biological tendency toward depression. There was little that could be done to make the stress go away; it was something that Carl was going to have to live with, to work through. Rather, Kristie's—and Carl's—focus needed to be on what he could do to bear the stress.

EXERCISE 19.1 Personal Cost-Benefit Analysis of the Effects of Your Depressive Symptoms

For each of your responses to depressive symptoms, you'll describe briefly how the upsides and downsides help or hinder your striving toward your life goals and toward living out your core values. To complete this exercise, refer to your personal responses to your depressive symptoms (module 18) and to your previously identified core values (module 4). Feel free to add additional items to the list of core values and goals.

Choose one or two responses to depressive symptoms from module 18 and exercise 18.1. Try to pick one response that most people would consider healthy and one response that most would consider not so healthy. Write them in the first column of the table after Carl's example. Write the positive effects (upsides) and the negative effects (downsides) of each response in the middle two columns. Fill in the last column by referring to exercise 4.1, where you identified several core values and life goals. Copy the blank form before filling it out so that you can come back and do the exercise with several responses.

Carl's Personal Cost-Benefit Analysis of the Effects of His Depressive Symptoms

Response to depressive symptoms	Positive effects (upsides)	Negative effects (downsides)	Impact on life goals and core values
A "healthy" response: *Hang in there by talking with my wife when I'm depressed, even though I still feel removed from the whole situation.*	*My wife continues to be supportive and doesn't get angry or ignore me like she would if I withdrew totally. Sometimes I can talk with her about what's bothering me, like how worried I am about José, and we can do some problem solving.*	*I feel like I'm dragging myself through molasses. I even feel like a phony because I'm trying to make conversation but I feel dead inside. I feel like I'm not being "real" with her and I feel guilty.*	*My family is the most important thing in my life, and my wife is the most important person in my life. I know that even "going through the motions" until this gets better is better than spiraling down into isolation and despair that will feel even worse.*
A "not-so-healthy" response: *Just focusing on whether my son has problems with depression like me and not talking with my wife, my coworkers, or the other participants in the Life Goals group.*		*My wife will get upset if I give her the silent treatment. If I don't talk with my coworkers, I may miss deadlines to complete my work assignments.*	*If I don't communicate with my wife or coworkers, I will end up creating stressful relationships with people I rely on every day.*

Personal Cost-Benefit Analysis of the Effects of Your Depressive Symptoms

Response to depressive symptoms	Positive effects (upsides)	Negative effects (downsides)	Impact on life goals and core values
A "healthy" response:			
A "not-so-healthy" response:			

Now that you've written a couple of examples, let's review how a personal cost-benefit analysis works:

▶ Step 1: Identify your responses to depressive symptoms. Honesty time: *Give equal time to the "bad" as well as the "good."*

▶ Step 2: What are the costs and the benefits of each? Honesty time: *Don't forget the upsides of the "bad" responses as well as the downsides of the "good" responses.*

▶ Step 3: How does each of these responses work for or against your core values and life goals?

Continue this exercise for all of the depressive symptoms that you can identify. Looking at how you respond in healthy and unhealthy ways to your depressive symptoms increases your awareness of how you make choices when depressive symptoms occur. As you practice and become more experienced in identifying these responses to depressive symptoms (step 1) and applying a personal cost-benefit analysis approach (step 2), you will gradually be able to choose purposeful—to *act* rather than to *react*—and to choose in ways that are consistent with your life's goals and values (step 3).

WHAT'S NEXT?

In the next two modules, you'll address in more detail two of the unwanted co-travelers with depression: suicide (module 20) and anxiety (module 21). Then, you will learn more about how to manage these troublesome symptoms, should they occur, in modules 22–24. Finally, in module 25, the last module on depression, you will pull together the information you've learned to construct a Personal Action Plan for Depression.

Module 20: Dealing with Suicidal Thoughts

> *In this module, you will address the difficult topic of suicidal thinking, which, unfortunately, occurs from time to time for people with bipolar disorder. As when dealing with other aspects of this condition, you will approach the issue of suicide by weighing the costs and benefits of the actions.*

SUICIDE AND BIPOLAR DISORDER

Studies indicate that suicidal thoughts and actions are not uncommon among people with bipolar disorder. By some estimates, up to one in fifty people with bipolar disorder attempts suicide each year (Baldessarini 2002). Research has also demonstrated a variety of risk factors for suicide among people with bipolar disorder, including depression, substance misuse, psychosis, anxiety, being older, being male, having chronic medical problems, or having chronic pain (Bauer 2003).

The term "suicidality" is often used to describe actions or thoughts related to suicide, such as deliberate self-harm, or thoughts or plans of self-harm or suicide. Current thinking considers suicidality and related self-harm to be "a complex behaviour that can be best thought of as a maladaptive response to acute and chronic stress, often but not exclusively linked with thoughts of dying" (Mitchell and Dennis 2006, 151). What does this mean? It means two things: (1) not all suicidality reflects a desire for death (though it can, sometimes) and (2) people are often brought to the point of considering suicide or self-harm when there seems to be no other response possible—that is, when the costs-and-benefits scale around living has tipped too far toward the cost side. People are in so much pain that they simply cannot see the benefits of living.

What leads people to consider giving up on life altogether? Sometimes it is simply a symptom of severe depression or mixed mania. At times it is a planned means of escape. Sometimes it is an angry act. Almost always it is an act of desperation, accompanied by a sense of helplessness (a feeling that the person cannot do anything to change things) and hopelessness (a feeling that things will never get better).

Virginia's Story

"It was a brutal time," Virginia told the other members of her Life Goals group. "That's the only way I can describe it. I couldn't sleep. I couldn't eat without getting nauseous. I was losing weight. I just wanted to be left alone, but when I was left alone, things were even worse. It was like I had the world's worst headache, only it was inside my brain—like someone was twisting and twisting a wet dishrag behind my eyes … tighter and tighter and tighter. Then, something snapped. I wasn't angry, really, or I didn't think so. More frustrated. There was nothing more to my life, and I'd sealed myself off from everything that was my life. I was really in a spiral and I was getting deeper and deeper, farther and farther away from anyone and anything I cared about. Then one night, it must have been about 3 A.M., a lightbulb went on in my head, and I said, 'I'm gonna end it all. This will all be over. I'll be in peace, and everyone around me will be better off.' I know I was fooling myself—or at least I was looking at only one part of the equation. Sure, my husband was hurting, and my kids were confused, and I think all of them were angry at me, but I see now that they still had some hope for me, even if only a glimmer. I couldn't see it. And then, I swear it went exactly like this: I had a fistful of my pills in my hand in front of the bathroom sink, the water glass was filled, and I'd written the note and taped it to the mirror … and then our thirteen-year-old fleabag of a cat walked in and nuzzled my leg. That's all, that was it—I burst into tears. I still don't know why, exactly. I just collapsed on the floor, sobbing. My husband heard me and got up and knew exactly what was going on. Before I knew it, I was in the hospital, and everything from then on seems like a blur. And still it all seems so unreal now, looking back. It was only two months ago, but it seems like a different world, like I was a different person. I'm not 100 percent yet, not by any means—I don't even know what that means anymore. But my husband is there for me, and my kids, and, yeah, that damn cat. They keep me tethered to this earth, somehow. Somehow we'll figure it out."

Virginia was so very close to taking her life and to doing incredible harm to her loved ones in the process. In her case, she was kept alive by the thinnest of threads—her cat—and yet it was a thread connecting her to the rest of her life: her home, her family, and their history together. The scale was back in balance.

WHAT MAKES LIFE WORTH LIVING?

In module 4, we talked about what makes life worth living—and also how bipolar disorder can get in the way of pursuing those things. There are a number of aspects of life that are important to most of us. Recall the concentric circles diagram (figure 4.1, repeated here as figure 20.1), with you at the center and with larger and larger circles around you.

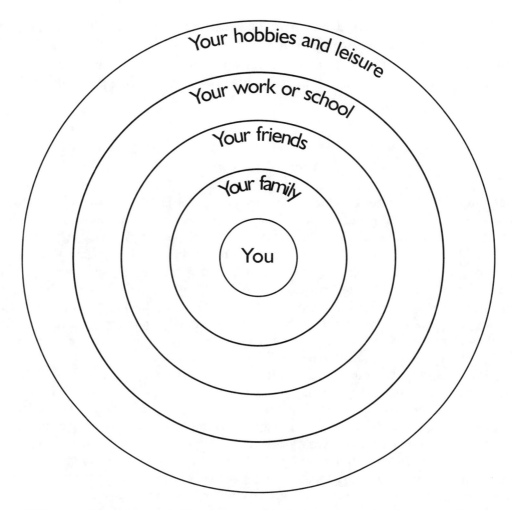

Figure 20.1 What makes life worth living: a series of concentric circles

For each of us, a sense of what makes life worth living includes these elements:

▶ Your own sense of self: your sense of self-worth, your values, and your goals, desires, habits, and quirks

▶ Your family, both family of origin and, if applicable, your adult family

▶ Your friends and acquaintances

▶ Your work or school

▶ Your hobbies and leisure activities

So, perhaps counterintuitively, in this module on suicide we will not spend much time discussing suicide or the ending of life. Rather, we will approach this from the other end of the scale—living life: *what makes suicide not worth it?*

EXERCISE 20.1 Tethered to Your World

This exercise should seem familiar: it's one half of a cost-benefit analysis. In this exercise, we're only going to look at the positive sides of the people and things in your world—those people and things that keep you tethered, really connected, to this world. The following categories map onto the concentric circles in figure 20.1. For each of these categories simply answer the question "What is it that keeps me going in my life even when I'm depressed? What are the counterweights to suicide?"

Now, it's quite possible—even likely—that not all of the categories below will represent positives in your life (e.g., you can't stand your boss at work or you and your spouse have separated). That's okay—just leave those items blank. We're focusing on the good, the positive things that you like in your life right now. Just as in real life, you'll work around the things that aren't positive, while recognizing and building up strength in other areas. Use additional paper as needed.

Self-image (values and life goals):

_____

_____

Family:

_____

_____

Friends:

_____

_____

Work or school:

_____

_____

Hobbies and leisure activities:

_____

_____

Now you have a catalogue of those aspects of your life that keep you going, even when you're in mental pain—the parts of your life that make it worth living. Tuck this list away for those really bleak times … or for those not-so-bleak times: it's worth remembering these positive aspects often.

SOME RESOURCES

Despite all the self-help work you can do on your own during a time when suicide seems like a reasonable—or the only—option, there are often times when you simply need someone else. Sometimes it's a family member or close friend. It's important to involve a trained professional, preferably the care provider you're in ongoing treatment with. Sometimes it's simply about getting to the nearest emergency room or crisis center. Sometimes all a person can muster is a call to an anonymous suicide prevention line—and we now have good scientific evidence that these can help (Gould et al. 2007). If you hit these hard times, remember to let someone know how you're feeling and let them help you.

In appendix A, we provide a Web-based list including two antisuicide resources. These in turn will direct you to more resources, to people who can help you.

So here's the question for you at this point: what resources are available to you—*you*, specifically—and how will you access them in times of need?

EXERCISE 20.2 Activating Your Resources

In this exercise, you will identify and list resources, both personal and professional, that you can activate in times of desperation. In addition, you'll answer what is perhaps the trickier question: "How do I know I need to activate this resource?" That is, what are the triggers and early warning signs for feelings of self-harm that should move you to action before things get serious? Fill in the blanks with the names and telephone numbers of people you can rely on. Then, briefly list some of your triggers that will remind you that it's time to call them.

Family member and/or friend

Who? _____

Telephone number: _____

What triggers or warning signs tell you to contact them? _____

_____

Clinician

Who? _____

Telephone number: _____

What triggers or warning signs tell you to contact them? _____

_____

Emergency room or crisis center walk-in

Where? _____

Telephone number: _____

What triggers or warning signs tell you to contact them? _____

_____

Anonymous telephone help line or hotline

Which one? _____

Telephone number: _____

What triggers or warning signs tell you to contact them? _____

_____

In this exercise, you identified a net of external resources to complement the list of positives in your life (expressed in exercise 20.1) to serve as internal resources. Together, these two lists can help you gain perspective. Take a minute to reread your responses. You may recognize a pattern emerging of triggers and warning signs that might prompt you to talk with a family member, friend, or a clinician earlier than you would have in the past. If the find yourself thinking about suicide, your first response might be to talk with someone who knows you personally. On the other hand, think about whether you would feel more comfortable getting immediate help from a trained professional who works at an emergency room, a crisis center, or an anonymous help line. The critical point is that you should never feel guilty, ashamed, or embarrassed to reach out for help.

Clearly, you must be alive to pursue your own life goals and live your own core values. Although for time-limited periods all may seem lost, remember always: that feeling, too, shall pass. Hang in there and act according to your goals and values.

WHAT'S NEXT?

At this point, you have identified internal supports—things and people that make your life worth living and so help tip the cost-benefit balance toward life—and you have identified external supports of people to call on who help tip the balance in times of your most significant need. In the next module, we'll explore how it feels for people with bipolar disorder to live with anxiety and we'll offer ways to cope with it.

Module 21: Anxiety—Another Unwanted Co-traveler

> *In this module, you will become familiar with the various types of anxiety disorders that may co-occur with bipolar disorder and you will learn some basics about how they are treated.*

WHAT'S ANXIETY DOING IN A BIPOLAR DISORDER WORKBOOK?

As we mentioned in module 6, anxiety is common in people with bipolar disorder, more common than in the general population (Bauer et al. 2005). Anxiety symptoms are also more common in people with *all* types of chronic medical conditions, including mood-related disorders (Bauer 2003). Perhaps that's not surprising, though we don't know exactly why this happens. Is it neurochemical? All mental activity is neurochemical, on some level. Is it due to stress in life from difficulties caused by medical conditions such as bipolar disorder? Sometimes it is, and sometimes anxiety appears to come on its own. For most people who experience them, both mood and anxiety symptoms are likely to be connected to both life stress and physiology, and the symptoms are most likely related to each other.

SPECIFIC ANXIETY DISORDERS

Anxiety symptoms come in a variety of "flavors," and there are several types of anxiety disorders that tend to co-occur with bipolar disorder. So that you can recognize them, this section lists some of these symptoms and disorders, including generalized anxiety disorder (GAD), panic disorder, post-traumatic stress disorder (PTSD), social anxiety disorder and phobias, and obsessive-compulsive disorder (OCD).

We describe some practical skills that are often taught for managing some of these anxiety symptoms. If you have these symptoms to the degree to which they interfere with your life, you'll want to talk to your providers about getting some focused help with implementing these types of strategies. Appendix A, Self-Help Resources, provides other resources.

Generalized Anxiety Disorder

Generalized anxiety disorder is a pattern of chronic worry about many different things, and more worry about a greater number of things than is realistic. GAD usually comes with significant muscle tension, and it disrupts sleep, causes fatigue, and preoccupies people's minds. Does it sound hard to separate from depression? It is: depression rarely occurs without some symptoms of anxiety, so a formal diagnosis of GAD usually isn't made unless the symptoms continue for months in the absence of depression.

Many of the medical treatments for depression (e.g., antidepressant medications), as well as many of the behavioral and cognitive techniques helpful for depressive symptoms (see modules 22–24), are also helpful for combating excessive worry and other symptoms of GAD. In addition, progressive muscle relaxation, which is described in this module, can help reduce tension.

Panic Disorder

Panic disorder is a striking, physical type of anxiety. A *panic attack* is a sudden onset of fear with physical symptoms—shortness of breath, nausea, shakiness, sometimes light-headedness, and even passing out. The attacks may last several minutes or sometimes over an hour. Then they go away. Observers usually don't know the person is having a panic attack, although the attacks are very uncomfortable. Sometimes the attacks come in response to stress, and sometimes they come out of the blue. If the attacks become so disabling that the person becomes afraid to leave the house, it's called *agoraphobia*. Panic attacks are frequently part of depression.

The discomfort of panic attacks can be part of a vicious cycle. It starts with increased arousal—having physical symptoms of tension such as a fast, racing heart. These symptoms are followed quickly by *catastrophizing*—scary thoughts such as "I'm having a heart attack," "I'm going to faint or lose control," or "I'm going crazy." This usually leads to overbreathing (hyperventilating), fidgeting, and pacing, and to self-reinforcing avoidance behaviors such as leaving a situation.

Post-Traumatic Stress Disorder

PTSD is a long-term impact of a life-threatening or harmful experience. People who suffer from PTSD had experiences such as sexual or physical trauma, combat, car crashes, or unexpected events such as the sudden death of a family member. PTSD may include nightmares or daytime *flashbacks*, which are like waking nightmares. Certain triggers in the person's environment may bring on unpleasant memories or even flashbacks. People with PTSD often tend to live their lives on guard either physically or mentally. PTSD can involve both physical and mental anxiety.

Social Anxiety Disorder and Phobias

Social anxiety disorder involves an unusual amount of nervousness in social situations or when you are the center of attention, as when you are giving a talk or a toast at a wedding. All of us experience some of this, and not surprisingly, it is often part of depression. As with GAD, the diagnosis of social anxiety disorder is usually not made unless the symptoms continue for months during a period when the person is not depressed.

Specific phobias were once also called *simple* phobias. They involve terror in response to something specific, such as spiders, heights, closed spaces, water, and so on.

Obsessive-Compulsive Disorder

Obsessions are thoughts that seem to push their way into a person's mind repeatedly and uncontrollably, and usually unpleasantly. *Compulsions* are rituals or habits that a person must do in order not to feel very anxious. An example of an obsession would be to have distasteful violent or sexual thoughts that one cannot control. Examples of compulsions include hand washing or checking locks many more times than is necessary. Treatment for this disorder usually involves practicing a combination of blocking the habitual response and substituting new thoughts and behaviors for the habitual ones.

WHEN DOES ANXIETY BECOME A PROBLEM IN BIPOLAR DISORDER?

Anxiety disorders frequently occur in people with bipolar disorder, and symptoms can be present at any time in any mood. For some people, anxiety symptoms may be present only during periods of depression. In that case, anxiety symptoms will improve when the depression goes away—depression seems to make everything worse. And, to turn this around, anxiety seems to make everything worse. So treatment for anxiety, either with medications or psychotherapy or both, can be an important part of treatment for bipolar disorder.

When does anxiety become a problem in bipolar disorder? It's a problem when it gets in the way of your life goals or works against your core values. One additional way anxiety can become a problem in bipolar disorder is when it leads to self-medication with alcohol or drugs. No doubt about it, alcohol and some drugs have some antianxiety effects—but at what cost? Even though anxiety can occur during mania, for some people mania brings relief from anxiety. Here there is a possible danger that people may stop treatment in order to become manic—that is, in order to lessen their anxiety. Again, you know the question: at what cost?

So managing anxiety can be an important part of your bipolar management. This module will provide suggestions for managing anxiety, and modules 22–24 will outline useful strategies alongside suggestions for managing depression.

Tim's Story

Tim had severe panic attacks during his first depressive episode when he was in his twenties. Thankfully, his depression and mania had been well controlled with medication over the fifteen years that followed. His clinician began to be concerned about Tim's drinking, which seemed to have increased over the previous six months. In fact, ever since Tim had gotten a promotion at work, he had been having "a drink or two" each day at lunch and more on the weekends. Tim began falling asleep at his desk after lunch and arguing with his wife at home on the weekends. Work at his new job began piling up. Tim and his clinician tussled over whether he was drinking too much, and Tim was unusually defensive. It later emerged that Tim's promotion meant substantially more responsibility and worries, and that his panic attacks had returned and occurred just about every afternoon. Despite his promotion being a "good stress" and despite Tim's mood symptoms being under control, panic was coming back into his life, and he was doing what he could to treat it. Medication adjustment and focused anxiety therapy brought the panic and, subsequently, the drinking under control. Tim learned to practice deep breathing every morning and afternoon and was able to slow his heart and breathing down instead of taking a nip when he began to feel tense at work. He began to get a lot more work done in the afternoons and started to have more confidence that he could succeed in his new position.

Tim's story illustrates how a very common coping response to anxiety symptoms—drinking alcohol—can have both seemingly beneficial and detrimental effects. It also illustrates that treatment for panic can be remarkably effective in relieving symptoms, which in turn helps people function better and make progress toward important life goals.

SELF-CARE FOR ANXIETY

Things that can help minimize the symptoms of most types of anxiety while also helping you minimize or abstain from use of alcohol and other drugs (e.g., marijuana), include reducing caffeine and getting regular physical exercise. Other helpful things include regular relaxation, meditation, or spiritual practice. You'll find an easy relaxation exercise to try below.

Managing Panic

Learning to manage panic or other anxiety symptoms involves practicing new ways of short-circuiting the vicious cycle we described above. The first step is learning that while the physical sensations caused by tension and hyperventilation are extremely uncomfortable, they are *not* in any way dangerous to you. Plainly written information about the physiology of panic symptoms is readily available (Barlow and Craske 2006).

The next step is to practice consciously substituting new, neutral thoughts—"These symptoms are harmless" and "No one can tell that my heart is racing"—for the scary thoughts about something awful happening. Immediately starting deep breathing or what is sometimes called *diaphragmatic* or *abdominal breathing* can prevent the hyperventilation from making you feel dizzy and will also slow down your heart.

Finally, continuing to do your usual activities rather than leaving the situation will help you get back on track and feel less afraid of future occurrences. Therapists will often ask people with panic attacks to practice deep abdominal breathing so that it becomes second nature. Being able to do this during times of stress can help prevent a full-blown panic attack from occurring.

EXERCISE 21.1 Coping with Anxiety Through Relaxation

This exercise will get you started learning to control some of the physiological parts of anxiety symptoms. The physical and mental effects of stress can reinforce each other. When your body is tense, you're more likely to be on the alert and to think fearful thoughts. And fearful or worried thoughts can cause physical changes—like tense muscles, churning stomach, or heart palpitations.

First, give a summary rating of your current level of anxiety by circling the number that best represents your feelings. Think of it as a ruler to measure your level of anxiety and rate how anxious or nervous you feel right now.

	1	2	3	4	5
I feel:	Not anxious or nervous at all	A little anxious or nervous	Neutral	Very anxious or nervous	Most anxious or nervous you've ever been

Progressive muscle relaxation, developed by Herbert Benson thirty years ago (Benson 2000), is one of the most commonly used relaxation techniques. As the name suggests, it focuses on progressively relaxing your muscles from your fingers down to your toes. Since it's not easy to force your muscles to relax, this method uses a repeated cycle of tensing and then relaxing groups of muscles. It's like a swing or pendulum—pushing it in one direction gets things started and gives it the momentum to swing back the other way. By first tensing your muscles, it makes it easier to feel the relaxation that follows. Each cycle is five to seven seconds of moderate tension followed by slow relaxation. You'll try to focus on the relaxation for twenty-five to thirty seconds before moving on to the next group of muscles. As you proceed from your fingers down to your toes, you'll feel a slow wave of relaxation traveling down your whole body.

Here's the sequence of muscle groups from fingers down to toes:

▶ *Hands and arms*—Tense by making two tight fists, and then relax.

▶ *Upper arms*—Tense by pulling your elbows in against your sides, and then relax.

▶ *Forehead*—Pull up your eyebrows to wrinkle your forehead, and then relax.

▶ *Upper face*—Squeeze your eyes shut tightly, and then relax.

▶ *Lower face*—Clench your teeth, pull back the corners of your mouth, then relax.

▶ *Neck*—Pull your chin down, and then relax.

▶ *Shoulders*—Pull your shoulders up and back, and then relax.

▶ *Chest*—Take in a deep breath, hold it, and then relax.

▶ *Abdomen*—Tighten your stomach, and then relax.

▶ *Thighs*—Lift your knees slightly and press them together, and then relax.

▶ *Calves*—Pull your toes up toward your head, and then relax.

▶ *Feet*—Curl your toes under, and then relax.

As you finish the last cycle of tension and relaxation, spend another thirty to sixty seconds focusing on the feeling of relaxation throughout your body. Now try the anxiety ruler again. Rate how anxious or nervous you feel right now by circling the number.

	1	2	3	4	5
I feel:	Not anxious or nervous at all	A little anxious or nervous	Neutral	Very anxious or nervous	Most anxious or nervous I've ever been

Relaxation is a skill that can be improved with practice. Like learning any other skill, learning to relax is easier for some than others. For a few lucky people, it's completely natural. For the rest of us, though, it's a skill we have to develop. As with other skills, it gets easier and easier with more practice—but you get rusty at it if you don't keep it up. We suggest that you begin with a regular schedule of ten to fifteen minutes every day. You'll want to practice for a week or two before deciding how useful it is for you.

WHAT'S NEXT?

In the next module, you will become familiar with additional techniques for managing symptoms of depression and anxiety. You will learn to think like a scientist in order to cope with these symptoms.

Module 22: Taking an Experimental Attitude Toward Working on Depression and Anxiety

In this module, you will plan some personal experiments—changing what you do and observing what happens—to help you get unstuck from depression and anxiety. You'll once again have the opportunity, as in modules 10 and 13, to think like a scientist by generating many new ideas and approaches to tackling a question and observing your own actions.

BREAKING THE CYCLE OF DEPRESSION AND ANXIETY

Many people living with bipolar disorder tell us that the hardest part is dealing with bouts of depression, which is often accompanied by anxiety. In this and the next two modules, we'll work in depth on some strategies that have helped many people effectively cope with depression and improve the quality of their daily lives. Anxiety is such a common co-traveler with depression that many of these strategies work with anxiety symptoms as well.

Not surprisingly, when you are depressed, and especially if you're also anxious, you don't have much energy or motivation to get things done or to take care of your health. You're probably waiting to feel better or more motivated before you become more active and start doing things that once brought you pleasure or a sense of accomplishment. As you know, though, getting yourself to feel better is not an easy thing to do … or you would have done it already! Sometimes the things you do to try to cope with depression actually make you feel even worse, and you get caught in a vicious cycle. You may remember this feeling from our discussion of panic attacks in module 21. In this case, if you don't feel like going out when friends invite you along to a movie and instead stay home and dwell on all the things that are bothering you, you are going to feel more depressed and anxious. Then you will be even less likely to initiate going out with friends because not only do you feel even worse, you feel guilty, and so on.

So we want you to try something different. We'd like to see you make a positive change in your everyday experience—to do something that will make even a small difference in how you feel, a difference that you can see. We believe that your thoughts and feelings are powerfully affected by how you behave, for example, how you act around friends and family and coworkers, spend your free time, or approach tedious tasks. Our idea is that spending more time doing positive things will spill over and begin to change how you think and feel. As you make progress and become active in shaping how you spend your time, the negative thoughts will seem less overwhelming. But you don't have to believe us; you can set up one or two personal experiments to see whether this idea works for you.

WHAT IS A PERSONAL EXPERIMENT?

As in module 10 (when you acted like a scientist to construct a long list of possible coping strategies before evaluating the value of each item), you will develop a personal experiment as a way to try out a new approach to doing things. We call it an experiment because we don't know in advance what the results are going to be, just as in module 13 (when you acted like a scientist who stated hypotheses and tested different possible explanations). We aren't sure just what will work best for you, so it is important to watch closely for the results. You may have to try a few experiments before you find what helps you the most. Because it's an experiment, you can keep what works and leave behind what doesn't.

We'll start with some modest experiments. When you feel down, even a small step in a positive direction can make a real difference in how you feel. Even if you don't think this will work for you, we ask you to give it a try in order to test this idea that trying a new activity could lift your mood. In fact, trying a personal experiment is probably most valuable if you are skeptical that it will really work.

WHAT HAS WORKED BEFORE?

For most people, knowing what's helped in the past can be the best way to find what is likely to help now. Following are some types of activities that have helped other people get out of a downward spiral and begin moving in a more positive direction.

▶ Enjoyable experiences that you haven't been doing lately (for example, spending time playing with your pet, taking time to take a bath, watching a ball game at the local park)

▶ Accomplishing something—like finishing something you've been putting off too long (for example, paying some bills, doing house repairs, cleaning out the refrigerator, signing up for a class)

▶ An escape or change of scene (for example, watching a movie, having breakfast out, reading the paper at a coffee shop, walking on a beach)

▶ Connecting with others (for example, calling a friend you haven't seen because you felt too down, calling old friends from the neighborhood whom you haven't heard from in a while)

▶ Physical activity (for example, walking, dancing, taking an exercise class)

▶ Something creative (for example, playing music, drawing, writing poetry)

▶ Something silly or playful (for example, playing games, dressing up in costume)

▶ Taking care of your health (for example, checking your blood pressure, creating weekly meal plans, getting overdue lab tests done)

▶ Working on anxiety symptoms with the strategies in module 21

EXERCISE 22.1 Mood Lifters

Think about examples in the list above (or better yet, other things not in the list) that have helped to lift your mood or lower your stress level in the past. Try to remember the things you enjoyed most when you were feeling better or the things you used to do that really made a difference in your life. You may want to use the following questions to get started.

What things have you enjoyed the most in the past?

_____

_____

_____

What things would your best friend suggest you try again?

_____

_____

_____

What things have you done that you're most proud of?

_____

_____

_____

What things have helped you to feel more confident or less anxious?

_____

_____

_____

What things would you most like to get off your plate?

_____

_____

_____

What have you always wanted to try but never made time for, or were too afraid to do?

_____

_____

_____

Now read over your list and think about which things you have done or want to do that can help you lower your stress level. It may be a new way of thinking that will improve your attitude or an activity that you can make happen during the next week.

EXERCISE 22.2 Simple Ideas to Get Moving

When you're getting started with this type of behavioral experiment, it's best to focus on things you can complete in a short time. Pick things from the list above so that you can begin right away—even today—to help give yourself an immediate mood lift. In other words, you don't have to plan big things like a trip to Hawaii. Write your ideas here:

1. _____

2. _____

3. _____

4. _____

Now look over your list. Circle the one or two things that look best to you. Focus on the things that you can make happen during the next week.

Larry's Story

Larry became sad and anxious shortly after his divorce from his wife of eight years. He was employed as an assistant supermarket manager and worked a rotating shift of odd hours. When he was married, his wife and neighbors were his most frequent social companions, and his wife maintained their social calendar. After his divorce, Larry didn't feel much like socializing with the neighbors because he was embarrassed about his divorce. He spent most of his nonwork hours watching TV, eating chips, and thinking about what a failure he was. A coworker who had been divorced for some time asked him to go to a local minor-league baseball game, but Larry didn't feel like he'd be very good company. Fortunately, the coworker was pretty insistent, and so Larry went to the game. Larry ended up getting caught up in the game and enjoyed scoring each play on the scorecard. When he got home that night, he realized he hadn't once thought about his marriage all evening.

Larry's experience illustrates the truism that "where your feet walk, your head will follow." That is, sometimes getting into motion physically and moving your attention to diversionary activities can lift your mood, if only for that time. But, hey, you deserve it! You deserve the opportunity to feel better regardless of how long the feeling lasts.

DEVELOPING AN EXPERIMENTAL ATTITUDE

When you're thinking of trying something new, many doubts and questions may come into your mind. You may even think, "This is stupid." Don't waste your time trying to combat all your doubts. This is supposed to be an experiment. It wouldn't be an experiment if you knew in advance exactly what was going to happen. You have to do the experiment to find out! Having an experimental attitude means that you keep doing it even if you feel unsure or you're afraid it won't work. Try to keep an open mind about how your mood can change in response to how you spend your time. In the next module, we'll examine your data and plan some new kinds of personal experiments.

Planning Your First Experiment

Now it's time to write your *experimental protocol*, or specific action plan. The goal is to identify a few specific experiments you'll try during the next week. The more specific you are, the more likely it is that your experiment will actually happen.

EXERCISE 22.3 Choose Your Experiment

Start by picking one thing from your list of things that have helped before in exercise 22.1. Think about a good time and place during the next week to try it out. Be as specific as you can: What day, what time, and where will you try it? Is there anyone else who can help you to follow through on your plan? Write your plans in the following worksheet. You will probably want to make several photocopies of this worksheet. You may want to try some of your experiments more than once; that's the most scientific way to find out how they work. You may also want to try more than one experiment. Remember, though, that it's more important to really follow through on a small number of plans than to plan a boatload of experiments at this point.

Next, gather your data from your experiment. Like a scientist, you'll write down what happens when you try something new or positive. As the time comes for each experiment, pay attention to what you're feeling and thinking and then use the second half of the worksheet to write what you notice. After you've tried your experiment, think about how it affected your mood. Also, write down any ideas about what you'd do differently next time.

Don't be surprised if you feel a little self-conscious about doing the experiment. You're planning to do something that doesn't fit with how you've been feeling. Depression and anxiety will try to keep you unmotivated and stuck, and it may take a bit of effort to get unstuck. That's why the advertising copywriters from Nike came up with a slogan about just doing it. Just remember to observe yourself and write down what happens. It's an experiment!

Personal Experiment Worksheet

Describe the experiment you plan to perform:

What? _____

When? _____

Where? _____

With whom? _____

What obstacles or internal roadblock might get in your way? How might you avoid them? _____

_____

Complete this section after you've done your experiment:

What happened as the time for the experiment approached? What did you think and feel about actually doing it? _____

_____

How successful were you at doing just what you'd planned? _____

_____

_____

What did you notice after you were done? _____

_____

_____

Rate the effect of your experiment on your mood by circling the number.

	1	2	3	4	5
I feel:	A lot worse	A little worse	Neutral	A little better	A lot better

WHAT'S NEXT?

In the next module, we'll look at the results of your experiment and plan some new experiments to keep you moving in a positive direction. We'll also talk about how your thoughts, positive and negative, affect your mood and impact the course of depression.

Module 23: Taking Action to Fight Depression and Anxiety

In this module, you will plan some additional personal experiments to fight depression and anxiety and will begin to construct an activity calendar to build on your success.

DEBRIEFING AFTER YOUR EXPERIMENTS

In the last module, you planned at least one personal experiment to see how positive activities would affect your mood. Now it's time to debrief and see what you learned from your data collection. This next experiment will be a little different from the others—it's a bit of an extended review and serves to organize and strengthen your coping responses, and also to identify any difficulties you may have had to date.

EXERCISE 23.1 Pause and Review

The first question concerns what happened when it was time to try your experiment. Here's an example:

"I said I would walk twice with my friend after work. On Tuesday we went, but on Thursday I just felt too tired to go."

What did you notice when the time came to do your personal experiment, and how close did you come to doing what you had written down?

_____

_____

_____

_____

The next question is about how things went when you did complete the activity or activities you had planned. Here's an example:

> "I said I would take my sister's kids to the zoo. I told my sister we would be gone for a couple of hours. Well, we all got so caught up in some of the new exhibits, that before I knew it, we were there over four hours. I really enjoyed the antics of the animals and the kids' rapture over it all. My mood really lifted, but when I came home, I thought about my problems at work again."

What did you notice about the effect of the experiment on your mood and thinking?

_____

_____

_____

_____

If you are like most of the people we've worked with, you probably noticed two things. The first is that when it came time to do one of your experiments, something "came up" that prevented you from carrying it through completely as planned. Perhaps a practical thing got in the way, like not having time or someone else not being available to do something with you. Or perhaps you were too tired or "forgot" or didn't see the point of the exercise. We call these experiences *internal roadblocks*—times when the depression has a powerful hold and gets in the way of completing your experiment. If you experienced these roadblocks, you're right on schedule. Again, if these changes were easy you would have done them already. So it will be helpful to look at these roadblocks out in the open to plan how to get around them. You will need to outsmart the "opposition"—depression.

The second thing you probably noticed after your first round of personal experiments was that when you completed your experiment as planned, there was a temporary change in both your mood and the chatter in your brain, and you could see this change. That's good; you can easily build on that. Let's go on to the next phase.

A NEW AND IMPROVED EXPERIMENT

Now it's time to plan the next round of experiments. Think about when you've tried to improve your mood in the past and about the kinds of things that seemed particularly helpful when it came to lifting your mood. Since we're still experimenting, also try to think of one or two more things to try that are completely new—that may even be a little outrageous. The idea is to think of things that don't match with being depressed. If you start giggling while you imagine yourself trying something, then you're getting the right idea!

Keisha's Story

Keisha had been feeling depressed and anxious and hadn't even left her house in a couple of weeks. She had barely bathed, much less made herself look presentable. Her friends had pretty much given up on her socializing with them by this time and had stopped calling her to come to church or out shopping. Keisha figured they probably all hated her by now. One day Keisha realized she really had to do something a bit outlandish to get her out of her extreme funk. She came up with the idea of inviting her friends over for a Saturday afternoon party where everyone had to wear the ugliest bridesmaid's dress they still had in their closets. She told her friends to not even worry if they couldn't completely fit in those dresses anymore. Her friends came over, and for several hours they ate cake and hooted over whose dress was the ugliest and tightest, Keisha laughing along with everyone else. Her friends were thrilled to see her and gave her lots of hugs and told her how much they had missed her.

Rather than continuing to avoid her friends, Keisha designed an experiment—to contact her friends and have a fun get-together, to overcome her isolation.

EXERCISE 23.2 Brainstorming Ideas for New Activities to Address Depression and Anxiety

What are some of your ideas for activities to try that are completely new and outside the box for you?

1. _____

2. _____

3. _____

So how do these ideas strike you? Are they a little bit outrageous, perhaps, or at least outside your comfort zone? That's not a bad place to be—having more strategies for depression makes you more resilient—and you're never too old to learn new tricks!

Here's a place for you to plan two new experiments—one building on the tried and true, and one kind of "out there," from the list above. This time you'll also plan ahead for those pesky internal roadblocks. Remember to make copies before filling in the worksheet, as you'll need at least two copies for this exercise.

Personal Experiment Worksheet

Describe the experiment you plan to perform:

What? _____

_____

When? _____

Where? _____

With whom? _____

What obstacles or internal roadblocks might get in your way? How might you avoid them?

_____

_____

Complete this section after you've done your experiment:

What happened as the time for the experiment approached? What did you think and feel about actually doing it? _____

_____

_____

How successful were you at doing what you'd planned? _____

_____

_____

What did you notice after you were done? _____

_____

_____

Rate the effect of your experiment on your mood by circling the number.

	1	2	3	4	5
I feel:	A lot worse	A little worse	Neutral	A little better	A lot better

EXERCISE 23.3 Activity Plan

Now that you've completed a new set of experiments, it's time to make a longer-range plan to keep up the momentum. Our new goal is for you to make a regular daily plan for several weeks for activities that will boost your mood and confidence.

Think about the activities you've tried in your experiments that you'd like to make part of a regular routine. What have you learned about the kinds of activities that make the most difference in how you feel? What has been most practical for you to accomplish? What do you have the most support from others for? Think about how many times each week you'd like to do each activity. Perhaps there is one activity that you could find time to participate in once a week or even every day. You may come up with an entire list of possibilities and can choose one or two to begin with. See what works for you. Here's an example:

What activity?   "Softball practice"

How many times per week?   "Twice—Tuesday and Thursday nights"

1. What activity? _____

   How many times per week? _____

2. What activity? _____

   How many times per week? _____

3. What activity? _____

   How many times per week? _____

4. What activity? _____

   How many times per week? _____

5. What activity? _____

   How many times per week? _____

6. What activity? _____

   How many times per week? _____

We've found it's most helpful for follow-through if you have specific plans like these. You are more likely to go to softball practice than to do a vague thing like "get more physical activity." You may find it helpful to get out a calendar, whether on paper or on a handheld PDA or computer, and write all your plans from above into your daily schedule. Fill in as much detail as you can, such as where and what time and with whom you will do each activity. Also, set goals that you imagine you will be able to reach—that is, don't overreach or try to do too much at once. It's more important to succeed. Succeeding at reaching smaller goals is more helpful for building your confidence than falling short of a bigger one, especially when you've been feeling depressed.

Finally, don't forget to anticipate the roadblocks that might pop up when you are getting ready to complete your activities. Expect both success and setbacks over the short term—and as you get more experienced and add new strategies to your toolbox for depression, you'll discover that the successes will outnumber the setbacks.

EXERCISE 23.4 Avoiding Setbacks

In this exercise, you'll write down three ideas about what may help you get back on track when you encounter a problem. What are some of your ideas about what you could try if you find yourself feeling discouraged or falling back into old, inactive patterns?

1. _____

_____

2. _____

_____

3. _____

_____

Just as it takes practice to adopt an experimental attitude, design your personal experiment, and have the courage to carry it out, it also takes skill to avoid setbacks and overcome them when they do happen. When things are going especially well for you, turn back to this exercise and add some positive strategies to the list.

WHAT'S NEXT?

In the next module, you'll learn some ways of taking a step back from negative thinking patterns that may also get in the way.

Module 24: Coping with Negative Thoughts in Depression and Anxiety

In the last module, you focused on action (behavior) strategies. In this module, you will practice taking a step back and observing your thoughts (cognitions) and you will plan some experiments for releasing the power that negative thoughts have over you.

TAKING A STEP BACK

When we feel depressed or anxious, most of us have characteristic patterns of negative thinking. For example, some people imagine the worst thing that could happen in any given situation and then they dwell on it. Some people think horrible thoughts about themselves whenever something goes wrong, and others focus on the hopelessness of even trying to feel better. All types of negative thoughts have some things in common. Typically, they are exaggerated or pretty extreme. They seem to happen automatically and they're embarrassing, so you don't share them with anyone. Negative thoughts tend to color your thinking so that you can't see anything good about yourself or a situation. They crowd out any more balanced thoughts and they tend to snowball—bringing an avalanche of other negative thoughts along with them.

The first step in combating negative thoughts is to put them on the table. Negative thoughts can be so familiar and so automatic that it's hard even to notice how they are controlling your mood and the way you behave, and how they are feeding into the vicious cycle of depression we described in module 22. So we have to make a special effort to take a step back and observe how our own negative thoughts work. A description follows of methods you might use to learn to see your typical negative thoughts for what they are. It's our hope that some of these methods sound like things you could try, or that they will help you become creative in designing similar strategies.

David's Story

When David got overwhelmed at work, his thoughts focused on how he could never get everything done: "It's hopeless; there's no way I can dig out of this" and "I'm such a loser. I'm sure I am going to get fired." David got more discouraged, more exhausted, and less able to plan ways to dig himself out of the pile at work.

For David, the trick to taking a step back from his situation was to imagine himself as a "thought scientist" standing to the side with a clipboard and white lab coat, observing his repeated negative thoughts. As each negative thought popped into his mind, he would write it down on his clipboard. He'd try not to get caught up in the content of the thought, but rather just note it and give it a rating as to how negative it was, like "That was a particularly virulent one, maybe the nastiest one all day."

Similarly, you can imagine yourself as any type of observer—maybe as a judge at the Olympics ("That negative thought was a 9.3!") or as a radio-show host ("And in the fifth position this week on the negative-thought countdown show is 'I'll never amount to anything!'") Others we've worked with picture their negative thoughts as moving across a computer screen like a screensaver—automatically running through their mind when they aren't distracted by something else.

EXERCISE 24.1 Writing Down Your Negative Thoughts

We'd like you to try to step back and observe your own pattern of typical negative thoughts. Putting them on the table—writing them down—can take away some of their power over you. Don't try to combat them or tone them down at this point; just jot them down here. It may be helpful to think about the areas or times in your life (at work, at home, with friends) where negative thoughts tend to occur. Here are some examples:

At work—"No one ever listens to me."
With friends—"Janey just pretends to like me."
At home—"I can't do anything right; I'm such a terrible father."

1. _____

2. _____

3. _____

4. _____

EXERCISE 24.2 Interrupting Your Negative Thoughts

The next step is to try some strategies that will help you get some distance from your negative thoughts in real time. We want you to be able to notice your thoughts in a new and different way than you have before. Instead of getting hooked into them, we want you to see them as just thoughts. The idea is to watch your thoughts as you would watch a movie or other people in a restaurant or animals in the zoo. Your thoughts can be fascinating to watch, but you don't need to get all caught up and interact with them. It can help to think about them in a humorous context—as if they were a puppet show—if that helps you to view them objectively.

What method or methods would you like to use to try to catch and observe your own negative thoughts in the next day or two? Here are some examples:

"I'll imagine someone calling me to say just what my own head is saying."

"I'll make a personal hit parade of my top ten negative thoughts."

_____

_____

_____

Set aside some time in the evening to write down what happens when you try to take a step back from negative thoughts.

Did you find there were times when it was easier than other times? What helped you to catch yourself? How did you feel afterward?

_____

_____

_____

CHALLENGING YOUR NEGATIVE THOUGHTS

Now that you've learned to notice your automatic thought patterns and take a step back from them, we'll offer you some strategies for more actively challenging negative thoughts. Our goal is not to get rid of *all* negative thoughts or worries, but to keep worries in their place and restore a healthier balance to your everyday thinking.

We'll present a few options below for you to try. We'll remind you here to try to hold on to your experimental attitude because it's likely you'll need to try out a few different methods before you discover what works best for you.

Thought Stopping

Thought stoppers are simple ways to short-circuit, or interrupt, negative thoughts before they start to control your mood. They can be things you say to yourself, mental images you think about, or actions you might take. Thoughts stoppers should be simple and quick—and should be something you can do any time or place. Here are a few examples:

▶ As soon as you catch yourself slipping into negative thinking, imagine a big red stop sign and yell "Stop!" inside your head.

▶ Wear a rubber band around your wrist and snap it every time you notice a negative thought crossing your mind.

▶ Imagine pushing a "mute button" to shut up the annoying negative thoughts.

EXERCISE 24.3 Thought Stopping

List some thought stoppers that you'll try in the next week:

1. _____

2. _____

3. _____

4. _____

Changing the Subject

Another strategy is simply to shift your attention to something else—"change the channel" from your negative thoughts, so to speak. Here are some examples:

▶ When you get caught up in worries or self-criticism, try a change of scene. Get up and move around or go someplace else. Physical activity can help to shift your attention from negative thinking.

▶ Call someone, especially somebody who is a positive influence for you.

▶ Remind yourself of better times. Carry a picture or a list of positive things you've accomplished that you can take out when you need to change the subject in your head.

EXERCISE 24.4 Change the Negative Channel

What are some methods for changing the subject that you'd like to try?

1. _____

2. _____

3. _____

4. _____

Being Logical with Yourself

The final type of strategy you may want to try is to take a step back from the way you are interpreting a situation and examine the evidence for your negative thought. As we mentioned earlier, negative thoughts are often exaggerated or extreme or even illogical. Luckily, irrational negative thoughts can only live on if we can't see the evidence that proves them wrong. Have you ever had the experience of having a friend help you to see or interpret a situation in a new way, one that was different from what your negative assumptions suggested? The key to this type of strategy is to act like that friend and think about other ways to see or interpret an upsetting situation.

EXERCISE 24.5 Pulling Negative Thoughts Apart

The following worksheet will help you be more logical about your negative thoughts. In the first column, write one of your typical negative thoughts. In the second column, jot some notes on what real evidence you have to support your negative or self-critical thought. What are the facts or behaviors that prove your view? How far did you have to "jump" (that is, how much did you have to imagine or fill in) to reach that negative conclusion? In the third column, describe how someone else might look at the situation. For instance, would a friend blame you as much as you are blaming yourself? And finally, in the last column, describe a few other explanations for the same situation or set of facts. How many of these other explanations are just as likely as the negative one you came up with?

Pulling Negative Thoughts Apart

Negative thought	Real evidence	Objective view of someone else	Other explanation of situation

When you used this logical approach, did it help to write down your thoughts and the answers to these questions? Somehow negative thoughts often look weaker and more illogical when you see them on paper.

WHAT IF MY NEGATIVE THOUGHTS ARE REALLY TRUE?

We must acknowledge here that while many negative thoughts are illogical or extreme, sometimes they are just simple facts. If you have just gotten divorced, it's hard to argue against the repeated negative thought "I couldn't make that relationship work." In these situations, you don't want to ask yourself whether the thought is true, but rather whether it makes sense to think that thought over and over and over again. If you are struggling with a true negative thought, try asking yourself these two questions: "Why now?" and "So what?"

Asking "Why now?" is a way of shifting your attention. The fact that your relationship didn't work out doesn't mean you need to remind yourself about it every second of the day! But if there's something useful to be gained—in pursuit of your life goals—by looking at some aspect of the issue, then it makes sense to do so … though in manageable doses.

Asking "So what?" can help you get to the negative interpretations you are making that lie underneath the facts. For example, the fact "I couldn't make the relationship work" may be a cover for other thoughts, like "I'm such a failure at relationships" or "No one would ever marry me." Often, the subtle message underlying the repetitive thoughts is that whatever it is, it is your fault also. And it is these interpretations, or *attributions*, that are often what affect your mood. After all, attributions are not really facts at all—they're opinions (and harsh ones at that) that can't predict any future experiences. You can't rely on a fortune-teller's crystal ball. Remember—you're a scientist! These negative thoughts can be combated with logic. For example, last time we checked, relationships depend on two people, not just one! So, in the example above, it doesn't make sense to take all the blame.

WHAT'S NEXT?

We hope that you'll try some of these thought-balancing methods in the coming weeks and discover what works best for you. In the next module, you'll select what you've learned works best and assemble it into a Personal Action Plan for Depression.

Module 25: Personal Action Plan for Depression

> *In this module, you will pull together everything you've learned to avoid, minimize, and cope with depressive symptoms. You will use this information to develop a Personal Action Plan for Depression, similar to the action plan you put together for mania.*

WHAT IS A PERSONAL ACTION PLAN FOR DEPRESSION?

As in part II on mania, an action plan is an outline of personal coping strategies to prevent or limit an episode, in this case, a depressive one. From your work with mania, you already know that it is most effective to anticipate difficulties and plan how you'll respond. You'll write your plan on a worksheet and also on a reminder card that you can refer to when depressive symptoms occur.

AVOIDING A DEPRESSIVE EPISODE

Over the past several weeks, you've put a lot of effort into experimenting with trying new activities and ways to watch yourself thinking. If you want to hold on to the progress you've made, you'll also need to keep practicing the things that have helped you so far. Practicing these depression-fighting strategies that helped you get better will also help you manage the rough times that will come up in the future. As we mentioned earlier in module 15, keeping things going well when you have bipolar disorder includes maintenance and sometimes a tune-up. It means you'll be using the tools you're learning in this workbook to attend to your symptoms as well as checking in with your care provider when needed.

Creating a written Personal Action Plan for Depression is the best way to pay attention to how you are feeling and to keep practicing the new skills you've developed. In this module, we will work on the various parts of an action plan aimed at helping you avoid depression altogether or take action early if things start to slip.

DEVELOPING PERSONAL ACTION PLAN FOR DEPRESSION

Now it's time to review your personal early warning signs of a depressive episode, the triggers that start episodes, and your positive or negative responses. All of this information is vital to the creation of your Personal Action Plan. So the next few exercises will help you to pull together your work in prior modules and will distill the information down into your Personal Action Plan.

Personal Early Warning Signs of a Depressive Episode

The first part of your Personal Action Plan for Depression is a summary of what you learned about your personal warning signs of depression. You may not be able to totally avoid becoming depressed again, but you can learn to see it coming. Catching yourself before depression goes too far will give you a better chance of staying healthy. Look back to module 16, where you constructed a list of signs and symptoms of depression in your Personal Depression Profile. These thoughts, feelings, and behaviors are your core symptoms. Everyone experiences the signs and symptoms of depression differently. By tracking your signs and symptoms over time, you will understand how your thoughts, feelings, and behaviors change when you're depressed.

EXERCISE 25.1 Identifying Your Personal Early Warning Signs of Depression

Let's return to your Personal Depression Profile in exercise 16.2, where you placed an "E" (for "early") in the column next to the symptoms you identified as your early warning signs. List them again here and add any other early signs you've noticed to this list. Whenever you have a new insight into your signs and symptoms, just add to these profiles and lists. Take a moment to update them now, if you have anything to add, and then summarize the most prominent early warning signs below:

1. _____

2. _____

3. _____

4. _____

It's also a good idea to keep track, in some routine way, of how you are doing. Some people look at their Personal Depression Profile every week and some check in with a friend or family member about symptoms or signs they may have noticed. The key is to be regular about it. Giving yourself routine checkups will help you notice depression sneaking up on you before it gets too bad.

Triggers of a Depressive Episode

When you recognize your early warning signs of a depressive episode, you become tuned in to the thoughts, feelings, and behaviors that develop in the beginning of an episode. You'll recall from the discussion about triggers in module 17 that something happens, either external to you (in terms of a stressful situation) or internal to you (in terms of what you think or how you behave in reaction to this stress) that may cause these signs and symptoms to emerge. The next step in managing depression is to become aware of and respond to these triggers, or high-risk situations.

EXERCISE 25.2 Identifying Your Triggers of Depression

Turn back to module 17, where you constructed your list of personal triggers of a depressive episode in exercise 17.1. Update that list of triggers in exercise 17.1, if you have anything to add, and then write down the most common triggers for your depressive periods below:

1. _____

2. _____

3. _____

4. _____

Responses to Depression: Beneficial and Not So Beneficial

How you respond to triggers and to symptoms of depression is the critical part of working through bipolar disorder to achieve your life goals: when you're in the middle of a depressive episode and feel like things will never get better, what do you do?

Look over the last few modules and review the strategies and coping responses, old and new, that have been more or less helpful for you. What worked for you and what didn't? What can work for you preventively? How can you plan in advance to react in a more positive way? Remember to think from the long-term, strategic perspective: what helps you reach your own life goals and what gets you sidetracked or heading backward?

EXERCISE 25.3 Focusing on Your Beneficial Responses to Depression

First, list the routine positive activities that you will practice regularly. Ideally, these are strategies you can use at least weekly, and preferably daily. The goal is to build these into your daily life so that you'll be more resilient when you encounter the daily hassles of life. Here are some examples:

"I'll go for long walks with the dog, catch up with friends by phone every evening, and pay bills as they come in so they don't build up."

"I'll wear a rubber band on my wrist to snap whenever I start beating myself up at work."

1. _____

2. _____

3. _____

Next, list specific responses that you can emphasize when you start to notice your early warning signs or are faced with a depression trigger. Here are some examples:

"When the cold and dark winter weather hits, I plan to take a warm bath every evening."

"I'll ask my work buddies to drag me bowling with them at least once a week no matter what excuse I give."

1. _____

2. _____

3. _____

List specific responses *not* to do. Here are some examples:

"When my boss comes down hard on me and I'm feeling sorry for myself, I won't drown my sorrows with beer."

"I won't let myself sleep until noon."

1. _____

2. _____

3. _____

A PERSONAL ACTION PLAN FOR DEPRESSION

As you did for manic symptoms, your next step will be to put all these components together in a wallet-sized card to keep with you as a part of your reminder system and to keep you focused on your life goals despite depressive symptoms—kind of like a medical alert bracelet, only in your wallet and as a signal for you, rather than anyone else. This does not mean that living your life with bipolar disorder reduces to a wallet-sized card or that that's all that's necessary to manage the disorder. No one wants to slip back into depression. Depression is really a pretty awful state to be in. It's so awful that no one wants to think about it very much. And that's part of the problem. Like ignoring a stop sign at a busy intersection, ignoring signs of depression is not good for your health. It's tempting to think that stressful times won't happen again, but that's unlikely. Be alert for thoughts like "That's all behind me now; I don't need to pay attention to how I'm feeling" or "Maybe I'll give my walking program a rest for the winter." If you start to slip away from your plan, that's probably a sign you need to whip out your wallet card and get back on track with good self-care.

Review and update your action plan regularly. If your plan never changes, then you are probably not using it regularly.

EXERCISE 25.4 Personal Action Plan for Depression

Now you can complete the wallet card below by pulling together all the information from the exercises in this section. Just write the key strategies on this card and don't forget to add your support person—your family member, friend, neighbor, coworker or even a health care professional—who you would call to assist you in an urgent or emergent situation.

You can photocopy this card and keep it with the card that you developed for mania in module 15.

Action Plan for Depression

Key early warning signs:	Responses *not* to do:
1. _____	1. _____
2. _____	2. _____
Triggers to avoid or manage, and how:	Contact provider: _____
1. _____	Phone: _____
2 _____	Contact support person: _____
Responses to do:	Phone: _____
1. _____	
2. _____	

WHAT'S NEXT?

You've completed the first phase of Life Goals treatment—laying the foundation for managing your life by understanding the basics about bipolar disorder, developing a picture of your own specific patterns of mania and depression and related co-travelers, and outlining coping strategies for symptoms.

In the next modules, we'll focus on physical wellness, that is, how your physical health impacts your ability to cope with symptoms of bipolar disorder. In modules 26–29, we'll explore issues relating to overall wellness, especially diet, exercise, tobacco use, and sleeping habits.

## PART IV

Working to Wellness: Physical Health

Module 26: Healthy Diet— Food and Mood Connections

In module 26, we'll work in depth on some strategies that have helped many people effectively improve their physical health by focusing on a healthy diet. We'll also explore the effect of mania and depression on eating habits.

HEALTHY DIET REDUCES RISKS

If you're like many people living with bipolar disorder, you may feel that it's difficult to eat a healthy diet in addition to managing your symptoms and the rest of your daily activities. Perhaps you have enough to do just recognizing your triggers and symptoms and then finding strategies to best manage your condition. But part of living with bipolar disorder is figuring out how you can retain real respect for yourself, feel in charge of your behavior, and manage your health. Caring for your physical health as well as your mental health is part of this taking charge. You may remember from our discussion on breaking the cycle of depression, in module 22, that you can make positive changes in how you think and feel by doing something different, by simply experimenting with new behaviors. In this module, you'll have the opportunity to evaluate your current diet, consider healthy eating habits, and choose new ways of approaching food choices. We'll also discuss ways to anticipate and avoid high-risk situations that may entice you to overeat or eat very high-calorie foods.

ANOTHER CO-TRAVELER: RISK OF HEART DISEASE

As you are aware from our discussion in previous modules, people with bipolar disorder have to deal with unwanted co-travelers—psychiatric conditions such as anxiety disorders, psychosis, and alcohol or substance use. Eating disorders, obesity, and metabolic disorders may also increase the burden of this condition, as there appears to be a relationship between mood disorders and being overweight. People with bipolar disorder may be at greater risk for being overweight than people in the general population (Keck and McElroy 2003) and for suffering from medical conditions related to excess weight, such as diabetes and heart disease (Richardson et al. 2005; Kilbourne, Rofey, et al. 2007).

This risk may be due to factors associated with the condition itself or with medications used to treat bipolar disorder. Some psychiatric medications may interfere with the ability to feel full or satisfied after eating. The list below provides information on eight of the commonly prescribed medications to treat bipolar disorder and their effects on weight. You can work with your care provider to select mood stabilizers that do not promote weight gain.

Medication	Effect on weight
Clozapine (Clozaril) and olanzapine (Zyprexa)	More weight gain than other antipsychotics
Risperidone (Risperdal), quetiapine (Seroquel), lithium (Lithobid), divalproex (Depakote)	Low-to-moderate weight gain
Ziprasidone (Geodon) and aripiprazole (Abilify)	Minimal weight gain

Source: American Diabetes Association et al. (2004).

People with bipolar disorder are vulnerable to other risk factors for heart disease (Kilbourne, Rofey, et al. 2007). Many people with bipolar disorder are at risk of having poor physical health, including metabolic syndrome. Metabolic syndrome, a set of medical disorders that may be associated with increased risk of heart disease, includes the following: impaired glucose tolerance or insulin resistance, high blood pressure, central obesity (around the waist), decreased HDL ("good") cholesterol, and elevated triglycerides. However, a healthy diet and a physically active lifestyle can reduce the risk of metabolic syndrome and the resulting poor outcomes from heart disease and diabetes. Your health care provider can help you reduce your risks by reviewing your medical history, giving you a physical exam, and monitoring the following key indicators (American Diabetes Association et al. 2004):

▶ Body mass index (BMI, the ratio of your height and weight) and waist circumference

▶ Personal and family history of obesity, diabetes, high cholesterol, high blood pressure, or heart disease

▶ Blood pressure

▶ Fasting glucose level

▶ Lipid profile (cholesterol levels and triglycerides)

▶ PRL (prolactin, a hormone involved in a variety of functions, including regulating stress hormones, which may be irregular in people with bipolar disorder)

RELATIONSHIP BETWEEN MOODS AND FOODS

Mood symptoms associated with bipolar disorder can also increase the risk of heart disease through poor eating habits and less-active lifestyles.

Effect of Depression on Physical Health

Depression and poor physical health often go hand in hand. Depression can interfere with a person's ability to take care of him- or herself. Depression can make people less active and either cause them to lose their appetite or encourage cravings for high-calorie foods. Not surprisingly, when you're depressed, you may not have much energy or motivation to stick to a healthy diet. You're probably waiting to feel better or more motivated, and in the meantime, you want to eat comfort foods, even if they contain many calories. Sometimes when you eat foods high in sugar, fat, or salt to feel better in the short term, they can make you feel like you have no energy in the long run. This type of diet can raise your blood pressure and weight, leading to the body's inability to process sugar (*glucose intolerance*), all of which can lead to heart disease. Unfortunately, people with bipolar disorder are more likely to report poor eating habits, including not eating many vegetables and fruits (Kilbourne, Rofey, et al. 2007). For all these reasons, people with depression are at a greater risk for heart disease than those without depression. By starting and maintaining healthy diet and exercise habits, you can reduce depressive symptoms and, in turn, reduce the health risks.

Effect of Mania on Health and Eating Habits

Stress and mania can make people eat more than they want to, or sometimes people are simply feeling too stressed to take care of themselves. Mania, anger, and constant negative thinking can trigger stress hormones in your body that then increase blood pressure and heart rate. This increase is due to the high energy levels during manic episodes, reaction to fears during periods of paranoia, anger or constant irritability, and the body's fight-or-flight response. Mania can also cause some people to overeat or binge eat unhealthy foods, such as junk foods that have a high fat or sugar content (chips, cookies, greasy food). These foods can raise blood sugar and cholesterol levels, causing your blood sugar to fluctuate and making you feel sick after you have eaten too much.

There is an association between bipolar disorder type II and eating disorders (McElroy et al. 2005), with a higher rate of binge eating occurring in people with bipolar disorder than in the general community (Krüger, Shugar, and Cooke 1996). People with binge-eating problems feel an uncontrollable urge to eat large amounts of food (beyond feeling full). Binge eaters often develop this a habit as a way to deal with stress and depression, finding comfort in eating but often feeling sad about their loss of control and resulting weight gain. These feelings cause them to eat more, continuing the vicious cycle.

GETTING STARTED WITH HEALTHY EATING

Our food choices are often linked to our childhood habits, our culture, or our current lifestyle, rather than to a logical calculation of calories and nutrients. This means that you can choose to take an active part in shaping your personal diet. Make changes that will reflect the tastes and smells that are appealing to you while meeting your health needs. It will take time to plan ahead to purchase and prepare healthy foods you can reach for when you're feeling stressed. The focus of this section is on spending more time planning healthy meals and snacks to help you feel in better control of your health.

When we talk about eating healthy foods, we're referring to a variety of foods from the basic food groups:

▶ Fruits and vegetables

▶ Grains and starches (e.g., bread, cereal, rice, potatoes)

▶ Dairy (e.g., milk, cheese, yogurt)

▶ Meat and meat substitutes

▶ Fats (e.g., oil, butter)—in limited amounts

Try to eat a variety of foods from each food group and concentrate on choosing foods that are naturally high in nutrients and low in calories, like fruits, vegetables, low-fat dairy products, and whole grains. It's best to tailor your diet to meet your own needs. You can consult your care provider to help you develop a personal plan. For general recommendations on serving sizes and total calorie requirements for men, women, and children, and depending on age and activity level, you can consult the *Dietary Guidelines for Americans*, published every five years since 1980 by the U.S. Department of Health and Human Services and the U.S. Department of Agriculture (HHS and USDA 2005).

Take a few minutes to think about your current eating habits. Do you often choose foods in each group? When you're eating, do you stop just before you feel full? Remember, it takes time for the body to release the hormones that turn off appetite and tell you you're full.

If you open your refrigerator right now, do you have a variety of fruits and vegetables on the shelves? If you have healthy foods to reach for when you're hungry, rather than cookies, candy, chips, and other high-calorie foods, then you are on your way to a healthy diet. Some tips for healthy eating that people have recommended include the following:

▶ Eat at regular times and eat breakfast.

▶ Eat when you are hungry and stop eating right before you are full.

▶ Reduce the amount you eat gradually and do not deprive yourself of food.

▶ Pay attention so as not to mindlessly eat at times when you are depressed or bored.

▶ Slow down when you eat.

▶ Write the name of each food you eat in a food diary or log.

▶ Prevent overeating at mealtime by eating small, healthy snacks in between meals.

▶ Eat a healthy snack before grocery shopping to avoid impulsive high-fat purchases.

▶ Eat a variety of foods (balance leafy vegetables, protein, and carbohydrates).

▶ Avoid saturated fats and trans fats (often found in baked goods), especially if you have heart disease. Learn to substitute olive oil, vegetable oils, and the like for high-fat items, such as butter. Replace fatty red meats with fish, nuts, chicken, and so on. Select grilled chicken and avoid fried chicken.

▶ Avoid meals with sugar and too many starches ("white foods" such as pasta or potatoes), especially if you have diabetes. Learn to substitute whole grains, brown rice, and so on for starches.

▶ Try to cut out the "empty" calories of sugary snack foods (candy and soda). Get your calories from healthy food rather than drinks.

▶ Select fresh fruits and vegetables whenever possible. Choose frozen foods rather than canned ones, as canned foods are usually high in sodium (making you retain water and possibly increasing your blood pressure).

▶ Look for canned fruit packed in its own juice rather than syrup, or canned tuna packed in water instead of oil.

▶ Include a minimum of 1,000 to 1,200 mg per day of calcium (in milk, cheese, and yogurt, for example) in a daily plan for women.

▶ Select five to six servings per day of fruits and vegetables and six servings per day of whole-grain products.

▶ Read nutritional labels carefully, noting the number of servings in a package and the number of calories for each serving. Ingredients are listed on the label in order from largest to smallest amount, so a product contains more of the first item listed than of any other item.

EXERCISE 26.1 Healthy Tips and Your Current Eating Habits

In this exercise, you'll review your eating habits and choose one recommendation to serve as a goal to work on during the next week. Keep in mind when you're setting goals that you have to determine small, achievable steps. Remember that rewards should not produce negative consequences. For example, choosing to celebrate reaching a goal of healthy eating by eating a high-fat food would not work. An example is included on the next page.

What is realistic for you to accomplish during the next week?

Current Eating Habit	Unrealistic Goal	Realistic Goal

Current Eating Habit	Unrealistic Goal	Realistic Goal
Eating unhealthy, sugary snack foods	*Stop eating or cooking unhealthy snack foods* *Stop snacking between meals*	*Not eat unhealthy foods three times next week (or even one day)* *Empty kitchen cabinets of unhealthy foods* *Eat sweet healthy foods at snack time, like fruit or raisins*
Buy unhealthy, high-fat, high-sodium foods at the grocery store and at restaurants	*Walk down grocery aisles past unhealthy foods and not purchase* *Go to favorite restaurants and not order favorite foods (if unhealthy)*	*Shop for fresh foods around the perimeter of the grocery store and avoid certain aisles* *Choose new restaurants and select healthier meals*
Celebrate by going out for ice cream	*Not celebrate something special*	*Get together with others to celebrate by doing something active, like throwing a frisbee or a ball*

Barbara's Story

Barbara is a twenty-seven-year-old who was recently diagnosed with bipolar disorder. Her psychiatrist prescribed an antipsychotic for her, and after several months, she had gained fifteen pounds. When Barbara brought up the issue of her weight gain with her care provider, her provider mentioned that it might be a side effect of the medication. Worried about gaining even more weight, Barbara stopped taking her medication without telling her provider. A few weeks later, she had a manic episode that included several nights in a row in which she binged on doughnuts, chocolate, and ice cream. After her manic episode, Barbara became depressed and continued to eat chocolate and ice cream to make herself feel better. As a result, she gained several more pounds over the next month. At her appointment, Barbara briefed her provider on her recent cycle of episodes and also noted that she had gained more weight. Realizing that Barbara had been reluctant to take the medication because of weight gain, and that this side effect had actually set off a chain of events that led to her rapid change in moods, her provider switched her to another antipsychotic medication that had less effect on weight gain. She also referred Barbara to her general practitioner for an evaluation with a nutritionist, who then worked with her to develop a diet and exercise plan to help with weight loss.

EXERCISE 26.2 Food Log of Current Eating Habits

One strategy that has helped many people to gain control over their eating habits is to record what they eat each day in a food diary, or on a logsheet located on the following page. The awareness a logsheet brings may make the difference between whether you gain or lose weight. On these logsheets, record the food you eat each day and the amount of each food. Try to write in the Food Logsheet every time you eat or drink something, as it is hard to remember later. This logsheet is for you to look at to help you recognize your current eating habits, and it can be as simple or elaborate as you'd like. You can count calories and carbohydrates or simply write the foods you eat in a notebook or on a daily calendar.

Sample Food Logsheet

	Monday
Breakfast	*Whole wheat toast, glass of orange juice*
Snack	*Banana*
Lunch	*Grilled chicken sandwich, diet cola, tortilla chips*
Snack	*Apple with peanut butter*
Dinner	*Pasta with meatballs, salad*
Snack	*Cookie (one)*

▶ Is the Food Logsheet a good way to help you keep track of healthy and nonhealthy eating habits? What patterns have you noticed during those times when it is easier to eat well? For example, is it easier to eat well at breakfast or right after payday? What is it about those times that makes it easier to make healthier choices? For example, are you eating the same thing every day because of what's available or are you able to buy out-of-season fruits that you enjoy?

▶ Do your food choices over the course of a week include foods from all of the basic food groups? Note that dietary requirements can differ for women versus men, older versus younger people, and pregnant women, depending on your activity level.

▶ Have you noticed that you eat less of certain unhealthy foods since you are using the Food Logsheet? For instance, if you were eating potato chips every night before writing in the logsheet, have you stopped eating chips every night or even stopped completely? Have you added yogurt as an afternoon snack to satisfy the dairy group?

Food Logsheet

	M	Tu	W	Th	F	Sa	Su
Breakfast							
Snack							
Lunch							
Snack							
Dinner							
Snack							

ANTICIPATE FOOD CHALLENGES

These are times when it's very likely that you won't eat properly. Below are some examples of high-risk situations that people have told us challenge their desire to eat healthy foods:

▶ Being at social events (parties, picnics, sports activities)

▶ Being in certain places or settings (work, home, restaurants, theaters)

▶ Experiencing emotions that trigger eating or drinking (anger, tension, boredom, happiness, excitement, depression)

▶ Being with certain people (family, friends, or neighbors who aren't aware of your diet encouraging you to eat foods that you shouldn't eat, or eating such foods in front of you)

▶ Experiencing stressors that trigger you to eat or drink (concerns about money, feeling hot or cold)

▶ Feeling tired and not wanting to eat or cook a nutritious meal

▶ Not having healthy foods on hand

▶ Dining out

▶ Preparing snack foods for children

▶ Being overloaded with too many activities or obligations and not having time to eat or prepare a proper meal

Please add any situations that are high risk for you that are not listed above.

1. _____

2. _____

3. _____

EXERCISE 26.3 High-Risk Eating Situations

In this exercise, please anticipate a problem that will make you eat in an unhealthy manner. Then identify the high-risk situation and possible solution. Here are two examples.

Examples of High-Risk Eating Situations

Problem	High-risk situation	Solution
Not eating breakfast	*I was feeling tired and running late in the morning.*	*At dinnertime, while I'm still in the kitchen, plan what I could eat for breakfast and prepare parts (e.g., place the bowl, spoon, and cereal on the table). Carry a healthy item (e.g., carrots and celery) with me as a snack.*
Ate ice cream	*I was depressed and I often eat ice cream because it helps me to feel better.*	*Begin a new habit when feeling depressed, perhaps taking a walk or phoning a friend.*

High-Risk Eating Situations

Problem	High-risk situation	Solution

Based upon your food records and the high-risk situations that cause problems for you, what would be one realistic goal for you?

_____

_____

WHAT'S NEXT?

One of the ways to improve your health may be to lose weight. In order to lose weight, you need to create a *negative energy balance*. In other words, you have to use more energy than you take in through eating. The two most highly recommended ways to lose weight are low-calorie eating and regular physical activity. So developing and maintaining healthy eating habits is only part of the solution to reducing risks of chronic conditions. In the next module, we'll explore the importance of increasing your physical activity levels (exercise) to prevent weight gain and to promote better physical and mental health.

Module 27: Get Moving for Maximum Physical and Mental Health

In this module, you'll assess your current exercise habits, set short-term and achievable goals to increase your level of physical activity, anticipate obstacles, and take pride in your results.

BEING ACTIVE IMPROVES HEALTH

Physical activity promotes mental and physical health and improves the quality of your day-to-day life, regardless of your age. Feeling better physically can positively influence all aspects of your life's work, which we explored in module 5. People who aren't physically active have a higher risk of developing heart disease, high blood pressure, diabetes, and other chronic medical conditions than people who are physically active (Richardson et al. 2005). As you know from module 26, people with bipolar disorder are at higher risk than the general population for developing these medical conditions. There is also evidence that people with bipolar disorder are more likely to report poor exercise habits, including doing less walking or fewer strength exercises than people who do not have serious mental conditions (Kilbourne, Rofey, et al. 2007). Regular physical activity reduces the risks associated with most chronic diseases, even among people who have already been diagnosed with disease (Blair et al. 1992).

Diane's Story

Diane is a thirty-four-year-old woman with bipolar disorder who enters claims information into a computer at an insurance agency. She had managed her bipolar symptoms with medication but felt depressed a lot of the time. To ease her stress at work, she usually took a break by driving to the main access road at the industrial office park, to one of the fast food restaurants. Although she enjoyed these breaks, she noticed that she was gaining weight. She decided to talk with her husband about weight gain, and he suggested that they start taking a walk together around the neighborhood after dinner. In addition, he wondered if her poor eating habits might be contributing to the way she felt and suggested that she talk with her care provider about ways to manage her depressive symptoms and weight gain. Diane agreed to go for walks after dinner after realizing that her job and her office location didn't present any opportunities for exercise time.

EFFECT OF DEPRESSION ON PHYSICAL ACTIVITY

Depression, as you know, can drain people of energy and the motivation to take care of themselves, lead to less active lifestyles and poor eating habits, and result in an increased risk of developing chronic medical problems. The benefits of exercise include reducing depressive symptoms by increasing self-esteem and reducing social isolation. There is some evidence that aerobic exercise (Newman and Molta 2007) and yoga therapy (Duraiswamy et al. 2007) are effective in reducing symptoms of people with serious mental conditions. Research also indicates that physical exercise can improve symptoms of depression (Frank 2007; Simon, Ludman, and Tutty 2006). People simply feel better when they are engaged in physical activity. Regular exercise helps to increase energy levels by boosting strength and fitness, relieving stress, and regulating moods. It is also one of the best ways to lose weight, coupled with a healthy diet.

EXERCISE 27.1 Current Exercise Habits

In this exercise, describe what type of physical activity, sport, or exercise you currently participate in, how long you spend on it, and how often you do it. Don't be concerned if you can't fill in the table. The point is to begin to seriously think about being physically active on a regular basis.

Type of physical activity	Duration	Frequency

As you know, awareness is only the first step. To take it to the next level, you need to choose an activity that you'll continue to do on a regular basis. After that, you can increase the amount of time you spend exercising and select a new activity when you're bored with the first one.

CHOOSE YOUR ACTIVITY

Many people get discouraged thinking about exercise because they believe that you need expensive equipment or a membership to a gym or yoga studio. But it doesn't matter what type of physical activity you choose. Sports, aerobic exercise, yoga, qi gong, walking, or yard work are all beneficial. The key factor is the amount of energy used and the amount of time spent to improve health and fitness. What we mean by *regular* exercise is something in which you participate at least three times a week. The American College of Sports Medicine and the American Heart Association recommend that in order to maintain health, all healthy adults need a minimum of thirty minutes, five days each week, of physical activity; or vigorous aerobic physical activity for a minimum of twenty minutes, three days each week (Haskell et al. 2007). Just walking in parks, shopping malls, or your own neighborhood can provide the thirty minutes you need. And exercising on a regular basis will make you feel less tired in the long run.

So let's come up with ways to increase your level of physical activity. Remember that physical activity might be a specific type of exercise, recreation, or sport that you enjoy, but it can also just mean increasing the demand you place on your body on a daily basis. Here are some tips on increasing your level of physical activity:

▶ *Set a consistent time:* exercise each day at a regular time.

▶ *Park and walk:* avoid parking spaces close to your office, grocery store, and so on.

▶ *Take the stairs:* walk instead of taking the elevator or escalator.

▶ *Exercise nearly every day:* exercise at least thirty minutes, five days per week; on a busy day, take three ten-minute "activity breaks."

▶ *Schedule time with a friend:* work out with a friend.

EXERCISE 27.2 Set an Activity Goal

In this exercise, you'll choose an activity that you would like to participate in three times a week. Once you decide on an activity, think about breaking the goal into small steps that will encourage you to begin exercising—just like we've talked about with your development of healthy eating habits. For instance, if you decide you want to play tennis or basketball, one of your steps would be making sure that you have a tennis racket or a basketball; another step would be finding a location at a local high school court or wherever you want to play. Keep in mind that each step takes you closer to beginning your new healthy activity.

Let's suppose you would like to organize a walking club because it's hard to become motivated to take a brisk walk each night by yourself. Perhaps you have family members or neighbors who might want to join you. Rather than feeling overwhelmed by the idea of organizing a group to walk with on a regular basis, break the overall goal into small steps. Each step is considered to be one goal that can be accomplished in a short period of time.

Step 1: Select friends, family members, or neighbors who might be available to join your walking club and construct a list containing contact information (telephone numbers and e-mail addresses).

Step 2: Determine a possible walking route, taking into consideration the terrain and time available.

Step 3: Call the people you have identified and determine their interest level, possibly scheduling a walk on weekdays or weekends at a specific time.

Step 4: Establish a time or place for the group to meet for the first walk. If necessary, establish a time or place to meet with prospective walkers before beginning the club.

Step 5: Have the walking club set a goal of walking a certain number of miles. Discuss with the group the idea of pretending you will all be walking from the starting point to a specific destination (e.g., a distant relative's home, a particular sightseeing location like the Grand Canyon, or an overseas location). You can use an Internet-based map service to calculate the actual number of miles between your starting point and this destination.

Step 6: Plan an activity to celebrate the completion of the goal.

Step 7: Chart daily or weekly progress toward that goal, noting number of miles walked and number remaining until you reach your "destination."

Step 8: Set a new goal or destination for the walking club.

Step 9: Brainstorm about ways to overcome any problems, including when members drop out, needing to change the route, and so on.

Now it's your turn to map out your exercise activity.

Overall physical activity goal: _____

Step 1: _____

Step 2: _____

Step 3: _____

Step 4: _____

Step 5: _____

Step 6: _____

Step 7: _____

Step 8: _____

Step 9: _____

RECOGNIZE YOUR ABILITY TO INCREASE YOUR PHYSICAL ACTIVITY LEVEL

Try to make small positive changes in your everyday experience that are measurable. After sticking to an exercise plan, how can you see what you're achieving? You may want to use a pedometer to count the number of steps you walk each day. Or you may choose to check your pulse or use a heart monitor to see the changes in your fitness level. Some people who want to see the difference in how they look rely on a measuring tape to see how many inches they've lost, or they check the size of a favorite pair of jeans or look at photos taken before and after weeks of exercising. Other people just know that they can do more sit-ups or housework or something else than they could do before. Notice your accomplishments, no matter how big or small they are, and take pride in your work. Giving up unhealthy habits and being motivated to adopt new behaviors requires dedication and should be rewarded. And once again, your rewards should not have a negative consequence, so rewarding yourself by taking time off from exercising or by eating something really high in calories or fat may not be the best choice.

PREPARE FOR OBSTACLES IN MAINTAINING PHYSICAL ACTIVITY

Keep in mind that there will be times that, for a variety of reasons, it won't be easy to keep up with the exercise or sport that you've chosen. Even if depressive or manic symptoms create barriers for you, continue your planned physical activity whenever possible. It's common to become bored and lose motivation. Less than half of the participants in organized physical activity programs continue with the program after six months (Dishman and Buckworth 1996). Those who don't will need to get back on track, select a new activity, and begin again.

Look ahead to the obstacles you might run across and try to think about how you can overcome them. An example might be anticipating that you won't be able to get outside to walk or play sports during the cold winter months. How can you continue to stay active in this situation? You may want to plan a fun alternate activity, like going swimming or taking a dance class at your local community center.

WHAT'S NEXT?

In the next module, we'll explore how smoking cigarettes or using other tobacco products will prevent you from achieving better physical health and we offer strategies to overcome negative habits.

Module 28: Managing Tobacco Use—It's Your Choice

In this module, you will continue to work on positive strategies that focus on wellness, this time with an emphasis on managing tobacco use. You will develop a plan to avoid triggers and high-risk situations that sabotage a healthy decision to stop smoking or using tobacco. This module is devoted to helping tobacco users cope with challenging issues that may interfere with attempts to quit and may be of value to you if you have other habits that negatively impact achieving better physical health.

WHY MENTION TOBACCO USE IN A BIPOLAR DISORDER WORKBOOK?

You may never have smoked or chewed tobacco or used snuff, or you may be an ex-smoker and keenly aware of the health benefits of your decision. As we mentioned briefly in module 5, people with bipolar disorder, depression, or certain other mental conditions become smokers at a much higher rate than other people (Compton, Daumit, and Druss 2006). Like alcohol and drug use, which we discussed in module 12, tobacco use can be an issue in any mood state—manic, depressed, or normal mood. Studies show that depression is associated with smoking; it is more common for people who are depressed to be smokers than it is for people who are not depressed. And smokers are more likely to be depressed than nonsmokers (Freedland, Carney, and Skala 2005). For reasons we don't completely understand, people with serious mental conditions are twice as likely to smoke as not, and they tend to smoke more cigarettes than other smokers, consuming an estimated 34 to 44 percent of all cigarettes smoked in the United States (Compton, Daumit, and Druss 2006). The good news is that they are just as likely to quit smoking as the general population (El-Guebaly et al. 2002).

Changing this one behavior, smoking, will dramatically help you achieve better physical health and live a longer, healthier life—and save an awesome amount of money! In the United States, cigarette smoking, which harms every organ in the body, is the leading cause of preventable death (HEW 1964). Quitting smoking will lower your risk of having a stroke, heart attack, or cancer (HEW 1964). Research indicates that if you have experienced these health problems, quitting will reduce your chances of having another episode. In fact, some studies have reported that among people who have heart disease, those who quit smoking reduce their risk of premature death by 36 percent compared with people who continue to smoke (Freedland, Carney, and Skala 2005). So, even if you have been smoking for years, your body starts to recover as soon as you finish the last puff or spit out the tobacco.

There are, of course, other reasons why you may want to quit using tobacco. Our patients have told us several reasons, for example, saving money, being a positive role model for younger relatives, smelling better, and having better skin. What benefits can you imagine for yourself? What are some reasons that make quitting smoking important to you?

Many people find it helpful to break down the overall goal of quitting into small, achievable steps and to reward themselves for each accomplishment. For instance, you can manage your habit by smoking fewer and fewer cigarettes each day rather than trying to quit all at once. Another strategy is referred to as *scheduled smoking*, where people smoke the same number of cigarettes they have always smoked but at times not connected with their usual habit patterns, in order to begin working on the behavioral aspects of addiction. As you might approach any other bad habits, just start thinking about how you can change your behavior. This means that if you typically smoke a cigarette when you drink coffee in the morning, just drink the coffee. Perhaps twenty minutes later, go ahead and smoke that morning cigarette. Since the act of drinking and smoking will occur at different times, it may be easier to drop the smoking habit once you have made that decision.

EXERCISE 28.1 Log of Your Typical Smoking Pattern

In this exercise, record the number of cigarettes or tobacco packets you consume each day of the week. After becoming aware of how much you currently smoke or the amount of tobacco products such as chewing tobacco or snuff you use, the next step will be to figure out what triggers your need to smoke, and then how you can reduce your intake. This logsheet gives you a place to record your changes during the first month. Keep in mind that logging these small steps will allow you to see some progress along the way while striving toward your goal of not smoking.

Tobacco Use Logsheet

Day	Week 1	Week 2	Week 3	Week 4	Total number of cigarettes per day (or number of tobacco packets)
Su					
M					
Tu					
W					
Th					
F					
Sa					

Being aware of your habit is the first step. Review the chart to see any pattern. For instance, do you smoke more on the weekends? When you recognize the reasons you use tobacco and the locations and times of day you use it, you can begin to manage your habit. By taking the next step in setting short-term, achievable goals to limit your use of tobacco, you can experience success firsthand. Your body can adapt to less nicotine. These small steps prepare you to consider quitting smoking once and for all.

You'll recall from our discussion about triggers in modules 9 and 17 that psychosocial triggers are just as significant as biological factors, in this case physical cravings. In fact, to achieve success in quitting smoking, you'll need to become aware of these triggers and avoid high-risk situations that stimulate your old habit.

TOBACCO USE TRIGGERS

If you are a smoker or use tobacco products, you are probably aware of the triggers that stimulate your cravings to smoke. Stress is often viewed as a trigger. Remember that people with bipolar disorder are more sensitive than others to stress and change. Some people smoke when they are driving by themselves in a car, watching TV, or talking on the phone. Others can't resist joining their friends when they smoke. Finding ways to cope with stress and with triggers so that you do not feel the urge to smoke is important. Some people have found that taking a hot bath, going for a walk, talking with friends, or reading a book helps to reduce stress. These methods can help distract you from smoking.

LEARN NEW BEHAVIORS OR HABITS

Throughout this workbook, we have recognized that behavior change is difficult. The key is to change the cues that trigger your desire to smoke. For instance, if you like to light a cigarette when you have a cup of coffee, start to drink tea or another beverage instead. When you first try to quit smoking, you may find it helpful to change your routine. Perhaps driving a different route to work or eating breakfast in a different place (even sitting in a different chair at the same table at home) may prompt you to behave differently. It may be helpful to move a chair that you sit in when you smoke to a different spot in the kitchen, living room, or office. That way your physical environment gives you a cue that there is a change occurring. In addition, remove the physical signs of your tobacco habit by tossing out every cigarette and tobacco product, ashtray, match, and lighter from every location in your house, car, desk, coat pocket, purse, and backpack. Then, clean the tobacco smell from draperies, upholstery, walls, and carpets in your home, office, and car.

Brigitte's Story

Brigitte began dreading each weekday morning when she had to get up for work. Her boss seemed to be giving her too many assignments recently, without giving her enough time to complete them. She was feeling stressed-out. Brigitte controlled her symptoms of bipolar disorder with medications and routine appointments with her care provider. Lately, she recognized that she had been smoking more. Every morning she had a cigarette with her coworkers in front of the building before going into work. When she was bored at work after lunch, she would take a cigarette break and smoke outside with the hope that she could then focus better. Two or three times a week, Brigitte would meet her coworkers for happy hour at a bar where she would smoke more. On other nights at home, Brigitte felt the urge to smoke after dinner. Brigitte discovered that she was buying packs of cigarettes more often and considered making an appointment with her care provider to deal with her stress at work and her increase in smoking. Brigitte recognized that her habit of smoking was getting out of control and she was prepared to get some help.

EXERCISE 28.2 Triggers of Tobacco Use

In this exercise, write down what triggers your urges and what makes it hard to resist smoking or using tobacco. Let's use Brigitte's case as an example.

Brigitte's Tobacco Use Triggers

Reasons for smoking or using tobacco	Triggers	Location	Time of day	Alone or with others	New behavior
1Relieves stress	Meet coworkers before work	Outside the main entrance at work	Morning	Alone and with others	Enter different door at work.
Improves concentration	Boredom, after lunch	At work	Late afternoon	Alone	Walk down the hall or the stairs.
Makes me part of a group in social situations	Happy hour after work in a bar	Bar	Early evening	With others	Avoid smoky restaurants or bars. Hang out with nonsmoking friends.
Helps manage weight	After-dinner snacking	Kitchen	Evening	Alone and with others	Go for a walk after dinner. Avoid walking into the kitchen after dinner.

Now it's your turn to analyze why, where, when, and with whom you smoke or use tobacco. Try to brainstorm new behaviors that will help you resist the temptation to continue smoking.

Your Tobacco Use Triggers

Reasons for smoking or using tobacco	Triggers	Location	Time of day	Alone or with others	New behavior

Achieving better physical health can become a reality when you avoid the triggers, substitute new positive behaviors, and stop smoking or using tobacco products. If you're a smoker, take a moment to consider what it would mean to you personally to quit smoking. Is your primary interest to save money, to be a positive role model for your children, or to avoid physical problems like coughing or cancer that may accompany prolonged smoking? Whatever your reason, you owe it to yourself to consider quitting.

CHOOSING THE BEST METHOD TO QUIT SMOKING

Since you're the one who places the cigarette or tobacco in your mouth, you'll need to be actively involved in choosing the method that will work best to stop this habit. If your past attempts to quit smoking haven't worked, you'll especially want to choose a program that has been proven successful and stick with it. Your care provider, family and friends, local health department, or the national hotline 1-800-QUITNOW may offer suggestions in terms of strategies, support groups, or counseling (individual, group, telephone, and Internet) to help you quit smoking.

Using any method, your body will adapt to a decrease in the level of the addictive chemical nicotine, the active ingredient in cigarettes and other tobacco products, and go through withdrawal. Most withdrawal symptoms peak within forty-eight hours, and your physical symptoms completely disappear within six months (WebMD 2005). Your care provider may recommend medication to assist you. The U.S. Food and Drug Administration (FDA) has approved six medications to help you quit smoking:

▶ Nicotine gum—available over the counter

▶ Nicotine inhaler—available by prescription

▶ Nicotine nasal spray—available by prescription

▶ Nicotine patch—available by prescription and over the counter

▶ Varenicline (Chantix)—available by prescription

▶ Bupropion SR—available by prescription (Note: This is the antidepressant bupropion, also marketed as Wellbutrin; be certain not to take this without consulting your mental health prescriber, even if another prescriber says it's okay.)

Essentially, these medications reduce the intensity of your physical or biological triggers to smoke. Talk to your care provider about which method might be best for you.

EFFECTS OF QUITTING ON MOOD AND APPETITE

When you quit smoking or stop using tobacco products, the withdrawal from nicotine can cause symptoms such as intense cravings, increased appetite, irritability, and depressed mood. Letting go of any routine is difficult and requires that you use effective coping strategies to improve your mood and your positive sense of self. Think back to the coping strategies you learned in modules 10 and 18 when dealing with symptoms of mania and depression. Pick one or two strategies that may help you cope with the mood changes you may now experience. If you find yourself feeling depressed, contact your care provider, who may adjust your psychiatric medication temporarily, help to monitor your moods, and offer encouragement to successfully change your habits.

When the nicotine is removed from your body as you stop using tobacco products, your metabolism slows down to a healthy level and you burn fewer calories. As your sense of smell and taste return, food tastes better, so you'll need to put into action the healthy habits you've learned (in module 26 on diet and module 27 on exercise) to avoid eating more and gaining weight. Your hands and mouth may need something else to do, such as playing with a straw, chewing gum, or eating celery or pretzels. Using the Food Logsheet in module 26 to monitor your overall diet and snacking habits, and maintaining a regular exercise routine, will help you to focus on becoming healthier.

GET SUPPORT FROM YOUR TEAM

As was the case with the other ways we've been discussing to help you achieve wellness, you have a better chance of being successful if you have support. Your family, friends, coworkers, and care providers can provide positive feedback to you during the process of quitting. It's important not to get too discouraged during this process.

Before successfully quitting, most people try to quit several times, with most relapses occurring in the first three months when the old habit is still fresh. If you quit and start smoking again, it doesn't mean you can't quit using tobacco products. It just means you need to choose a better plan that will work for you. Even when you recognize your triggers and anticipate and avoid the high-risk situations that make it difficult to cope with not lighting up, the urge to smoke may overwhelm you. Don't be discouraged; you just need to learn to apply effective, positive coping strategies and to rely on the support of your family, friends, coworkers, and care providers. Write a detailed description of the situation in a logbook so that you can avoid that situation next time.

PULLING IT ALL TOGETHER: GET READY … GET SET … GO

Perhaps you're ready to set a date to quit. Now you're aware of how much you smoke, the reasons you smoke, and why you might want to stop. You've tossed out the cigarettes or tobacco products, removed the tobacco smell, and changed your routine to help avoid triggers that will encourage cravings. Your friends and care providers may have helped you select a smoking cessation plan that has been proven successful. And you have some coping strategies and new positive habits to call on when the going gets rough. As you achieve each step, remember to congratulate yourself for how far you've come. After you quit, don't tell yourself that you can control your smoking habit and just smoke one cigarette. Just don't smoke at all.

Reminder Checklist

▶ **Get ready: decide that you're going to quit.**

_____ Reduce the number of cigarettes (or tobacco packets) you consume each day.

_____ Remove every cigarette (or tobacco product), ashtray, match, and lighter from every location in your house, car, desk, coat pocket, purse, and backpack.

_____ Clean the tobacco smell from upholstery, walls, and carpets in your home, office, and car.

_____ Consider ways to avoid triggers, such as by moving your favorite chair in your home or office, or by taking a new route to work.

_____ Plan to maintain a healthy diet and exercise routine.

▶ **Get set: set the quit date** (not a stressful day like a holiday, birthday, or anniversary).

_____ Alert your support team of family, friends, coworkers, and care providers of your quit date.

_____ Choose a smoking cessation plan that has been proven to be successful.

_____ Select coping strategies to call upon as your body withdraws from nicotine.

▶ **Go: become a nonsmoker.**

_____ Adopt new behaviors or habits.

_____ Reward yourself, even spending some of the money not spent on tobacco.

_____ Inspire other smokers by sharing your healthy commitment to stop smoking and by not allowing people to smoke in your home, car, or work space, or at your restaurant table.

▶ **False start: Get ready … get set … and go again.**

_____ Review what helped you and what hurt you in your last attempt to quit.

_____ After you quit smoking, don't smoke even one more cigarette.

Source: Adapted from _You Can Quit Smoking Consumer Guide_ (HHS 2000).

WHAT'S NEXT?

In the next module, we will discuss how your sleep habits affect your mental and physical health, and we will suggest methods that will help you recognize changes in your sleep patterns.

Module 29: Sleep to Keep Your Life in Balance

In this module, you will learn how sleeping well on a consistent basis will improve your mental and physical health. You'll also learn how your sleep patterns can influence the symptoms of bipolar disorder.

SLEEP INFLUENCES YOUR HEALTH

Having a good night's sleep will help you to stay healthy, feel better, be less stressed, and maintain a healthy weight. The link between poor sleep and physical illness is strong. People who sleep fewer hours each night tend to have higher blood pressure and a higher risk of heart attack, weight gain, and diabetes (Kase 2007). Sleep deprivation also produces higher levels of stress hormones, affecting moods. People who experience such deprivation have problems in concentration, problem solving, memory, judgment, reaction time, and other functions (Kase 2007). The age-old doctor's advice to get a good night's rest makes sense, as sleep helps the body regulate metabolism and fight infections and inflammation. A lack of sleep changes the metabolism and levels of growth hormones, both of which affect the skin and muscle mass, just as in the normal aging process. In addition, your appetite increases as metabolism lowers, and hormones that make you feel hungry also increase, while levels of the hormone that makes you feel full after eating decrease. There is evidence that sleep loss increases cravings for high-calorie foods due to decreases in sensitivity to insulin, which in turn increases the risk of developing diabetes. (Kase 2007). It's a big challenge to follow the suggestions in modules 26 and 27 on diet and exercise, but you may want to address one more health factor: now it appears that getting a good night's sleep, many nights in a row, can help you maintain a healthy weight (Kase 2007).

REGULATING THE BODY'S CLOCK

People with bipolar disorder are particularly sensitive to the effects of sleep loss. In ways we are just beginning to understand, our sleep-wake cycle is regulated by a *circadian rhythm*—the cycle of physiological or behavioral processes that occur during a twenty-four-hour period. This rhythm is affected by daylight and darkness, social contacts, activities of daily living, and other environmental factors (e.g., seasonal changes), which act as cues to signal the brain to set our biological rhythms (body clock). A variety of stimulants and medications can change the sleep-wake cycle as well; for instance, caffeine, nicotine, amphetamines, and methylphenidate (e.g., Ritalin) can disrupt sleep and your biological clock.

There appears to be a relationship between the interruption of these rhythms and the onset of mania and depression. People with bipolar disorder are often more sensitive than others to changes that influence the body's clock (Goodwin and Jamison 2007). Recall in module 2 that we discussed that all thoughts, feelings, and behaviors are regulated by brain cells. The brain system that regulates these thoughts, feelings, and behaviors is related to another system in the brain that regulates circadian rhythms, known as the *biological clock*. You learned in previous modules that stress can affect these systems and cause symptoms. By maintaining these rhythms with a routine of daily activities and a regular sleep pattern, you may be able to regulate your body's clock and thus to manage the mood swings experienced in bipolar disorder.

As you know, positive and negative life events cause stress and may disrupt the amount of time that you can sleep peacefully. There is evidence that people with bipolar disorder may have a predisposition to problems in their circadian rhythm and sleep-wake cycle that may be partially responsible for the development of bipolar symptoms (Frank, Swartz, and Kupfer 2000).

ROLE OF THE BRAIN IN SLEEP

The body's clock regulates our sleep and wake times. It isn't an actual clock, but rather a tiny structure in the brain that contains thousands of neurons. As we noted in module 2, neurons communicate by secreting chemicals called neurotransmitters, which act on different groups of nerve cells in this and other parts of the brain to control whether you are awake or asleep. However, the brain is just as active during the time you are sleeping as when you are awake. It is unclear whether it is the sleep-wake rhythm or the restorative nature of sleep that is most important in helping to manage symptoms of bipolar disorder.

SLEEP PATTERNS

Relaxing routine activities before bedtime signal your body to prepare for sleeping. At bedtime, try to avoid any activities that may cause excitement or tension: this is not the time to solve tough family or work problems or address financial concerns. Some people unwind from the day's stress by listening to soothing music, reading a book, soaking in a hot bath, or doing relaxation or deep breathing exercises. Other people simply brush their teeth, wash their face, and slip under the covers. Any routine you follow will serve as a cue to your body's clock to switch to a sleep period.

More than half of adults in the general population who were surveyed by the National Sleep Foundation (2002) reported *insomnia* (an inability to sleep) at least a few nights a week. Insomnia is very common in people with psychiatric conditions, including bipolar disorder. Care providers always assess sleep issues as part of a diagnostic evaluation for bipolar disorder. In fact, sleep problems are warning signs of both mania and depression. Symptoms of mania include less need for sleep, while symptoms of depression include insomnia or sleeping too much. Lack of sleep may be a possible trigger for the onset of manic symptoms in people diagnosed with bipolar disorder (Barbini et al. 1996). Mania then may cause insomnia, although a person may not feel disturbed by sleeping less, which sets up a vicious cycle. Changes in the sleep pattern, specifically those of more than three hours, may mean that a significant mood change could occur the day following the lack of sleep (Bauer, Grof, et al. 2006).

MONITORING SLEEP PATTERNS

It's essential to become aware of the number of hours you typically sleep and the quality of your sleep so that you can recognize any changes. The amount of sleep each person needs depends on a number of things, including physical health and age. You need enough sleep to feel rested and not sleepy during the day. You may begin to notice that you're sleepy when you want to be alert. Or you may notice that you have a lot of energy even though you haven't had much sleep. Both of these experiences are cues that your sleep pattern is changing and that you need to be aware of any early warning signs of mania or depression so you can employ the coping strategies you identified in modules 10 and 18. Some people are keenly aware of this sleep change. Others may want to use a logsheet to track the time spent sleeping so that they can then share the information with a care provider. In either case, a standardized sleep-wake log may help.

EXERCISE 29.1 Sleep-Wake Log—One Week

Use the following Sleep-Wake Log to record when you have been asleep, awake, or awake in bed (trying to sleep). Fill in the time blocks for each day for up to a month indicating when you were asleep. Place a slash in time blocks when you were awake in bed, fill in the block completely when you were asleep, and leave the block blank when you were awake and not in bed. This will give you a snapshot of your overall sleep pattern. Feel free to make copies of the Sleep-Wake Log so you can keep track for additional months to determine your typical pattern. (*Source:* Permission to reprint the Sleep-Wake Log from Peter C. Whybrow, MD.)

Sample Sleep-Wake Log

Month			Day	Morning												Afternoon												Evening												
ISS Mania	Dep	Mixed		1	2	3	4	5	6	7	8	9	10	11	12	1	2	3	4	5	6	7	8	9	10	11	12	1	2	3	4	5	6	7	8	9	10	11	12
			1																																					
			2																																					
			3																																					
			4																																					
			5																																					
			6																																					
			7																																					
			8																																					
			9																																					
			10																																					
			11																																					
			12																																					
			13																																					
			14																																					

Sample Sleep-Wake Log

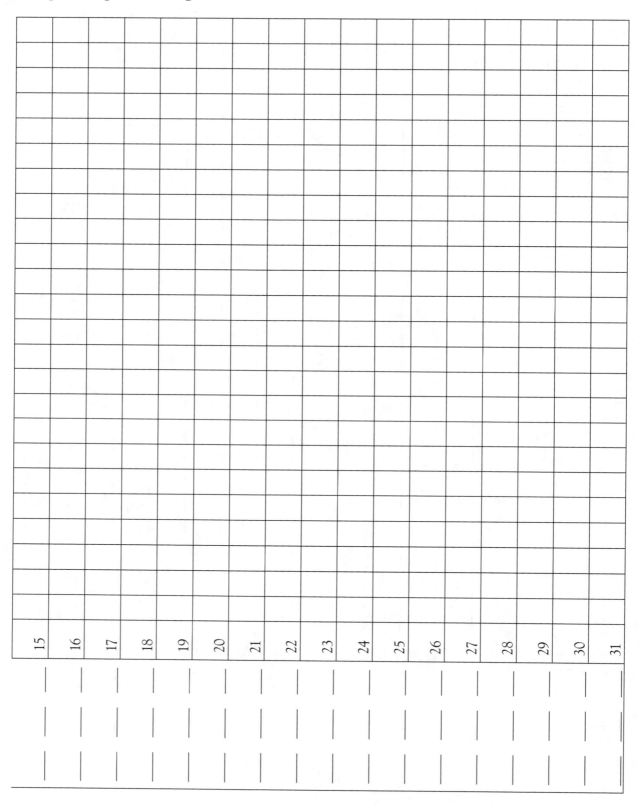

EFFECTS OF FOOD, EXERCISE, AND TOBACCO USE ON SLEEP

The amount of food you eat or what you drink close to the time you go to bed may make you feel uncomfortable and affect your sleep. Large meals, lots of fluids, and alcohol, caffeine, or tobacco may lead to a less restful sleep. Also keep in mind that vigorous physical activity or stimulants like caffeine and nicotine at bedtime awaken the body.

GOOD SLEEP HABITS

Learning to reduce and manage stress will help you sleep better. Some people find it helpful to write a to-do list or a journal entry describing all of their worries and possible solutions before going to bed. Rather than reviewing the issues over and over again in your mind while lying in bed, you can attack the list feeling refreshed the next day. If you can't avoid stress, try some of the relaxation techniques mentioned in module 21.

If you experience sleep problems, turn your bed into a cue for sleeping by only lying in bed when you're ready to fall asleep. Not everyone wants to sleep in a cool, dark, quiet place, unless they're a hibernating bear. The key point is to create the conditions *you* need to sleep comfortably: a reasonable room temperature, limited or no noise, no interruptions, and a comfortable mattress and pillow that provide lots of support. Most importantly, turn down the lights, as bright light signals your body's clock to keep you awake. Feeling well rested will allow you to feel better mentally and physically and help you regulate your mood. The following sleep tips may help you.

Daytime Routine

▶ Set a regular wake time; use an alarm if necessary.

▶ Don't have any caffeine (coffee, tea, soda) after noon.

▶ Exercise moderately during the day, daily.

▶ Don't take naps.

▶ Don't have alcohol—especially if you take sleeping medications.

Bedtime Routine

▶ Avoid large meals for four hours before bedtime.

▶ After-dinner exercise helps some people but hinders others: just experiment.

▶ Use the bedroom only for sleep and sex: no TV, reading, and so on.

▶ Don't use nicotine for four hours before bedtime or during the night.

▶ Use relaxation tapes for five to fifteen minutes of deep breathing exercises or meditation before bed and if you awaken at night.

▶ Restrict your sleep by staying in bed no more than fifteen minutes longer than your current sleep time. (Do not doze and wake.) Also, increase your time in bed only as the time sleeping increases, that is, make bedtime earlier by small (fifteen-minute) increments until you reach a sleep period that leaves you feeling well rested.

Here's an example of how to restrict sleep:

▶ Estimated sleep period: 11:00 P.M. to 4:00 A.M.

▶ In bed: 11:00 P.M. up at 4:15 A.M.

▶ Adjust bedtime to fifteen minutes earlier the next night, if necessary: 10:45 P.M. to 4:15 A.M.

EXERCISE 29.2 Using Your Sleep-Wake Log to Address Sleep Problems

Now try some of these sleep tips and find out if they are working by tracking your sleep habits for a week on the Sleep-Wake Log. After you have logged your sleep pattern for at least a week, experiment with ways to improve your sleep pattern. It's like the personal experiments in module 22, where you try out a new way of doing things and don't know in advance what the results are going to be. You may need to try a few experiments by using tips from the list above or coming up with other options before you find what best helps you get the most to get a restful sleep.

In this exercise, list the dates you try an experiment and describe how the experiment worked. Here's an example.

Sample Sleep Habit Concerns

Date(s)	Experiment	Results
2/10–2/17	*No caffeine after noon and exercising thirty minutes a day*	*Sleep came one hour earlier. Sleep time increased one hour overall.*

Sleep Habit Concerns

Date(s)	Experiment	Results

Roberto's Story

Roberto never had problems falling asleep at night. It was only Monday nights that he found himself waking up in the middle of the night, switching on the TV while he was lying in bed, and feeling exhausted in the morning. He assumed his sleep troubles stemmed from not wanting to start the workweek or get up to go to his job at the paint store. His friend Judy suggested that his weekly tennis game and big dinner with his buddies at a local sports bar on Monday nights might be impacting his sleep. He had to admit that he played tennis only once a week, and then played until nearly nine o'clock and afterward ate greasy appetizers and a full dinner with French fries, and topped it off by sharing a pitcher of beer with his friends. So Roberto asked his friends to meet at the courts at an earlier time and pick a restaurant with a menu of healthier and lighter choices, and he opted to drink water with dinner. To his surprise, Roberto wasn't feeling bloated by alcohol and excess food and could sleep through the night.

WHAT'S NEXT?

In the next module, you'll continue working toward your life goals by addressing those aspects of your life that make life worth living, like family, friends, work, and leisure activities.

## PART V

Working to Wellness: Your Life Goals

Module 30: Working Through to Your Life's Goals

In this module, you will be introduced to a method for working on your life's goals, a process that may have been disrupted by bipolar disorder. Using this method, we draw on some of the skills you learned in prior modules that focused on optimizing management of the condition and apply those skills to key areas that make life worth living: family, friends, work, and hobbies and leisure activities.

YOUR LIFE'S GOALS: WHAT IT'S REALLY ALL ABOUT

The majority of the modules in this workbook have focused on managing signs and symptoms of bipolar disorder and its unwanted co-travelers. Although a smaller portion of this book, page-wise, is devoted to managing your life's goals, this is really what all the effort is about. The work in this module builds on the work you've done on your core values (module 4) and the "concentric circles" of your life's riches (figure 4.1)—family, friends, work, and hobbies and leisure.

Whether or not a person is affected by bipolar disorder, no one is completely satisfied with all these spheres of life all the time. And for people with conditions like bipolar disorder, depression, and the like, it is very typical to have a significant gap between where you are in life and where you want to be. In bipolar disorder, for instance, loss of spouse and job are not uncommon and "re-creative" leisure activities tend to fall by the wayside. Life begins to feel impoverished … and sometimes, in given moments, to feel not worth living.

WORKING TOWARD YOUR LIFE'S GOALS: A METHOD

How, then, do you get back on track toward your life's goals? You know already that there is no easy answer. Perhaps you've tried and failed, often, to reignite your love life or to land that job you've wanted. Perhaps you've tried and failed often enough that you've stopped trying—and even trying to try seems overwhelming. You're not alone—this is a common situation for people working through bipolar disorder, and it is a reasonable place to start.

While this workbook doesn't provide a cure-all, it does provide an *approach*, a method to get you started and to guide you on your way. The method derives in part from our work in the Life Goals group psychoeducation program (Bauer and McBride 2003)—which is, of course, why we called it "Life Goals"! In the workbook you have in your hands, we have adapted that basic method, presenting it in a format that you can use either on your own or with a care provider. As with our approach in prior modules of this workbook, you will find an emphasis on (1) taking things that at first seem overwhelming and breaking them down into their component parts and (2) dealing with the components step-by-step.

THE STEPS TO PROGRESS ON YOUR LIFE'S GOALS

It is probably not surprising to you that a key step in working on your life's goals (a process that may have been disrupted by bipolar disorder) is to identify a goal to work on. We'll get to that momentarily, but we want first to lay out a prior step—in fact, let's lay out all of the five steps we have identified in goal attainment and explain them each in turn. Follow along with Fred, LaToya, and Carmen in their stories, and fill out the chart in exercise 30.1 as you go through the steps.

Step 1: Describe the challenge.

Step 2: Identify the specific goal.

Step 3: Break the goal down into subgoals.

Step 4: Construct specific steps and monitor progress.

Step 5: Troubleshoot roadblocks.

STEP 1: DESCRIBE THE CHALLENGE

Before you try to identify a specific goal, it is often helpful to describe, in somewhat free-form fashion, the lack you feel in your life, or where you see a need to work on a goal and why. It's okay at this point to be general and somewhat vague—out of this vagueness will come one or more individual and fairly specific goals.

Fred, LaToya, and Carmen's Life Goals Session

Dr. Tom began the first Life Goals session by having group members describe areas of their lives that they wanted to work on, ones that bipolar disorder had impacted: "Describing the challenges bipolar disorder has brought to your life is sometimes not easy. It can be overwhelming and hard to find a place to start—or once you start thinking about this, it may be hard to stop! What's most useful at this point is to think a moment and then, using the Life Goals Worksheet, jot down a few sentences on the area of your life that you'd most like to improve. Recall that the main areas we usually think about are family, friends, work, and hobbies and leisure-time activities." After some writing, some discussion, and some erasing, and some more writing and some more discussion, several of the group members offered to read aloud what they had written. Fred read, "Ever since my divorce, my life has seemed empty, without love. I rarely see my kids. I don't date and I spend every evening after work and most weekends at home alone." LaToya shared her most important challenges: "I feel like a little kid. Ever since I lost my job, I've had to move back in with my mother, and she treats me like I'm fourteen again. I spend as much time out of the house as I can, and she worries even more and gets on my case, seems like every day." Carmen said, "I was about to start classes at culinary school when this whole thing hit. I want to get my career on track and become a chef."

As you can see, Fred, LaToya, and Carmen all had very understandable gaps in their lives. Each described the gaps with a somewhat different tone and level of specificity, but each pointed in a particular direction—or in several directions.

EXERCISE 30.1 Constructing Your Life Goals Worksheet and Beginning Your Work

As you read through the steps in this chapter, we'd like you to begin to fill out your own Life Goals Worksheet. We provide a blank version here that can be photocopied and used over time and for multiple goals. At this point, simply follow the lead of Fred, LaToya, and Carmen and at the top of the sheet describe an area of challenge that having bipolar disorder has led to. There may well be several, and that's okay. Just be brief and specific. Then, keep this challenge in mind while reading the description of the next steps and before completing the remainder of the worksheet.

Life Goals Worksheet

Date started: _____

Description of the challenge: _____

_____

_____

_____

Overall goal: _____

Subgoal 1:	Subgoal 2:
Date written: _____	Date written: _____
Step 1: Date completed: _____	Step 1: Date completed: _____
Step 2: Date completed: _____	Step 2: Date completed: _____
Step 3: Date completed: _____	Step 3: Date completed: _____
Step 4: Date completed: _____	Step 4: Date completed:_____

STEP 2: IDENTIFY THE SPECIFIC GOAL

Now you will work from this challenge toward a specific overall goal. There may be several possible overall goals within a challenging area. In fact, in Fred's case, he identifies the loss of his marriage as the greatest challenge, and this has impacted several areas of his life including his love life, his role as a parent, and his leisure time. LaToya's area of challenge, losing her independence and becoming dependent on her mother again, is related to job loss and also has led both to family conflict and to a sense of lack of self-worth. Carmen, on the other hand, has presented a very focused, narrow area that leads directly to a goal: getting to culinary school. In each of the first two cases, choices must be made to find a place to start—otherwise things will quickly get overwhelming.

> ### *Carmen, Fred, and LaToya's Story Revisited*
>
> Carmen had no trouble specifying a very specific overall goal: getting into culinary school. Fred and LaToya, on the other hand, had some thinking and discussing to do. As Dr. Tom expected, Fred seemed overwhelmed by his loss—and in fact, Fred was in a depressive episode during this time. LaToya, on the other hand, was angry at her mother and at times had difficulty focusing on goals for her own life as opposed to complaining about her mother. Dr. Tom didn't think she was hypomanic—just angry. The group did some processing of Fred's and LaToya's situations, and with some discussion, each focused on a single, most important overall goal. Fred was able to articulate the following overall goal: "Spend time with my kids that is enjoyable for at least one day each week." LaToya knew that getting a job was the ticket out of her mother's house and back to independence, but at the same time she knew that she was not ready for this. Her overall goal was more realistically oriented toward managing her current situation, however much she didn't want to be there: "Carve out some personal space and time in my life even though I'm living in my mother's house."

THE FOUR PRINCIPLES FOR GOAL DEVELOPMENT

In working with the group, Dr. Tom kept in mind the four principles of goal development. In our experience, there are a number of pitfalls in specifying and working on goals. Not attending to these can lead to confusion, failure, demoralization, and giving up. Let's lay these out and discuss each briefly in turn.

Principle 1. Make goals personally meaningful.

Principle 2. Make goals specific enough so that progress can be measured.

Principle 3. Make goals that depend primarily on you and not upon the cooperation of some other person.

Principle 4. Make goals that can be broken down into a series of small, realistically attainable steps.

Principle 1: Make Goals Personally Meaningful

The goal must be important, and important to *you*, not to your therapist or clinician, not to your spouse, and not to your kids. You will be the one expending the effort on this, so you are the one who chooses where to start. There are, of course, many places to start. What is most important to you? (Recall Fred's goal.) But also, what is realistic, given your current circumstances? (Recall LaToya's goal.) It is important to remember to have aspirations that lead to "stretch goals"—goals that take you a bit beyond what you think you can do. Remember to also honor where you presently are in terms of energy, optimism, skills, and the like. *We can all learn from failure, but no one benefits from demoralization!*

Principle 2: Make Goals Specific Enough So That Progress Can Be Measured

"'Progress?' 'Measurement?' What are they talking about? This isn't science. This isn't business—it's my life!" Well, we agree with you on the last point, but not so much on the first two. Life *is*, in a sense, a science and a business. The behavioral therapists among us would say that a key part of getting your life on track with a mood disorder—with all of life's complexity and richness and emotional coloring—is, yes, to specify and measure. Set out a goal and see where you are in relation to it. This means, simply, if you've achieved a goal, you deserve to know! How can you know? By specifying the goal in a way that you can tell if you've made it or not. And, by this logic, it makes sense to specify the intervening steps as well.

Principle 3: Make Goals That Depend Primarily on You and not the Cooperation of Some Other Person

It is a common temptation to rely on someone else to make one's life worth living. It's easy to lampoon those who wait to hit the lottery to have all their problems solved, but this type of depend-on-others mind-set can sneak quite easily into our lives.

On the other hand, as John Donne famously wrote in the seventeenth century, "No man is an island," and just about everything worth living for brings us closer to other people—it's part of what makes the world go around.

So, realistically, a goal should be developed that will depend *primarily* on your own efforts. Can LaToya guarantee that her mother will respond well to her limit setting? No, but her goal is to set the limits. Can Fred guarantee that his kids—or he—will have a fulfilling time together each weekend? No, but his focus is on setting things up so that a fulfilling time is more likely. And as for Carmen, clearly she can't guarantee admission to culinary school—but she can do her best to apply and get in. Specifying a goal with a focus on your own efforts and capabilities, even if others are involved as they usually are, should lead to a sense that you will at the very least fight the good fight—and, at the end of the day, have enough emotional energy, and newly honed skills, to try again.

Principle 4: Make Goals That Can Be Broken Down into a Series of Small, Realistically Attainable Steps

No one jumps from the first floor to the second; we walk up the stairs, and sometimes pause on a landing. Goals should be sufficiently important to you that you will work hard to reach them and will take the time to achieve each step along the way. The steps need to be specific enough that they can be broken down into action steps. We'll proceed to do this in the following section.

STEP 3: BREAK THE GOAL DOWN INTO SUBGOALS

This section and the next suggest that an overall goal be broken down into subgoals and steps that follow the same principles. Even apparently simple tasks can be broken down into component steps. Doing this helps in two ways. First, it can provide a useful road map showing how to get from here to there, and in doing so, also provide a way to check that you *can* get there. Second, specifying realistically achievable subgoals and steps is a guard against demoralization—which so very often comes with taking on too much, or with not taking on anything because the task at hand seems so overwhelming when viewed as a whole.

There is nothing magic about having two subgoals, even though two of these Life Goals participants broke down their overall goals into two groupings, and the Life Goals Worksheet for exercise 30.1 has two columns for subgoals. But if there are more than two or three subgoals, things get too complicated too fast. If there is only one subgoal, it simply becomes the overall goal or a step.

Fred, LaToya, and Carmen's Subgoals

Fred specified an overall goal of spending enjoyable time with his kids at least one day per week, and that seemed straightforward. But it led to a variety of tasks, as he quickly realized. With some thought, he realized that these tasks fell into two main categories—and these were his subgoals: "First, negotiate a regular time with my ex-wife. Second, figure out what I can do with a four- and a six-year-old that will be fun for them and won't drive me crazy with boredom." LaToya's subgoal was simpler, at least at this stage: "Have a discussion with my mother about what I don't like about her meddling." Dr. Tom, as you might imagine, worked with her to soften that a bit and create a second subgoal—to tone down the emotion, which wouldn't serve her well in the discussion—and to focus more on LaToya herself being assertive: "Have a discussion with my mother where I can calmly express what I need in terms of coming and going from the house." Carmen quickly specified two subgoals: "Fill out the application for culinary school and start looking for a job or volunteer experience that will make me a more attractive candidate."

STEP 4: CONSTRUCT SPECIFIC STEPS AND MONITOR PROGRESS

Subgoals and steps are very similar. The main difference is that subgoals are *groups* of steps. Steps are usually carried out sequentially—one after another—while you can work on the steps within a couple of subgoals at the same time.

Fred, LaToya, and Carmen's Steps

Fred specified a variety of steps within his two subgoals to work on. The first was difficult emotionally, as he and his ex-wife had not parted on good terms and their conversations as often as not ended in either shouting matches or silent freeze-outs. His steps looked like this:

▶ Step 1: Write down exactly what I want to ask for, as specifically as possible.

▶ Step 2: Talk with Jim [an old friend who knows both Fred and his ex-wife well] and get his advice about what I'm asking for and how he thinks I should handle the conversation.

▶ Step 3: Make a call and leave her a message, or send an e-mail so I don't have to talk with her, just to find a time that's good for her to talk about this so neither of us is rushed or preoccupied (may need to be persistent here if she's evasive).

▶ Step 4: Make a negotiating list of what I want most, what I'm willing to give up, and where I draw the line in the sand and argue for what I want.

His second subgoal's individual steps were much less fraught with negative emotion; it consisted mainly of making an inventory of what he liked to do, recalling what the kids enjoyed, and listing resources and ideas from the newspaper, phone book, and Internet about local activities. LaToya's steps involved a similar listing of what she wanted from her mother, a prioritizing of the list, and also some discussion (and in her case even some role-playing) with a friend to prepare for the discussion. Carmen, in methodical fashion, listed what she needed to do to get the culinary school's application and fill it out, as well as steps she'd need to take to get some volunteer experience.

In each person's case, these steps—as with the overall goals and subgoals—consisted of what Fred, LaToya, or Carmen were supposed to do by themselves—not what they were supposed to get someone else to agree to do. Whatever the outcome of taking these steps, they will have tried their best.

A Grab Bag of Goals and Subgoals

To flesh out this goals-subgoals-steps structure, we thought it might be useful to give you a few examples of goals or subgoals—some good, some not so good, and some reasons why. This will give you a better idea of the level of specificity and concreteness that will help you to succeed. Then, we'll move on to roadblocks.

Goals that probably won't work so well	Why these goals aren't so good	Better versions of these goals (and why)
Get married.	*Overwhelmingly complex, depends on someone else*	*Begin to date again (more concrete, depends less, though still somewhat, on others).*
Have a better relationship with my spouse.	*Too vague*	*Begin to discuss with my spouse our differences in child discipline (more specific).*
Have a better relationship with my husband.	*Too vague*	*Set out Friday night as "date night" with my husband (more concrete.*
Play some professional football.	*Too grandiose*	*Begin a regular exercise program (more realistic, depends less on outside factors).*
Get a raise at work.	*Depends on others*	*Set specific work goals (depends less on others, more realistic).*
Stop feeling depressed.	*Too vague; but could be a good example of an overall challenge (refer to the Life Goals Worksheet)*	*Plan to do at least one thing each week that I used to enjoy, like I learned in module 22 (more specific.*

STEP 5: TROUBLESHOOT ROADBLOCKS

If everything were as straightforward as goals-subgoals-steps-1-2-3-and-presto-all-is-fine, well, that would be great—and this would be a much shorter book. But the world doesn't always fall into line, and we ourselves are not so simple either.

It's natural to run into roadblocks to progress, both external and internal, along the way. While you can deal with external roadblocks by changes in strategy and tactics, it's actually more challenging to deal with the *internal* roadblocks—aspects of ourselves that get in our own way despite our best intentions.

In this section, we lay out two types of aids for dealing with roadblocks. First, we list some themes to keep in mind when the going gets tough. Second, we offer a brief list of roadblocks that can come up when working on goals and we suggest some ways to deal with them.

Four (+ One) Key Themes in Working on Life Goals

Key theme 1: Having mixed feelings (ambivalence) is a normal part of life.

Key theme 2: We all act in our own perceived best interest.

Key theme 3: We all learn from our failures, but none of us benefits from demoralization.

Key theme 4: Fake it till you make it.

Key theme 5: Balance key themes 3 and 4!

A Few Principles to Keep in Mind When Dealing with Roadblocks

When dealing with roadblocks, remember that having mixed feelings is a normal part of life. Keeping your best interest as your top priority, you can continue to work on your life goals and learn from all of your experiences along the way.

Having Mixed Feelings

A key theme in working on life goals is to remember that ambivalence—having mixed feelings about something—is really quite natural. We want to reach a goal, but we don't want to risk failure. We want X, but we don't want to give up Y. Accept that you will have some degree of mixed feelings about many, if not most, things in life. Don't beat yourself up about it.

Acting in Your Own Best Interest

Another key theme, related to this, is that we all act in our own perceived best interest—what seems to make the most sense to us. If you look closely even at many types of self-destructive behavior, there's usually at least a kernel of self-interest—often self-preservation—tucked away deep in there. What is instructive—as was the case in dealing with responses to manic and depressive symptoms (modules 10 and 18)—is trying to clarify the costs and benefits of particular choices. Working on your life goals is really no different from working on better managing your manic or depressive symptoms.

Learning from Experience

A third key theme is that we can all learn from occasional failure, but none of us benefits from demoralization. That is, in constructing goals and subgoals and steps, and dealing with roadblocks, you need to set yourself up for success wherever possible. "Stretch goals" are good, but if you find yourself getting demoralized, give yourself a break and wait a while or try a different strategy or get some outside help from a friend or a clinician.

Move Your Feet, Your Head Will Follow

The fourth key theme, which is common in the literature on addictions, is "Fake it till you make it." That is, even if you sometimes *feel* lousy when you're working on your life goals plans, *do* what you have to do. Or, as athletes have learned, playing with pain often pays off. Again, it's a balance between the third and fourth key themes—and you have to find the right balance between stretching your muscles and tearing them.

SOME ROADBLOCKS TO CONSIDER

This section presents a brief list of some common roadblocks that people encounter while working on their life goals and some strategies for working through or around them. An exercise follows where you will list some of your own roadblocks and develop strategies for overcoming them.

Roadblocks	Some strategies for working on (or around) roadblocks
It's hard to identify goals because you've never done this before.	▶ Go back to your challenge at the top of the Life Goals Worksheet. What is one thing—just one and no more—that would make this area of your life better (no, we said *just one!*).
Goals are too imprecise, so you don't know if you've reached them or not.	▶ Picture an imaginary or real friend or a guardian angel or your own therapist or some other benign and friendly and helpful observer watching from a distance. What would those observers be looking for to know if you have reached this goal?
Goals depend primarily on others.	▶ Pretend the person in question would never in a million years cooperate or come through. Could you, at the end of the day, at least say, "Well, I learned something from this that moved me closer to my goal. Now I need to move on to try something else."?
Goals are overly ambitious.	▶ Sure you're impatient—but are you setting yourself up for success? You can repeat the process infinite numbers of times, but you can only take one step at a time. ▶ Time for a self-check for manic symptoms? (See module 8.) ▶ Is there someone who can give you some feedback?
No goals are identified due to demoralization or depression.	▶ Try a personal cost-benefit analysis: What's the benefit of staying put, of not doing anything to improve the situation? What's the cost of trying? ▶ Time for a self-check for depression? (See module 16.) ▶ Watch for irrational thinking even if you're not clinically depressed—review module 13. ▶ Who can be a support for you both with feedback and, as we all need at times, some plain old cheerleading?
I've got a goal, but what about these subgoals and steps?	▶ Have there been other times when you have found that approaching a task step-by-step—in the workshop, in the kitchen, in school—has been useful and necessary? That approach can work here too.

EXERCISE 30.2 Your Own Personal Roadblocks

Everyone has their own personal roadblocks—and some sense of how to deal with them. Here's your opportunity to list some of your own.

Roadblocks	Some strategies for working on (or around) roadblocks

We imagine the first column was easier to fill in than the second one! Don't give up! Imagine yourself on a good day—or imagine that you are your own ideal therapist: what is at least one decent strategy?

Carmen's Story Revisited

Carmen had been going full speed ahead with her application to culinary arts school. She'd gotten a volunteer job at a soup kitchen and had sent for the admission forms. However, there was a downside to all this productive concentration on getting her career on track: her boyfriend had told her they should start to see other people. She'd had less time for him, she'd been preoccupied when they were together, and she was, overall, driven and cranky. Their relationship had become an innocent-bystander casualty in her intense career work. Now that he'd distanced himself, she was hurting. She hadn't realized how much the relationship had meant to her and how much of a support he'd been, in his own understated, laconic way. She began to get depressed and, remarkably to her, even began to think again that life wasn't worth living. She'd not been in this bad a mental space for several years. Not surprisingly, her career work itself began to seem overwhelming. She began to feel incredible self-loathing that took all sorts of bizarre forms, from tearing up all her drafts of her personal statement for the application and erasing the files from her computer to skipping her volunteer work because she felt she was in worse shape than other people. Some glimmer of her old self remained, however, and she realized that only she could pull herself out of this tailspin. To think about her relationship was overwhelming, so she decided to keep focusing on making decisions about her career work and let the relationship evolve in due time, or not. The most pressing, first issue now was that she was ready to give it all up, and so she decided to do a personal cost-benefit analysis on that—just as she had for her depression and mania coping skills.

Carmen's personal cost-benefit analysis follows. Notice how she stated the problem and the choices and how she approached costs and benefits.

Carmen's Personal Cost-Benefit Analysis of Roadblocks

Choice	Positive effects (upsides)	Negative effects (downsides)	Impact on life goals and core values
Give it all up—it wasn't that important anyway, and working at Biggie Burgers wasn't that bad.	*This is safe, safe, safe, safe! I know the routine, I can't fail, and I won't be any worse off than I am now. I'll probably end up doing myself in anyway at some point, so what's the use?*	*Deep down, I really hate Biggie Burgers. It's a nowhere job, and this is my chance to make my break. If I don't now, I know I'll hate myself even more.*	*I'm back where I started, not where I want to be as an independent, employed professional.*
Finish my application and send it off.	*This is what I really want deep down. At least I'll know I tried my best. Sometimes it takes a couple of applications to get in, and if I get rejected, at least this will be practice.*	*I'm sure I'll screw it up, just like I did my relationship. They'll see through me and reject me anyway. Why put up with one more failure? My life has been one long string of failures anyway.*	*Being an independent, employed professional is my goal—I can't forget that!*

You can see the truly depressive and self-critical spin Carmen put on a lot of her analysis—"I'm sure I'll screw it up. My life has been one long string of failures.... I won't be any worse off than I am now." After reading her personal cost-benefit analysis, she concluded that the positives outweighed the negatives. Carmen then decided to try to recover the application she'd deleted, and that was enough for one day. She went to talk with her friend Pam and confided in her all that had gone on. Pam was maybe not the greatest therapist, but at least she meant well. Just being with someone else who wasn't as critical of Carmen as she was of herself was helpful to some degree, and she slowly got back to work on her application—more slowly than before, with many breaks, and with some fits and starts, but back to work nonetheless.

EXERCISE 30.3 Personal Cost-Benefit Analysis of Roadblocks

Now it's your turn. Try applying your personal cost-benefit analysis skills to a roadblock to working on your life goals, just like you did for coping skills for mania and depression. Copy the blank form before filling it out so that you can come back and do the exercise for other roadblocks.

Personal Cost-Benefit Analysis of Roadblocks

Choice	Positive effects (upsides)	Negative effects (downsides)	Impact on life goals and core values

WHAT'S NEXT?

In the next—and final—module of the workbook you'll complete your skills-acquisition course with a trip to your health care provider's office. We know it's not necessarily obvious how to use the time with your provider. We provide some hints!

## PART VI

Managing Your Care

Module 31: Working Collaboratively with Your Providers

In this module, we will go over the principles of collaborative practice with your care provider. These ideas will help you make the most of your time with your provider by preparing and advocating for treatments that work for you and that are the best fit with your important life goals.

WHAT IT MEANS TO BE COLLABORATIVE WITH YOUR CARE PROVIDER

One of the most important relationships you have is with those who provide your treatment. Throughout this book we've talked a bit about what each of you brings to the table in this relationship.

Basically, it all boils down to this: While your provider has specialized clinical skills, you—and no one else—are the expert on your own life. You alone determine what's important to you and how you want to live your life. You are unique in your values and dreams. We sometimes say, "Your provider is the technical expert; you are the values expert" or "Your provider is the expert in conditions like yours; you are the expert in your condition."

Keeping in mind this collaborative perspective, we don't tend to think it helps much for care providers and therapists to be too *paternalistic*—telling you that they know what's best for you, or even *maternalistic*—feeling overly responsible for making sure you take care of yourself in a certain way. At the same time, mental health providers do know a great deal. They have a lot of experience with things that have helped other people they've worked with, and they hold a vast store of knowledge about the latest science concerning treatments that can help people to manage their condition and get on with their lives.

It has been our experience that the most effective and satisfying treatment relationship occurs when patients and providers work collaboratively to manage bipolar disorder. To *collaborate* means that both patient and provider actively participate in recognizing symptoms and making decisions about the patient's mental health treatment. Collaborating means you're using assertiveness skills to inform your providers about what's important to *you*. Relationship building is a process that takes time, effort, patience, and maybe even a little "training" of your care provider. We've begun a list of the essentials of a collaborative treatment relationship below. Are there any essentials we've left out? We've left blank spaces for you to add any essential ingredients you think are missing.

EXERCISE 31.1 Building Blocks of a Collaborative Treatment Relationship

Look over the list of core components of a collaborative treatment relationship and write down specific examples that are important to you. For instance, under "Effective communication" you could add *specific, observable* behaviors that you would like to see your provider do, like "Repeats or feeds back what I've said, so she makes sure that she understands me correctly." Under "Mutual respect" an example might be "Uses a calm voice and hears me out even when not agreeing with my ideas." At the bottom of the list, just add any essential ingredients that you think we haven't highlighted.

Effective communication

The patient understands the meaning of what the provider is communicating. The provider understands the meaning of what the patient is communicating.

Example: *I will stop from time to time and ask my clinician, "Do you see what I'm saying?" and wait for an answer.*

_____

_____

Complementary skills and division of responsibility

The patient and provider recognize each other's knowledge, skill, and ability. Providers encourage patients to take responsibility for their own behavior.

Example: *I ask my clinician about the side effects of each treatment option and then I ask to make the final choice.*

_____

_____

Mutual respect

The patient and provider both avoid stigmatizing behavior.

Example: *I will speak up calmly if I feel my clinician is talking down to me and will listen calmly to her response.*

_____

_____

Clearly defined treatment goals

The patient and provider are working together to achieve a common purpose and jointly set realistic goals.

Example: *My primary care doctor takes my blood pressure and tells me what it is at each visit. I will ask my mental health clinician, "How will we measure so we'll both know if I'm getting better?"*

Your ideas

_____

_____

GETTING THE MOST OUT OF A VISIT WITH YOUR PRESCRIBING PROVIDER OR YOUR THERAPIST

Visits with your prescribing provider (the person who prescribes your medication and testing) or therapist may not always go as you hope. Sometimes it's difficult to schedule more than a few minutes of time with your provider. Sometimes you may feel nervous and pressured, or afraid you may be judged for something you say. It may seem like your provider has an agenda, and it's different from yours. You may not feel like your care provider really sees how you are doing. Frequently it may seem like he or she is in a hurry. It can be hard to summarize and remember all the information and questions you have that are important for your provider to address.

There are a few things you can do to improve what happens in the limited time you have with your care provider.

▶ Keep track of how you've been doing between visits, using your personal depression and mania profile sheets or with the mood rating system introduced in the next exercise.

▶ Write down your visit goals and priorities before each visit. Your agenda could include things like a new problem or symptom you've been having or a side effect that's been bothering you and interfering with progress you'd like to make toward important goals. There may be specific help you need, for example, with a form to be filled out or a letter to be mailed.

▶ Complete a Visit Preparation Form (see exercises 31.3 and 31.4) to help you make the most of your time together and help the two of you devise a treatment plan tailored for you. Bring two copies to your visit—one for yourself and one for your provider. The forms in exercises 31.3 and 31.4 contain what we think are the key elements for discussion during an effective visit to address bipolar disorder concerns:

▶ Current medications (specify dose and side effects)

▶ Mood rating and symptoms you've been experiencing for the last month

▶ Rating of satisfaction with benefits or antidepressant effects of current medications

▶ Rating of satisfaction with side effects of current medications

▶ Questions you'd like answered at this visit

▶ Current life goals you're working on

EXERCISE 31.2 Rating Your Mood Status

Measuring your current mood can help you keep tabs on how you're feeling over time. Often when we're in a particular mood today, it's hard to recall how we felt yesterday. So it's helpful to check in and record your mood in real time. The following simple metric comes from the Internal State Scale (ISS; adapted from Bauer et al. 1991 and Glick, McBride, and Bauer 2003) and can give you a general idea of how to record your mood state on an ongoing basis. Like the screening tools we introduced earlier for bipolar disorder, the ISS doesn't diagnose a mood episode, but rather *suggests* or might give you reason to suspect a particular mood episode.

To use these ISS items, simply blacken the square that most closely reflects how you've been feeling over the past twenty-four hours. Although there may have been changes during the day and night, try to select one answer for each item. Then, add the totals in the two sections separately (well-being items 1–3 and activation items 1–5) and write them in the table that follows.

Internal States Scale—Short Version

Well-Being Items

1. Today I feel like a capable person.

0	10	20	30	40	50	60	70	80	90	100
☐	☐	☐	☐	☐	☐	☐	☐	☐	☐	☐

Not at all   Very much
Rarely   Much of the time

2. Today I actually feel great inside.

0	10	20	30	40	50	60	70	80	90	100
☐	☐	☐	☐	☐	☐	☐	☐	☐	☐	☐

Not at all   Very much
Rarely   Much of the time

3. Today I feel energized.

0	10	20	30	40	50	60	70	80	90	100
☐	☐	☐	☐	☐	☐	☐	☐	☐	☐	☐

Not at all   Very much
Rarely   Much of the time

Activation Items

1. Today I feel impulsive.

0	10	20	30	40	50	60	70	80	90	100
☐	☐	☐	☐	☐	☐	☐	☐	☐	☐	☐

Not at all   Very much
Rarely   Much of the time

2.   Today my thoughts are going fast.

0	10	20	30	40	50	60	70	80	90	100
☐	☐	☐	☐	☐	☐	☐	☐	☐	☐	☐

Not at all   Very much
Rarely   Much of the time

3.   Today I feel overactive.

0	10	20	30	40	50	60	70	80	90	100
☐	☐	☐	☐	☐	☐	☐	☐	☐	☐	☐

Not at all   Very much
Rarely   Much of the time

4.   Today I feel "sped up" inside.

0	10	20	30	40	50	60	70	80	90	100
☐	☐	☐	☐	☐	☐	☐	☐	☐	☐	☐

Not at all   Very much
Rarely   Much of the time

5.   Today I feel restless.

0	10	20	30	40	50	60	70	80	90	100
☐	☐	☐	☐	☐	☐	☐	☐	☐	☐	☐

Not at all   Very much
Rarely   Much of the time

ISS Mood State Summary Table

Add scores from the three well-being items and write the total in the box to the right.	Well-being total score =
Add scores from the five activation items and write the total in the box to the right.	Activation total score =

Let's interpret your ISS scores by answering simple questions and by summarizing the total number of days you experienced specific symptoms:

1. Depression score: If well-being total is less than 125, consider talking with your care provider about depressive symptoms.   Yes   No

2. Mania score: If activation total is more than 155, consider talking with your care provider about mania symptoms.   Yes   No

3. Mixed symptom score: If both are yes, consider talking with your care provider about mixed symptoms.

In addition to using the Internal States Scale, it's important to become aware of the number of days you experience bipolar symptoms. On a monthly basis, keep track of how many days you experience bipolar symptoms. Then determine whether your mood was manic, depressed, or mixed.

You can track your ISS results on your monthly sleep wake log (exercise 29.1). Simply record the score for your manic, depressive, and mixed ratings on the line on the left next to the date. Take this worksheet to your care provider to review your pattern in a one-month period.

EXERCISE 31.3 Visit Preparation Form: Your Prescribing Provider

Fill this form out as completely as you can before your next visit with your prescribing provider. Make two copies and hand one to your provider at the beginning of the visit. Although it may feel weird at first to have a written agenda, we think you will be surprised at how much more satisfying your visit will be. Make copies of the blank form to fill out so you can continue to use this form for future visits.

Current medication(s) and dose(s)

What's been prescribed	What you're actually taking

Current medication side effects:

_____

_____

_____

Satisfaction with benefits of current medications (circle one number).

1	2	3	4	5	6	7	8	9	10

1 = Not
satisfied
at all

10 =
Completely
satisfied

Satisfaction with side effects of current medications (circle one number).

1	2	3	4	5	6	7	8	9	10

1 = Not
satisfied
at all

10 =
Completely
satisfied

Questions you'd like answered at this visit:

_____

_____

_____

Major life goals:

_____

_____

_____

How the current treatment is helping or hindering progress toward these goals:

_____

_____

_____

Other agenda items:

_____

_____

_____

EXERCISE 31.4 Visit Preparation Form: Your Therapist

Just as you prepared for a visit with your prescribing provider, you also can prepare for a visit with your therapist. Again, make two copies and hand one to your provider at the beginning of the visit. Make copies of this form to fill out so you can continue to use this form for future visits.

Aspects of therapy that help you and parts that don't seem to help:

_____

_____

_____

The goals you want therapy to help with:

_____

_____

_____

Concerns you have about something your therapist said or didn't say:

_____

_____

_____

Questions about what you can work on between visits:

_____

_____

_____

Shannon's Story

Shannon liked the psychiatrist she had talked with during her hospitalization for her first manic episode. Dr. Lind was kind and did not make her feel ashamed about how she had behaved before she came to the hospital. She continued to see him after her discharge and faithfully took the medicine he prescribed. Unfortunately, one of the side effects Shannon experienced was a tremor in her hands. When she first told Dr Lind about it, he said it was minor and that she shouldn't worry about it.

At the next meeting of her Life Goals group, Shannon mentioned to the group that the shakiness in her hands interfered with quilting, which she had enjoyed for many years, and that she feared she wouldn't be able to continue with this important activity. Her fellow group members reminded her that her responsibility in a collaborative relationship with her provider was to tell her provider how her treatments helped or hindered her progress toward her personal life goals. While someone else might find the tremor merely annoying, for her it was more than a minor inconvenience. At her next visit, Shannon explained to Dr. Lind that these side effects were getting in the way of something very important to her life. Dr. Lind was understanding and suggested that Shannon switch to a different medication regimen.

WEIGHING THE COSTS AND BENEFITS OF TREATMENTS

Asking questions helps you to make informed decisions. What are some questions you would ask yourself or your provider when discussing the selection of medication, "natural treatments," or other therapy to treat your bipolar disorder? We suggest some below:

- ▶ Where did you or your care provider hear about this treatment? Was it from a reliable source?

- ▶ Was proof of the benefit determined in scientific studies?

- ▶ Were the results published in a reputable journal or a supermarket tabloid?

- ▶ Were the people in the study similar to you (in age, gender, or lifestyle)?

- ▶ Does the treatment require that you stop another medication or treatment, or change your diet?

- ▶ Is information listed about the potential dangers or downsides associated with the treatment?

- ▶ What is your provider's recommendation about this treatment?

EXERCISE 31.5 Cost-Benefit Analysis of Proposed Treatments

One way to organize this information that we've found helpful is to fill out—yes, you guessed it—a cost-benefit analysis. Feel free to make multiple copies of this exercise. For example, positive responses to your medication can be listed under the benefit column and side effects under the cost column. How does the *new* treatment balance out in a cost-benefit analysis?

Personal Cost-Benefit Analysis of Treatments

Costs (side effects of medication)	Benefits (positive effects of medication)
Type of treatment #1:	
Type of treatment #2:	

So now you've taken the reins and have become an expert self-manager of your personal experience with bipolar disorder. You have the tools and experience for managing the work of dealing with your condition and, more importantly, for carrying out the work of living a meaningful life.

We wish you all the best on your continued journey.

APPENDIX A

Self-Help Resources

General and Mood Disorders Resources

Child and Adolescent Bipolar Foundation (CABF) 1000 Skokie Blvd., Suite 570 Wilmette, IL 60091 Phone: 847-256-8525 Website: www.bpkids.org	*National Alliance on Mental Illness (NAMI)* Colonial Place Three 2107 Wilson Blvd., Suite 300 Arlington, VA 22201-3402 Phone: 703-524-7600 or 800-950-NAMI (6264) Website: www.nami.org
Depression and Bipolar Support Alliance (DBSA) formally known as the National Depressive and Manic-Depressive Association (NDMDA) 730 North Franklin St., Suite 501 Chicago, IL 60654-7225 Phone: 800-826-3632 Website: www.ndmda.org	*Mental Health America (MHA)* 2000 N. Beauregard St., 6th Floor Alexandria, VA 22311 Phone: 703-684-7722 or 800-969-6642 Website: www.mentalhealthamerica.net
National Institute of Mental Health (NIMH) Science Writing Press and Dissemination Branch 6001 Executive Blvd., Room 8184 MSC 9663 Bethesda, MD 20892 Phone: 866-615-6464 Website: www.nimh.nih.gov	*Partnership for Workplace Mental Health* American Psychiatric Association 100 Wilson Blvd., Suite 1825 Arlington, VA 22209-3901 Website: www.workplacementalhealth.org

Bipolar Disorder's Unwanted Co-travelers

Alcoholics Anonymous AA World Services P.O. Box 459 New York, NY 10163 Phone: 212-870-3400 Website: www.alcoholics-anonymous.org	*National Eating Disorders Association* 603 Stewart St., Suite 803 Seattle, WA 98101 Phone: 206-382-3587 or 800-931-2237 Website: www.nationaleatingdisorders.org
Cocaine Anonymous (CAWSO) 3740 Overland Ave., Suite C Los Angeles, CA 90034 Phone: 310-559-5833 Website: www.ca.org	*Anxiety Disorders Association of America (ADAA)* 8730 Georgia Ave., Suite 600 Silver Spring, MD 20910 Phone: 240-485-1001 Website: www.adaa.org
American Association of Suicidology 5221 Wisconsin Ave., NW Washington, DC 20015 National Suicide Prevention Lifeline 1-800-273-TALK Phone: 202-237-2280 Website: www.suicidology.org	*Suicide Prevention Action Network USA (SPAN USA)* 1025 Vermont Ave., NW, Suite 1066 Washington, DC 20005 Phone: 888-649-1366 or 202-449-3600 Website: www.spanusa.org
Recovery Resources Online Website: www.soberrecovery.com	*Kristin Brooks Hope Center suicide hotline* Phone: 800-SUICIDE Website: www.hopeline.com

Psychotropic Drugs Commonly Prescribed for Bipolar Disorder

Note that this table does not indicate whether or not a medication is officially approved by the U.S. Food and Drug Administration (FDA) for treatment of bipolar disorder. It only indicates medications that you are likely to encounter in general clinical usage for the indicated symptoms. (OCD refers to obsessive-compulsive disorder.)

Generic	Brand name (example)	Depression	Mania	Psychosis	Panic	Anxiety	OCD	Sleep
Tricyclics								
Amitriptyline	Elavil	X			X			X
Clomipramine	Anafranil	X			X		X	
Desipramine	Norpramine	X			X			
Doxepin	Sinequan	X			X			X
Imipramine	Tofranil	X			X			
Nortriptyline	Aventyl	X			X			
Protriptyline	Vivactil	X			X			

Generic	Brand name (example)	Depression	Mania	Psychosis	Panic	Anxiety	OCD	Sleep
Selective serotonin reuptake inhibitors (SSRIs or SRIs)								
Citalopram	Celexa	X			X	X		
Escitalopram	Lexapro	X			X	X		
Fluoxetine	Prozac	X			X	X	X	
Fluvoxamine	Luvox	X			X	X	X	
Paroxetine	Paxil	X			X	X	X	
Sertraline	Zoloft	X			X	X		
Monoamine oxidase (MAO) inhibitors								
Phenelzine	Nardil	X			X			
Tranylcypromine	Parnate	X			X			
Serotonin-norepinephrine reuptake inhibitors (SNRIs)								
Mirtazapine	Remeron	X						X
Venlafaxine	Effexor	X				X		
Other antidepressant agents								
Bupropion	Wellbutrin	X			X			
Nefazodone	Serzone	X			X			
Trazodone	Desyrel	X			X			X

Generic	Brand name (example)	Depression	Mania	Psychosis	Panic	Anxiety	OCD	Sleep
Benzodiazepine and related agents								
Alprazolam	Xanax				X	X		X
Chlordiazepoxide	Librium				X	X		X
Clonazepam	Klonopin				X	X		X
Diazepam	Valium					X		X
Flurazepam	Dalmane				X			X
Lorazepam	Ativan				X	X		X
Oxazepam	Serax				X	X		X
Temazepam	Restoril							X
Triazolam	Halcion							X
Zaleplon	Sonata							X
Zolpidem	Ambien							X
First-generation antipsychotics/neuroleptics or typical antipsychotics/neuroleptics								
Chlorpromazine	Thorazine	X	X	X				
Chlorprothixene	Taractan	X	X					
Fluphenazine	Prolixin/ Permitil	X	X					
Haloperidol	Haldol	X	X					
Loxapine	Loxitane	X	X					
Mesoridazine	Serentil	X	X					
Molindone	Moban	X	X					
Perphenazine	Trilafon	X	X					
Pimozide	Orap	X	X					
Thioridazine	Mellaril	X	X					
Thiothixene	Navane		X	X				

Generic	Brand name (example)	Depression	Mania	Psychosis	Panic	Anxiety	OCD	Sleep
Second-generation antipsychotics/neuroleptics or atypical antipsychotics/neuroleptics								
Aripiprazole	Abilify		X	X				
Clozapine	Clozaril		X	X				
Olanzapine	Zyprexa		X	X				X
Quetiapine	Seroquel		X	X				X
Risperidone	Risperdal		X	X				
Ziprasidone	Geodon		X	X				
Lithium and anticonvulsants								
Carbamazepine	Tegretol		X					
Divalproex, valproate, valproic acid	Depakote		X					
Lamotrigine	Lamictal	X						
Lithium	Lithobid, Eskalith	X	X					
Oxcarbazepine	Trileptal							
Other medications								
Buspirone	BuSpar					X		
Gabapentin	Neurontin	X				X		
Thyroxine, T4 L-Thyroxine	Synthroid	As an add-on to antidepressants for depression or to various medications for rapid cycling						
Triiodothyronine, T3 Liothyronine	Cytomel	As an add-on to antidepressants						

Guide for Clinicians

BUILDING FROM THE ORIGINAL LIFE GOALS PROGRAM

Overcoming Bipolar Disorder represents an extension of our previously developed Life Goals Program, a group-based psychoeducation program (Bauer and McBride 2003). It is an extension of this important work in two key ways—accessibility and breadth of coverage—to address the needs of individuals with bipolar disorder.

Accessibility

This workbook provides an extension to the Life Goals Program in terms of accessibility. When we first developed the program, we designed it with a group-based format for several reasons. We thought that it would provide an opportunity for mutual support among members. Meeting others with this condition would allow for mutual learning and also help combat stigma, as many of our group members had never met anyone else with this condition. Further, since we were working in the public sector, we wanted to reach out to as many people as possible. A group format where one therapist worked with five to eight people at a time rather than one-on-one counseling would make this more feasible. Subsequent work indicated that this group format was indeed feasible and that it also supported improvements in clinical status, social function, and quality of life when used in the context of a responsive, collaborative-care setting (Bauer, McBride et al. 2006a, 2006b; Simon et al. 2006).

With those encouraging signs, we decided to expand the scope, and our thinking progressed further. We now hope to get these illness management and life management skills into the hands of everyone with bipolar disorder. With this goal in mind, we have developed a self-directed workbook that contains the basics needed to improve these skills, even if a person does not have access to a therapist. This does not mean, however, that a therapist is not necessary—quite the contrary! We spell out below the ways in which *Overcoming Bipolar Disorder* can be used with a clinician, either individually or in a group setting.

Comprehensive Coverage

Overcoming Bipolar Disorder also extends our original Life Goals Program approach with the addition of several enhancements in content that we felt needed to be addressed if we were to optimally assist those working through bipolar disorder.

First, we made more explicit our foundation of working from a person's core values as the true touchstone for any kind of management of that person's medical conditions: no one strives to be the perfect patient—they strive to live full lives *despite* having to be a patient. The approach of this workbook—working from a person's core values—acknowledges this and emphasizes it for individuals and for clinicians as well.

Second, the eclectic nature of our approach, drawing on behavioral, cognitive, and motivational interviewing techniques, has become more evident in the "laboratory" aspects of this method. For instance, since it has become clear that many with bipolar disorder suffer persistent low-grade or even severe depressive symptoms (Goodwin and Jamison 2007; Bauer 2008a), we have enhanced our cognitive and behavioral strategies for dealing with depression in modules 22–24. In addition to enhanced cognitive and behavioral strategies, we've expanded the Life Goals approach to include techniques of motivational interviewing (Miller and Rollnick 1991). To begin with, we clarified our assumptions throughout the modules that those with bipolar disorder, and in fact all of us, (1) are often ambivalent about choosing among a variety of ways to cope with adversity or opportunity and (2) ultimately can find the solution within ourselves. Additionally, techniques similar to motivational interviewing (MI) are in evidence in a number of specific workbook methods such as the personal cost-benefit analysis.

Third, research conducted since the publication of the most recent edition of the Life Goals manual has highlighted the multifaceted needs of people with bipolar disorder. We have therefore expanded the content to assist in managing the "unwanted co-travelers" that often accompany bipolar disorder. These include both mental health issues (substance use, anxiety, psychosis, anger/irritability, and suicidality) and physical wellness issues (diet, physical activity, tobacco use, and sleep), which are increasingly being recognized as a source of excess morbidity and perhaps even mortality for those with this condition (Kilbourne, Rofey, et al. 2007).

THE CLINICIAN'S GUIDE TO USING *OVERCOMING BIPOLAR DISORDER*

Overcoming Bipolar Disorder broadens and deepens coverage of the needs of individuals with bipolar disorder, and it puts these tools directly in the hands of those who have this condition. This new format enhances, rather than replaces, the therapist's work. Therapists can use the workbook in two modes: individually or in groups.

Using *Overcoming Bipolar Disorder* in Individual Sessions

Overcoming Bipolar Disorder adapts well for use either in therapy sessions of thirty to sixty minutes or as part of shorter medication-management sessions with mental health or primary care prescribers. In either case, the key principle articulated in the introduction must be kept in mind: this kind of education is less like a lecture and more like a hands-on workshop—a practical step-by-step approach by which you develop specific, personalized knowledge and specific skills to live better with bipolar disorder. We recommend a discussion, early on, of the contents of module 31, Working Collaboratively with Your Providers. This will support both your and your client's efforts to build a common agenda for your work together during the sessions.

We also recommend familiarizing yourself with the relevant modules of the workbook prior to the session. At the beginning of each session, we suggest that you review the purpose and orientation of the module and why it may be important to the individual. You can then go over the content and specific exercises and assign homework to be reviewed at the next session. The responses to some of the exercises will undoubtedly surprise you.

How much should be covered in a session, and how much homework should be assigned? This depends on two factors: the amount of time you have in the session and the capabilities of the individual with whom you are working. Clearly, you can cover more ground, and jointly do more exercises, in a fifty-minute therapy session than in a fifteen-minute medication check; the latter, for instance, might be limited to a brief overview and assignment of homework. For an individual who appears relatively more impaired at that time, some direct teaching and a single exercise might be realistic.

A person can succeed in developing a skill set for managing bipolar disorder by working through each of the modules in order. However, we have been champions of "local adaptation" of mental health interventions (Kilbourne, Neumann, et al. 2007) and recognize that each person has individualized needs. *Overcoming Bipolar Disorder* contains a core curriculum that maps onto the original Life Goals content, plus specialty modules that reflect augmented content (see the table in this appendix). The core curriculum should be covered by everyone with bipolar disorder. This provides the basic information about the disorder and its impact on a person's life, introduces the management of mania and depression, addresses social role function difficulties, and supports collaborative management of one's clinical care.

Specialty modules expand the core content of the original Life Goals Program, and in some cases introduce completely new content. These modules will be relevant to some but not all individuals you will be working with—or, more likely, relevant to all individuals at some time or another during treatment. These latter modules cover such topics as the unwanted co-travelers (in terms of both mental health and physical well-being) and additional strategies for managing depression. The specialty modules can be covered when the clinical situation warrants.

Using *Overcoming Bipolar Disorder* in the Life Goals Program Group Intervention

The Life Goals group intervention consists of two parts. Phase 1 originally consisted of five sessions and was expanded to six sessions in the second edition (Bauer and McBride 2003) to accommodate a greater focus on managing care collaboratively. In both editions, Phase 2 focuses on achieving specific life goals (i.e., addressing social role function difficulties) that are identified by each group member. Phase 2 consists of an agenda-driven, open-ended process that lasts as long as the individual is working on a specific, identified life goal.

Phase 1: Core Curriculum (Life Goals "Classic") and Specialty Modules (Life Goals "Plus")

Mapping the Phase 1 modules onto individual Life Goals Phase 1—or "classic"—sessions is a fairly straightforward process, as the flow of the workbook follows the flow of the group-based program. You can consult the table in this appendix (adapted from Bauer and McBride 2003) to identify the exercises that map particularly closely onto the content of the previously developed Life Goals "classic" package.

However, since *Overcoming Bipolar Disorder* includes substantially expanded content for several topics—which we believe are essential to optimizing outcome for those with comorbid disorders or severe, persistent depression (i.e., most people with bipolar disorder)—several additional sessions will certainly be needed to cover this added material. Again, the therapist should be ready to tailor the agenda and flow of the group sessions to the needs of the individual group. While the core curriculum should be covered with all individuals, some of the supplementary—or "plus"—modules may be deferred if there is no clinical need. On the other hand, substantial time—and repetition—might be spent on relevant modules if, for example, suicidality, anger, or sedentary lifestyle are causing problems in group members' lives.

Core Curriculum and Specialty Modules

	Life Goals group session number	Module	Focus	Key exercises based on Life Goals manual
Core curriculum: Life Goals "classic"	1	1–7	Overview	4.1, 4.2, 4.3, 4.4, 5.1
	2–3	8–11, 15	Mania	8.2, 8.4, 9.1, 11.1, 15.4
	4–5	16–19, 25	Depression	16.2, 16.4, 17.1, 19.1, 25.4
	6	31	Managing care collaboratively	31.1, 31.2, 31.3, 31.4
	Phase 2	30	Social role function difficulties	30.1, 30.2, 30.3 (for each social role goal identified)

Specialty modules: Life Goals "plus"		12	Substance use	
		13	Psychosis	
		14	Anger/irritability	
		20	Suicidality	
		21	Anxiety	
		22	Introducing cognitive and behavioral strategies for depression and anxiety	
		23	Behavioral strategies for depression and anxiety	
		24	Cognitive strategies for depression and anxiety	
		26–29	Physical wellness	

*Adapted from Bauer and McBride 2003).

The Open-Ended Work of Phase 2 Life Goals

As noted above, Phase 2 of the Life Goals Program focuses on achieving functional goals, and it maps directly onto module 30, Working Through To Your Life's Goals. Since functional challenges are part of the lives of most individuals with bipolar disorder, substantial time will likely be spent on module 30. This module is designed to be used iteratively and in open-ended fashion. A person works on a specific, behaviorally identifiable goal until it is reached, and then, if desired, he or she develops and works on additional goals. In doing Phase 2 work, the basic approach for the therapist that is outlined in the second edition of the manual (Bauer and McBride 2003) is identical to that articulated in module 30.

Finally, note that separating self-management skills into Phase 1 and Phase 2—illness management and life management—is artificial. Part of Phase 2's work is reiterating, practicing, and relearning the skills developed in Phase 1. We separate them conceptually and operationally, but they are not truly separate chronologically. To put this another way, no one is ever done working on modules 1–31. Expect that a good deal of work will be done on illness management skills during ongoing work on life goals. This is not remedial work and the person has not failed—it is a natural part of skill development and illness management. Take whatever time is necessary to go back over and review, revise, and redo exercises and the content from any of the thirty-one modules whenever needed. Recall that the goal is not to finish the workbook, but to achieve one's life goals and live one's values.

A NOTE FOR RESEARCHERS AND ADMINISTRATORS

We have been working for some time on developing a range of products for implementation of this workbook in structured settings. These are typically research settings, where protocols need to specify what, exactly, will be covered, and administrative settings, where work flow issues dictate what can be covered and when. Feel free to contact us for assistance in developing such packages:

—Mark S. Bauer, MD at mark.bauer@va.gov

—Amy M. Kilbourne, PhD, MPH at amykilbo@umich.edu

References

Akiskal, H. S., and M. Tohen. 2006. *Bipolar Psychopharmacotherapy: Caring for the Patient*. West Sussex, UK: Wiley.

American Diabetes Association, American Psychiatric Association, American Association of Clinical Endocrinologists, and North American Association for the Study of Obesity. 2004. Consensus development conference on antipsychotic drugs and obesity and diabetes. *Diabetes Care* 65(2):267-272.

American Psychiatric Association. 2000. *Diagnostic and Statistical Manual of Mental Disorders*, 4th ed., rev. ed. Washington DC: American Psychiatric Association.

Aubry, J. M., F. Ferrero, and N. Schaad in collaboration with M. S. Bauer. 2007. *Pharmacotherapy of Bipolar Disorder*. West Sussex, UK: Wiley.

Baldessarini, R. J. 2002. Treatment research in bipolar disorder: Issues and recommendation. *CNS Drugs* (16)11:721–729.

Barbini, B., S. Bertelli, C. Colombo, and E. Smeraldi. 1996. Sleep loss, a possible factor in augmenting manic episode. *Psychiatry Research* 65(2):121–125.

Barlow, D. H., and M. G. Craske. 2006. *Mastery of Your Anxiety and Worry*, 2nd ed. New York and Oxford: Oxford University Press.

Barondes, S. H. 1998. *Mood Genes: Hunting for the Origins of Mania and Depression*. New York: W. H. Freeman.

Basco, M. R., and A. J. Rush. 2007. *Cognitive-Behavioral Therapy for Bipolar Disorder*, 2nd ed. New York: Guilford Press.

Bauer, M. S. 2003. *The Field Guide to Psychiatric Assessment and Treatment*. Philadelphia: Lippincott, Williams, and Wilkins.

———. 2008a. Bipolar (manic-depressive) disorders. In *Psychiatry*, 3rd ed., edited by A. Tasman, J. Kay, J. Lieberman, M. B. First, and M. Maj. Oxford: Wiley.

———. 2008b. *A Mind Apart: Poems of Melancholy, Madness, and Addiction across Seven Centuries*. New York: Oxford University Press.

Bauer, M. S., L. Altshuler, D. R. Evans, T. Beresford, W. O. Williford, and R. Hauger, for the VA Cooperative Study #430 Team. 2005. Prevalence and distinct correlates of anxiety, substance, and combined comorbidity in a multi-site public sector sample with bipolar disorder. *Journal of Affective Disorders* 85(3):301–315.

Bauer M, P. Crits-Christoph, W. Ball, E. Dewees, T. McAllister, P. Alahi, J. Cacciola, and P. Whybrow. 1991. Independent assessment of manic and depressive symptoms by self-rating scale: Characteristics and implications for the study of mania. *Archives of General Psychiatry* 48(9):807–812.

Bauer, M. S., P. Grof, N. Rasgon, T. Bschor, T. Glenn, and P. C. Whybrow. 2006. Temporal relation between sleep and mood in patients with bipolar disorder. *Bipolar Disorders* 8(2):160–167.

Bauer, M. S., and L. McBride. 2003. *Structured Group Psychotherapy for Bipolar Disorders: The Life Goals Program*, 2nd ed. New York: Springer.

Bauer, M. S., L. McBride, W. O. Williford, H. A. Glick, B. Kinosian, L. Altshuler, T. P. Beresford, A. M. Kilbourne, M. Sajatovic, G. R. Brown, S. G. Eilers, D. Evan, H. Fenn, R. Hauger, G. F. Kirk, A. Mayeda, J. Tekell, H. S. Akiskal, J. F. Collins, and P. Lavori, for the VA Cooperative Study #430 Team. 2006a. Collaborative care for bipolar disorder, part I: Intervention and implementation in a randomized effectiveness trial. *Psychiatric Services* 57(7):927–936.

———. 2006b. Collaborative care for bipolar disorder, part II: Impact on clinical outcome, function, and costs. *Psychiatric Services* 57(7):937–945.

Benson, H. 2000. *The Relaxation Response—Updated and Expanded (25th Anniversary Edition)*. New York: HarperTorch.

Blair, S. N., H. W. Kohl, N. F. Gordon, and R. S. Paffenbarger Jr. 1992. How much physical activity is good for health? *Annual Review of Public Health* 13:99–126.

Bush, K., D. R. Kivlahan, M. B. McDonell, S. D. Fihn, and K. A. Bradley. 1998. The AUDIT alchohol consumption questions (AUDIT-C): An effective brief screening test for problem drinking. *Archives of Internal Medicine* 158:1789–95.

Carlson, G., J. Kotin, Y. Davenport, and M. Adland. 1974. Follow-up of 53 bipolar manic-depressive patients. *British Journal of Psychiatry* 124(579):134–149.

Colom, F., E. Vieta, M. Reinares, A. Martinez-Aran, C. Torrent, J. M. Goikolea, and C. Gasto. 2003. Psychoeducation efficacy in bipolar disorders: Beyond compliance enhancement. *Journal of Clinical Psychiatry* 64(9):1101–1105

Compton, M. T., G. L. Daumit, and B. G. Druss. 2006. Cigarette smoking and overweight/obesity among individuals with serious mental illnesses: A preventive perspective. *Harvard Review of Psychiatry* 14(4):212–222.

Deckersbach, T., K. H. Perlis, W. G. Frankle, S. M. Gray, L. Grandin, D. D. Dougherty, A. A. Nierenber, and G. S. Sachs. 2004. Presence of irritability during depressive episodes in bipolar disorder. *CNS Spectrums* 9(3):227–231.

Dishman, R. K., and J. Buckworth. 1996. Increasing physical activity: A quantitative synthesis. *Medicine and Science in Sports and Exercise* 28(6):706–719.

Duraiswamy, G., J. Thirthalli, H. R. Nagendra, and B. N. Gangadhar. 2007. Yoga therapy as an add-on treatment in the management of patients with schizophrenia—a randomized controlled trial. *Acta Psychiatrica Scandinavica* 116(3):226–232.

El-Guebaly, N., J. Cathcart, S. Currie, D. Brown, and S. Gloster. 2002. Smoking cessation approaches for persons with mental illness or addictive disorders. *Psychiatric Services* 53(9):1166–1170.

Ewing, J. A. 1984. Detecting alcoholism: The CAGE Questionnaire. *Journal of the American Medical Association* 252(14):1905–1907.

Fagiolini, A., E. Frank, J. A. Scott, S. Turkin, and D. J. Kupfer. 2005. Metabolic syndrome in bipolar disorder: Findings from the Bipolar Disorder Center for Pennsylvanians. *Bipolar Disorders* 7(5):424–430.

Fenichel, O. 1945. *The Psychoanalytic Theory of Neurosis*. New York: Norton.

Frank, E. 2007. *Treating Bipolar Disorder: A Clinician's Guide to Interpersonal and Social Rhythm Therapy*. New York: Guilford Press.

Frank, E., H. A. Swartz, and D. J. Kupfer. 2000. Interpersonal and social rhythm therapy: Managing the chaos of bipolar disorder. *Biological Psychiatry* 48(6):593–604.

Freedland, K. E., R. M. Carney, and J. A. Skala. 2005. Depression and smoking in coronary heart disease. *Psychosomatic Medicine* 67(Suppl. 1):S42–S46.

Ghaemi, S. N., C. J. Miller, D. A. Berv, J. Klugman, K. J. Rosenquist, and R. W. Pies. 2005. Sensitivity and specificity of a new bipolar spectrum diagnostic scale. *Journal of Affective Disorders* 84(2–3):273–277.

Glick, H. A., L. McBride, and M. S. Bauer. 2003. A manic-depressive symptom self-report in optical scanable format. *Bipolar Disorders* 5(5):366–369.

Goodwin, F., and K. R. Jamison. 2007. *Manic-Depressive Illness*, 2nd ed. New York: Oxford University Press.

Gould, M. S., J. Kalafat, J. L. Harrismunfakh, and M. Kleinman. 2007. An evaluation of crisis hotline outcomes, part 2: Suicidal callers. *Suicide Life Threat Behavior* 37(3):338–352.

Harrow, M., J. Goldberg, L. Grossman, and H. Y. Meltzer. 1990. Outcome in manic disorders. A naturalistic follow-up study. *Archives of General Psychiatry* 47(7):665–671.

Haskell, W. L., I.-M. Lee, R. R. Pate, K. E. Powell, S. N. Blair, B. A. Franklin, C. A. Macera, G. W. Heath, P. D. Thompson, and A. Bauman. 2007. Physical activity and public health. Updated recommendation for adults from the American College of Sports Medicine and the American Heart Association. *Circulation* 116(9):1081–1093.

HEW (U.S. Department of Health, Education, and Welfare). 1964. *Smoking and Health: Report of the Advisory Committee to the Surgeon General of the Public Health Service*. PHS Publication no. 1103.

Washington, DC: U.S. Department of Health, Education, and Welfare, Public Health Service, Centers for Disease Control.

HHS (U.S. Department of Health and Human Services, Public Health Service). 2000. *You Can Quit Smoking Consumer Guide.* Washington, DC: U.S. Department of Health and Human Services, Public Health Service. www.surgeongeneral.gov/tobacco/consquits.htm.

HHS (U.S. Department of Health and Human Services) and USDA (U.S. Department of Agriculture). 2005. *Dietary Guidelines for Americans,* 6th ed. Washington, DC: U.S. Government Printing Office.

Hirschfeld, R. M., J. B. Williams, R. L. Spitzer, J. R. Calabrese, L. Flynn, P. E. Keck Jr., L. Lewis, S. L. McElroy, R. M. Post, D. J. Rapport, J. M. Russell, G. S. Sachs, and J. Zajecka. 2000. Development and validation of a screening instrument for bipolar spectrum disorder: The Mood Disorder Questionnaire. *American Journal of Psychiatry* 157(11):1873–1875.

Jacobs, E. 1994. *Impact Therapy.* Lutz, FL: Psychological Assessment Resources, Inc.

Johnson, S. L. 2005. Life events in bipolar disorder: Towards more specific models. *Clinical Psychology Review* 25(8):1008–1027.

Kase, L. M. 2007. Magic Power of Sleep. *Reader's Digest,* October, 110–115.

Keck, P. E., and S. L. McElroy. 2003. Bipolar disorder, obesity, and pharmacotherapy-associated weight gain. *Journal of Clinical Psychiatry* 64(12):1426–1435.

Kilbourne, A. M., M. S. Neumann, H. A. Pincus, M. S. Bauer, and R. Stall. 2007. Implementing evidence-based interventions in health care: Application of the Replicating Effective Programs framework. *Implementation Science* 2(December):42.

Kilbourne, A. M., D. L. Rofey, J. F. McCarthy, E. P. Post, D. Welsh, and F. C. Blow. 2007. Nutrition and exercise behavior among patients with bipolar disorder. *Bipolar Disorders* 9(5):443–452.

Kraepelin, E. 1899. *Psychiatrie: Ein Lehrbuck für Studierende und Aerzte.* Liepzig: Barth.

———. 1989. Manic-depressive insanity and paranoia. In *Classics of Psychiatry and Behavioral Science,* translated by R. M. Barclay and edited by G. M. Robertson. Birmingham, AL: Classics of Psychiatry and Behavioral Sciences Library. (Orig. pub. 1921, Edinburgh: E&D Livingstone.)

Krüger, S., G. Shugar, and R. G. Cooke. 1996. Comorbidity of binge eating disorder and the partial binge eating syndrome with bipolar disorder. *International Journal of Eating Disorders* 19(1):45–52.

Ludman, E. J., W. Katon, T. Bush, C. Rutter, E. Lin, G. Simon, M. Von Korff, and E. Walker. 2003. Behavioural factors associated with symptom outcomes in a primary care-based depression prevention intervention trial. *Psychological Medicine* 33(6):1061–1070.

Mammen, O. K., P. A. Pilkonis, K. N. R. Chengappa, and D. J. Kupfer. 2004. Anger attacks in bipolar depression: Predictors and response to citalopram added to mood stabilizers. *Journal of Clinical Psychiatry* 65(5):627–633.

Mayo Clinic. 2007. www.mayoclinic.com/health/anger-management/MH0073.

McElroy, S., P. Keck, H. Pope, J. L. Hudson, G. L. Faedda, and A. C. Swann. 1992. Clinical and research implications of the diagnosis of dysphoric or mixed mania or hypomania. *American Journal of Psychiatry* 149(12):1633–1644.

McElroy, S., R. Kotwal, P. Keck Jr., and H. Akiskal. 2005. Comorbidity of bipolar and eating disorders: Distinct or related disorders with shared dysregulations? *Journal of Affective Disorders* 86(2–3):107–127.

Miklowitz, D. J., M. W. Otto, E. Frank, N. A. Reilly-Harrington, S. R. Wisniewski, J. N. Kogan, A. A. Nierenberg, J. R. Calabrese, L. B. Marangell, L. Gyulai, M. Araga, J. M. Gonzalez, E. R. Shirley, M. E. Thase, and G. S. Sachs. 2007. Psychosocial treatments for bipolar depression: A 1-year randomized trial from the systematic treatment enhancement program. *Archives of General Psychiatry* 64(4):419–426.

Miller, W. R., and S. Rollnick. 1991. *Motivational Interviewing: Preparing People to Change Addictive Behaviour.* New York: Guilford Press.

Mitchell, A. J., and M. Dennis. 2006. Self harm and attempted suicide in adults: 10 practical questions and answers for emergency department staff. *Emergency Medicine Journal* 23(4):251–255.

National Sleep Foundation. 2002. *Sleep in America Poll.* Washington, DC: National Sleep Foundation.

Newman, C. L., and R. W. Motta. 2007. The effects of aerobic exercise on childhood PTSD, anxiety, and depression. *International Journal of Emergency Mental Health* 9(2):133–158.

Richardson, C. R., S. A. Avripas, D. L. Neal, and S. M. Marcus. 2005. Increasing lifestyle physical activity in patients with depression or other serious mental illness. *Journal of Psychiatric Practice* 11(6):379–388.

Simon, G. E., E. J. Ludman, M. S. Bauer, J. Unützer, and B. Operskalski. 2006. Long-term effectiveness and cost of a systematic care program for bipolar disorder. *Archives of General Psychiatry* 63(5):500–508.

Simon, G. E., E. J. Ludman, and S. Tutty. 2006. *Creating a Balance: A Step by Step Approach to Managing Stress and Lifting Your Mood.* Victoria, BC, Canada: Trafford Press.

Simon, N. M., M. W. Otto, S. R. Wisniewski, M. Fossey, K. Sagolvyo, E. Frank, G. S. Sachs, A. A. Nierenberg, M. E. Thase, and M. H. Pollack. 2004. Anxiety disorder comorbidity in bipolar disorder patients: Data from the first 500 participants in the Systematic Treatment Enhancement Program for Bipolar Disorder (STEP-BD). *American Journal of Psychiatry* 161(12):2222–2229.

Tohen, M., C. Waternaux, and M. Tsuang. 1990. Outcome in mania: A 4-year prospective follow-up of 75 patients utilizing survival analysis. *Archives of General Psychiatry* 47(12):1106–1111.

Waxmonsky, J. A., M. R. Thomas, D. J. Miklowitz, M. H. Allen, S. R. Wisniewski, H. Zhang, M. J. Ostacher, and M. D. Fossey. 2005. Prevalence and correlates of tobacco use in bipolar disorder: Data from the first 2000 participants in the Systematic Treatment Enhancement Program. *General Hospital Psychiatry* 27(5):321–328.

WebMD. 2005. Understanding nicotine withdrawal: The basics. www.webmd.com/smoking-cessation/understanding-nicotine-withdrawal-basics.

Winokur, G., P. J. Clayton, and T. Reich. 1969. *Manic-Depressive Illness*. St. Louis: C. V. Mosby.

White, R. C., and J. P. Preston. 2009. *Bipolar 101: A Practical Guide to Identifying Triggers, Managing Medications, Coping with Symptoms, and More*. Oakland, CA: New Harbinger Publications.

World Health Organization. 1994. *International Statistical Classification of Diseases and Related Health Problems*, 10th ed., rev. ed. Geneva: World Health Organization.

Mark S. Bauer, MD, is professor of psychiatry at Harvard Medical School and director of the Harvard South Shore Psychiatry Residency Training Program. He received his bachelor's degree from the University of Chicago and his medical degree and psychiatry residency training from the University of Pennsylvania. He is an internationally recognized educator, researcher, and clinician, with particular expertise in bipolar disorder.

Amy M. Kilbourne, Ph.D., MPH, graduated from the University of California, Berkeley, with a double major in molecular biology and rhetoric. She has both a master's degree in public health with a concentration in epidemiology and a doctoral degree in health services from the University of California, Los Angeles. Kilbourne's research is focused on improving outcomes in individuals with mood disorders through integrated general medical and mental health care strategies, and translating effective treatment models for mood disorders into community-based settings.

Devra E. Greenwald, MPH, received her bachelor's degree from Vassar College and her master's degree in public health from Yale University. She conducts research in mental health at the Center for Health Equity Research and Promotion at the VA Pittsburgh Healthcare System.

Evette J. Ludman, Ph.D., received her bachelor's degree from Brown University and her doctorate from the University of Oregon. She is a clinical psychologist and researcher at Group Health Cooperative, where she motivates people to make positive life changes, from quitting smoking to overcoming depression.

Linda McBride, MSN, received her master's degree in nursing from the University of Rhode Island. She has lectured internationally and is a recognized educator, researcher, and clinician with expertise in bipolar disorder, patient education, and collaborative treatment for people seeking mental health care. She is affiliated with the graduate program in the college of nursing at the University of Rhode Island. She was awarded the Administrator's Excellence in Nursing award by the Department of Veterans Affairs.

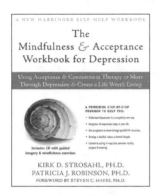

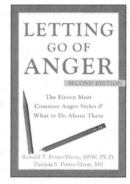

DATE DUE

Sep 25			
FEB 0 1 2009			
NOV 0 1 2012			
SEP 2 7 2022			
NOV / 2 2023			